AND THIS IS ME!

AND T

Mike Yarwood

HIS IS ME!

Jupiter Books

Acknowledgments

Mike Yarwood and the publishers wish to thank Mr Paul Forrester, Miss Ann Howard, Mr Michael Holder, Mr Ron Land, and Miss Valerie Dunne for their kind assistance in the preparation of this book.

Additionally they would also like to thank the following companies and individuals who graciously granted permission to reproduce copyright material: Syndication International Ltd, Lancashire and Cheshire County Newspapers Ltd, London Express News and Feature Services, Clifford Elson (Publicity) Ltd, The Press Association, Associated Newspapers Group Ltd, Forrester-George Ltd, John Lomas Ltd, Doug McKenzie, Terry O'Neill, the *Radio Times*, the *Sun*.

A very special debt of thanks is also owed to Mr Allen Andrews.

First published in 1974 by
JUPITER BOOKS (LONDON) LTD.,
167 Hermitage Road, London N4.

SBN 904041 14 X

AND THIS IS ME – Set in 12/14 pt. Monophoto Baskerville by Keyspools Ltd., Liverpool, and printed by R. J. Ackford Ltd., of Chichester.

I Dedicate This Book

to

The Most Sincere Sector of Show Business

THE PUBLIC

on whom I totally and gratefully depend.

Mike Yarwood.

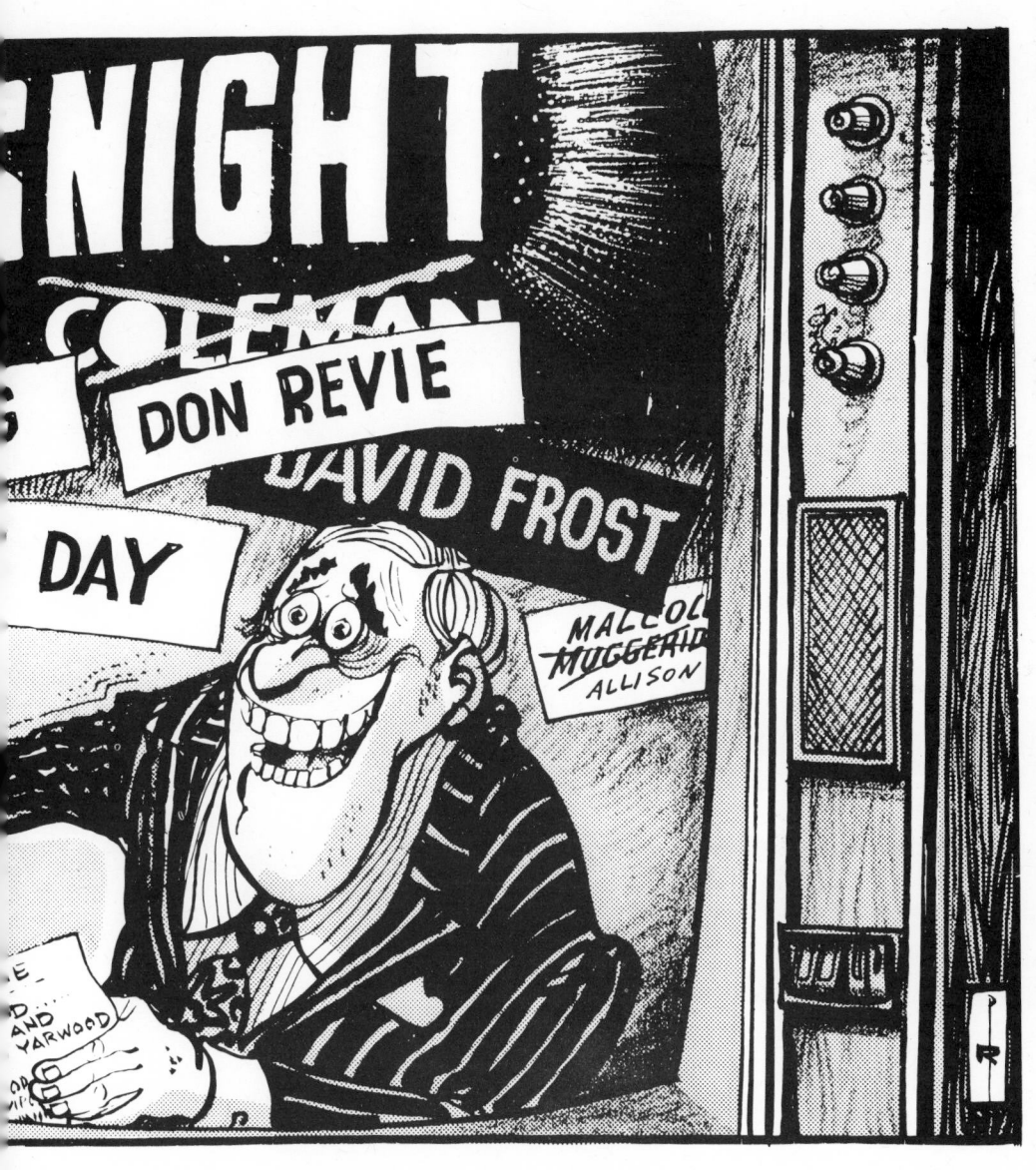

'And NOW!!... here's Mike Yarwood, to do the lot!'

(Ribgy in the *Sun*).

CONTENTS

AND THIS IS ME!
By way of an Introduction...

1. A Short Voyage Round Yarwood

2. Yarwood - A Mum's Eye View

3. Stories of My Life...

AND THIS IS ME!
By way of an Introduction...

From the Right Honourable Edward R. G. Heath, Esq., MBE, MP, to Mike Yarwood:

'WHY DON'T YOU GET OFF MY BACK?'

Speaking at the Men of the Year Luncheon in the Silver Room of the Savoy Hotel, London, on the 7th of November 1973, the Rt. Hon. Edward Heath said:

'*My Lord Mayor, Your Excellency, My Lords, Gentlemen . . . er . . .*
    (then, to Mike Yarwood, seated beside the Lord Mayor of London)
. . . Prime Minister and Leader of the Opposition. (laughter*) Look, he's actually blushing. He must be human after all! Well, if either Mr Wilson or myself should disappear under a bus, we have a ready-made substitute without the expense of an election. However I do wish he would get off my back by finding someone else to take the mickey out of.'*

Said Mike Yarwood, named Humourist of the Year, when he was finally granted Mr Heath's handshake:

'*Sir, thank you for being you. Without you I should probably be out of a job!*'

A message from the Right Honourable J. Harold Wilson, Esq., OBE, FRS, MP, to Mike Yarwood:

'YOU HAVE BETTER SCRIPT-WRITERS THAN I HAVE!'

Speaking on the 29th of November 1973 at the Labour Party Conference in Blackpool, the Rt. Hon. Harold Wilson said to Mike Yarwood:

'Mary always calls me to watch the box when you come on. You've better script-writers than I have. What about sitting in for me at the National Executive tomorrow? Some of your scripts are better than my party political broadcasts'.

Said Mike Yarwood in reply:

'Yes, Sir, but that's not the intention. Maybe when you are in power some Heath sketches work as party political broadcasts. As I see politics, the humour of knocking the other side is the only worth-while thing it's all about'.

WHO AM I?

I'M NO FOOL . . . though I'll play the fool to prompt the healing gift of laughter!

I'M THE QUEEN'S MAN WHEN COMMANDED!

And here you can see Sovereign and subject after a Royal Gala at the London Palladium in 1968. You must read about the very human encouragement she gave me when I tell the story later . . .

I'M NO MOTHER'S BOY . . .

. . . though I've always been very close to my parents, Wilf and Bridget Yarwood. I'm proud of them and, as you can see here, they were proud of me when I showed them the Variety Club of Great Britain Award as BBC TV Personality of 1973. (The design is of floodlights trained upwards on a heart, it isn't a harp, though Lord 'Ted' Willis did say when he got his, 'I must learn to play this instrument!).'

I'VE THREE GREAT GIRLFRIENDS . . .

. . . and their names are Sandra, Charlotte, and Clare. In case you're in any doubt, I'm married to the one in the middle, lovely Sandra, and she gave me Charlotte and Clare.

24

1. A Short Voyage Round Yarwood

ANYONE who writes about himself must risk being thought a big-head. I'll cheerfully take the risk because I have the courage of one of my deepest convictions. And that belief is—if you're not interested in my story, you won't read it.

GOODBYE, GROANERS!

So goodbye, groaners, and sincere thanks for having even picked the book up. But do drop it before you leave your thumb-prints on the page. Nobody is forcing you to take it, not even as required reading. I have word on very good authority that this work is unlikely to be scheduled as a set book for the General Certificate of Education. I leave that to *Hamlet* and *Cider With Rosie*. And I should remind you that you are dealing with one of the few comedians who never wanted to play Hamlet—though I can't say with my hand on my heart that I never wanted to drink cider with Rosie.

CHEER UP, WE'RE STILL A CROWD

In the days when the British Army wore scarlet, and used to advance into battle in a broad 'thin red line', they used to get potted at unmercifully by artillery and enemy sharp-shooters. When men fell, leaving gaps in the ranks, the sergeants used to roar 'Close the ranks!' so that the thin red line could continue as a forceful band of comrades, though sadly shortened. 'Close the ranks!' is all I can call now. For you—my friends—are the survivors. Don't feel too lonely. My memorable television audiences have been 22 million strong, and they weren't conscripts.

IF I CAN HELP SOMEBODY...

I hope my story is interesting. I believe it can be helpful. For this reason: I am not a great brash extrovert showbiz character. I am shy. I am petrified before a performance. I don't want to live it up afterwards, or show off to mainly uninterested people how 'star glamour' is supposed to register. I like the company of my family and my friends. Don't you?

Yet I am a performer. I was bitten by the bug of the theatre— which, you don't have to remind me, includes the music hall or the strip club or, if you like, the sawdust patch of the circus clown or the fairground buffoon. You can't insult us performers. Whatever you throw at us, we'll catch. Because we know we have the fever of artistic expression, however inadequate we may be, and shy as we often are.

28

I was a performer from a very early age, because my act started as mime. I got appreciation, but never the slightest encouragement to think of using any performing talent I had as the basis of a profession. I was 21 years of age before I even admitted to myself that such an ambition was permissible for a chap of my education and circumstances. And I still hadn't the slightest idea how to start being a professional performer. That was not very long ago. All which has happened to me has occurred in a very few years.

By telling my story, perhaps I can help others who are in the same hopeless position that I was in. It's encouraging to know just that *it can be done!* It's even better if you can follow just *how* it was done.

But this isn't a handbook for the stage-struck. Some people badly need encouragement for its own sake. Some people who are very well known to me desperately need encouragement to convince them that *anything* can be done—even such 'simple' actions as boiling a kettle or going upstairs. Handicapped people, distressed people, crippled children—sometimes cruelly depressed because of the difficulties they are in—are very well known to me because I have made it my business to get to know about them, and do a little for them in what ways I can. Think about them occasionally, all the rest of you millions, because they need the practical friendship of your thought.

And YOU are the kindest and most reliable people in my life, you know. I am now going to loose off my big mouth about YOU, the Public, and if you are feeling all modest and delicate, kindly leave the room or you will be offended.

MY DEDICATION

Why do you think I dedicated this book, as I said in my notice a few pages back,

29

To

The Most Sincere Sector of Show Business

THE PUBLIC

ON WHOM I TOTALLY AND GRATEFULLY DEPEND.

Answer: Because I meant it.

Show business has been very good to me, but the nicest people in show business are the public. They are the really reliably sincere people. It has got to be sincerity with them, because they are not going to buy a ticket unless they want to, they are not going to applaud unless they like you, they are not going to ask for your autograph unless they consider the trouble is worthwhile. They've got to be sincere, and they are what is lovely about show business, not all the backbiting and backstabbing, which exists—and don't let's pretend it doesn't.

A lot of people in our business like to cut themselves off from the public. Some people never sign autographs. They never answer fan mail. I answer every letter I get—except the anonymous ones! My wife Sandra is a great help to me in this. Mind you, it takes some time, but the letters eventually get answered, even though I sometimes think that by the time some of the writers get a reply they must have gone off me. But I cannot shrug off my deep debt to my audiences.

I never felt this more strongly than on the one occasion when I was quite ill. I had to leave a summer show for two weeks because of nervous exhaustion. I was suffering from a terrifying, inexplicable fear. When I went back, I still had the jitters in the daytime. But as soon as I walked through the stage door I felt fine. And once I was on stage there were no more problems. Because I felt that up to 2000 people sitting in that audience were on my side. I felt the protection of those people. There are times when I want to go down and shake everybody's hand in the audience. To think they've paid, to see me, I really feel a great affection for them. This is very, very genuine. It is not something I'm saying because I feel I ought to be syrupy towards you readers. The public are really the only people I care about in the business. If they didn't like me, they wouldn't come. If they didn't find me funny, they wouldn't laugh. We do mean something to each other.

NORTHERN CLUBLAND AND ALL THAT

In this chapter I am just taking you on a short voyage round Yarwood, a half-day trip to get to know the landmarks. So I'll tell you a story or two about Northern Clubland, the area where I started and to which I always return. Then I'll give you an honest taste of both triumph and disaster in my career. That will probably be enough for starters until we know each other better.

You have probably seen me putting over my impression of the Concert Chairman of a Yorkshire and Lancashire Working Men's Club. This was a strictly Yorkshire ambience which I did not penetrate during the first few months after I went professional. My very early engagements were with the theatre clubs around Manchester and within Lancashire. But as I got more widely known, I was invited into Yorkshire. Not always at a very princely fee.

I remember a Yorkshire working men's club which I played in my early days. I had been approached by the club chairman (and talent scout) after another performance and he asked me how much I would want to play a Sunday night at his place. I said the fee would be eight pounds. 'No!' he said, 'Too much, too much. I'll give you six.' I explained politely that eight pounds was the fee I had been getting for such an engagement. 'Well, I'll give you seven,' said the concert chairman. I accepted this. 'But,' he added, 'I'll have to put in a quid out of my own pocket, because six pounds is what I'm budgeted to.'

I couldn't really be bothered with his balance sheet, and forgot his calculations until the night I actually appeared.

I was waiting in the wings that Sunday night, and I heard the chairman introduce me. 'Now, ladies and gentlemen,' he said, 'you've seen this young man on *Comedy Bandbox*, he wanted eight quid tonight, any road we're giving him seven but only because I'm putting in a pound out of my own pocket . . . Here he is—Mike Yarwood!' It was the most unorthodox build-up I have ever received, and the figure for my fee was well and truly driven home in order to emphasise the chairman's generosity—which was embarrassing at the time but I have always got a good laugh out of it since.

There are a number of stories about mishaps or misunderstandings at Yorkshire working clubs, which people tend to dismiss as inventions. Yet they are true. I remember one double act arrived to appear at the club they were booked at, and they couldn't get in past the doorman because they weren't members. They insisted 'But we're the artists!' Back came the sturdy reply: 'I don't give a beggar who you are. If you're not a member, you don't get in.' And these performers never did that show.

There was the concert chairman who went up to a ventriloquist before his second show and requested: 'When you go on again, do you mind putting the dummy a little nearer the microphone, because they can't quite hear him at the back.' And perhaps my classic concerns the concert chairman who sternly warned a comedian at the band call: 'Whatever you do, we don't want any blue material, no mucky stuff, because we've a nice family audience here, so keep it clean.' Two minutes before the comic was due on, the chairman himself went on stage to make the following announcement: 'You'll be pleased to know that the new toilets have now been provided, so from now on would members please refrain from p---ing in the car park.'

32

CATCH PHRASE FOR DICKIE VALENTINE

You may recall a line from my impression of the concert chairman: 'Now we have tried to book Barbra Streidland [the mispronunciation is deliberate], any road she won't work Sunday noons and she wants too much money and I've seen her: she's rubbish.' I put the 'Sunday noons' gag in as a deliberate reminder of a longstanding joke with Dickie Valentine. There's a famous Yorkshire club in Rotherham called the Greasborough Social Club. Greasborough were in the van when the clubs started booking big names, and even their second top billing was a name, which means that I myself was quite well known by the time I was booked in there as second top to Dickie Valentine.

Greasborough was one of the Yorkshire clubs where the artists had to work on Sunday lunchtime—in fact that was the first show of the week: not exactly the most glamorous way to make your entry. Dickie had travelled up from London and was sharing a dressing room with me. Dickie was grumbling about having to work the Sunday noon show, and I agreed it was awful. Dickie was of course the top of the bill, the star attraction. The concert chairman came hustling in to the dressing room and started to explain the running order for the Sunday noon show. 'Now,' he said, 'the acrobat will go on first, you don't have to do your full act, because we don't have as long as at night, you see. And after that we'll have the speciality dancers, and then a house of bingo, and then you go, Mike.' There was a pause while Dickie worked all this out, and then he asked 'Well, what time will I be on, roughly?' 'Errr,' said the chairman, 'Oooh, errr, well we might not get to you!' The thought of arranging a variety programme so that it might be over before the star came on so amused me that for years afterwards I used it as a paper dart against Dickie. Whenever I saw him and we chatted about his engagements, or on the other

33

occasions when he and I were working together, I always managed to work in the catch phrase: 'Oooh errr, they won't get to you tonight, Dickie!'

THE QUEEN SHARED HER SECRET

I said I would give you a taste of the happy times and the bad times. A really memorable year for me was 1968 when, to get the details of my career straight, I celebrated my fifth anniversary in show business by being asked to appear in the Royal Gala. It was also the year I met Sandra, so you'll understand that it stands out brightly on my calendar. It was an Olympics year, and Sir Lew Grade (as he was shortly to become) put on a Royal Gala at the Palladium, guaranteeing from ticket receipts and television rights the sum of £40,000 to help finance the British Olympics team. He had seen me somewhere in cabaret, and he asked me if I would go into the bill at the Palladium. Jimmy Tarbuck and Des O'Connor were the comperes, and the stars included Tom Jones, Bruce Forsyth, Norman Wisdom and Dusty Springfield. Besides the Queen, Prime Minister Harold Wilson was to be in the audience.

I was already doing fairly meaty political references in my act, which included impressions of Edward Heath and Harold Wilson. When I got to the Palladium rehearsal. Lew Grade asked me about my intentions. 'What are you going to do with this Harold Wilson?' he queried. 'Oh,' I said, with intentional vagueness, 'I've got a script.' But I didn't get away with that. 'No,' he said. 'Don't do anything political, because the Queen's here and we don't want to embarrass anybody. Just come on with your pipe and raincoat and say "Good evening, nice to see you" or whatever, and leave it at that.'

Well, Lew Grade is the governor and you don't argue with him. But I was a bit unhappy over my instructions, and I moaned a bit as I discussed the act with Jimmy Tarbuck.

'This is ridiculous,' I said. 'What am I going to do? If I just come on and say Good evening, that is not going to get a laugh, and it is the climax of my act. Anyway, Harold is sitting six rows back.'

Jimmy thought for a moment and said: 'Well, put the raincoat on and the pipe, and just look down at him and say "Snap!"' I thought that was a suggestion that I could work up, so I thanked Jimmy and kept it up my sleeve. I didn't say any more about what I would do, in case I was told 'No, you can't do that.'

I went on early in the bill, in what I told the audience was a warm-up spot, but I enjoyed myself. Fortunately the audience enjoyed me, too. I did impressions of various comics, and began to get some more gamey political humour when I did a double act of Malcolm Muggeridge interviewing Edward Heath. That set the Queen laughing, as I learned from the newspaper reports next day: I didn't check at the time, because I am not one of those performers who keep shooting glances at the Royal Box to see how the act is going down.

Then I came to my last spot. At that time, Harold Wilson was still constantly sporting his Gannex raincoat, so I had to slip out of sight to get that on before my last appearance. I came on, pipe in mouth, to the usual laughter, and very deliberately walked down to the front of the stage, amid the chuckles of an audience anticipating some fireworks. Then I pretended to be caught short by the sudden sight of Mr and Mrs Wilson sitting in the stalls, although, of course, I well knew where they were. In my Wilson manner I looked fixedly at the Prime Minister, and then I said in my Wilson voice:

'As for you, Sir, I've just one thing to say to you—SNAP!'

The house exploded, and I walked off, having kept my bargain with Lew Grade and still made something of the act.

After the long show, Her Majesty made one of her very rare appearance back-stage to talk with the artists. We were lined up on the stage, and I knew that this was a magic moment in my life. The presentations went on, and she was getting nearer and nearer to me, and I was getting very scared. Finally she was talking to Bruce Forsyth, and I was next, and I was altogether terrified.

I was looking at Her Majesty, and the first time you see the Queen you never take your eyes off her. I was so fascinated. And suddenly I could see that this rather petite lady was really quite nervous. I felt that the one thing I must do must be to put her at her ease, because I thought she must be under tremendous pressure, carrying out this stately social role which I knew I could never have the grace to do.

The Queen came to me and she said 'It was most enjoyable. How long have you been doing this?' I told her, and she said 'It was very good, and it must be marvellous to be other people.' I said 'It was marvellous to do it for you, Ma'am. She said 'Well, it was very enjoyable,' and she passed on. And then she came back, almost with an air of amused conspiracy in her glance. 'Oh, by the way,' she confided, 'don't worry. The Prime Minister was laughing!' I was so moved by this little aside she gave me: as if to say 'Don't worry, you're not in any trouble.' What fascinated me as I thought about it afterwards was that, as I came on with the Gannex and pipe, she must have looked down from the Royal Box at how the Prime Minister was taking it, and she shared with me later her secret that it had been successful.

Next morning I knew just how successful it had been.

BOUQUETS AND BRICKBATS

I'm not going to bore you-all with constant quotations from my better press notices, and in any case I'll try and redress the balance by quoting a bad one for every good one. But I can't resist recording the thrill I got when I read in the *Daily Mirror* next morning:

YOUNG MIKE 'STEALS' THE BIG SHOW

Young Northern comedian Mike Yarwood 'stole' a Royal variety TV show at the London Palladium last night.

He did a brilliant 'take off' of Prime Minister Harold Wilson— with Mr Wilson sitting in the stalls and applauding him.

Yarwood, 25-year-old impressionist from Stockport, Cheshire, came on early in the show and joked: 'I'm only here in a warm-up spot.'

But he went off seven minutes later to cheers of 'more.'

Mike was later congratulated by the Queen . . .

The *Daily Express* reported: 'I've never seen the Queen so obviously enjoying herself. She fairly rocked at Mike Yarwood cutting short his impersonation of the Prime Minister when he spotted Mr and Mrs Harold Wilson in the stalls . . .'

And now, in order to keep my hat-size under control, I'll quote you one of my less appreciative notices. It was not, in fact, about the Royal Gala. It was a review of an appearance I made in the Tom Jones Show about eighteen months earlier. And this is what the *Sheffield Star* had to say about me:

'That man they pushed in front of the cameras to get the audience in a gay, happy mood! Corn wasn't the word.

'Mike Yarwood they call him. It's difficult to make out whether he's a comedian or an impressionist, he does both so badly.

'And the material he tried to pass off as jokes—I think his barber wrote his script.'

Talk about good, sturdy hatchet-work! If that man knew of a barber who wrote scripts, I reckoned that he could also pressurise a butcher into working as his private secretary.

38

TED HEATH'S SHAKING SHOULDERS

I have had plenty of time to analyse my work as an impressionist, and I know that I must use three gifts. I must be able to observe accurately. I must be able to reproduce what I observe in many aspects—the voice, the features, the stance, the mannerisms. And I also need that touch of art which good caricaturists have: the ability to isolate a feature or gesture or a characteristic turn of speech which I see to be significant in my own interpretation of the subject—and then to exaggerate it slightly so that it is more dominant in my impression than it is in real life. In this way my subject becomes instantly recognisable, but I am also making some comment on him—preferably good-humoured, as any cartoonist of stature does.

I find that I need to watch my subjects continually. I didn't do Ken Dodd until I had the opportunity to appear on the same show with him, and stand in the wings to watch him every night. I found this a great help. I think that practically every impersonation I am doing at the moment—and I have been 'living' with some of my subjects for ten years—gets better as it goes along. My subjects are like created children, and I need to live with them so that I can influence them. When I do them initially, I know that they're not as good as they could be. They can get better, and this only comes with practice, and working with an audience.

Some people say that I observed Ted Heath's shaking shoulders first, perhaps even before he did, and that he possibly becomes more self-conscious about it and perhaps does it more often. On the contrary, I think that my subjects exercise their mannerisms less once they have had their attention drawn to a trait by me. I know that since I first imitated Michael Parkinson he has stopped picking his nails and scratching his head.

Ted Heath's shaking shoulders are really a very rare pheno-

*'My dear boy, you capture me so per-fect-ly!' Malcolm
Muggeridge shares a joke and a little Pauline
philosophy over a cuppa with Mike Yarwood.*

menon. He doesn't do it often. It happened that the first time I
saw him do it, I had just made him laugh uproariously, and I
suppose it was his bad luck that I was there to note it—because,
like a caricaturist, I have exaggerated it.

It was rather a special occasion. After Sir Francis Chichester
had sailed round the world in 1966–7, a dinner was organised
to honour him. I was asked to perform at the after-dinner
cabaret. Edward Heath was the guest speaker who was to

pronounce the eulogy on Chichester. He was Leader of the Opposition at the time, but obviously he was there for his reputation as a sailor.

Unfortunately, parliamentary business kept Mr Heath away from the dinner. But he still engaged himself to make the speech afterwards. The cabaret was slotted in before his speech. And he arrived in the middle of it. He actually came into the banqueting chamber at the moment when I was doing an impression of him. Obviously he did not want to interrupt that, and he stayed by the door until he thought it was over.

But what he didn't know was that, at that time, I used to follow my impression of the Leader of the Opposition (as he was then) with one of the Prime Minister as the finale of my act. Also, I did what we call in the business 'false tabs' at the end of the Heath impression. This meant that I actually went off stage, and the band played. Psychologically, this helps to release a little pent-up applause, but it was also technically necessary in this case, because I had to put on the Wilson rain-coat before my last appearance.

Well, you couldn't expect Mr Heath to have any familiarity with all these theatrical details. I finished my Ted Heath and went off, and the band played, and the applause came. Mr Heath began to walk towards his place at the top table. And just at that moment I came in again doing Harold Wilson with his pipe and Gannex.

It was a terribly long walk for Mr Heath. Everything went quiet, and I just stood and watched him, speculatively, in the Wilson manner. All the diners could see both sides of the game, but they were very quiet, waiting to see what was going to happen.

I didn't say a word. I just stood there with my pipe and waited until he had sat down. Then I said, in the gravelly Wilson voice: 'I sincerely hope that that latecomer hasn't come here to heckle.' That released the tension. Everyone collapsed

'Pull yourself together, Harold, he hasn't a hope of every becoming Prime Minister — Mike Yarwood NEVER impersonates him!'

(Emmwood in the *Daily Mail*)

with laughter, and none more heartily than Mr Heath. But I noticed that he had gone quite red first, and I'm sure I hope I didn't embarrass him. But it was a situation that had to be crowned with a dominant riposte, or I should never have maintained control of the stage—which is always essential for a stand-up comedian. Anyway, Mr Heath really had a good laugh, and that was the first time I ever saw his shoulders shake. I suppose it's a clue to my cool (or crafty) character that I was able to note it at the time, and later to reproduce it. Really, this shoulder-shaking is a thing that Mr Heath does not do very often, only when he's really letting himself go in a laugh. I have played the caricaturist and exaggerated it, and I'm sure he finds it very boring if anybody remarks on it, because it is not a constant mannerism.

But this is an illustration of the way in which I feel I have to involve myself with my subjects through constant observation. I have been to many political meetings, and quite often to the House of Commons. I find that to watch and listen attentively while one of the political leaders makes a speech for perhaps an hour is a great help to me, and much better than brief flashes on the television news.

As a result, I do feel that I know my subjects very well. Even when I have met them socially for the first time, I have felt that I already knew them personally. When I met Harold Wilson at the Imperial Hotel, Blackpool, before a Labour Party Conference, I felt like an old acquaintance and I fancy he felt the same. He kept on quoting passages from work I had done, particular sketches that he had enjoyed, and from my side I found him absolutely identical with the image I had already constructed of him.

HEATH SWEEPS IN TO HIS REVENGE

Anyway, if I had inadvertently made Mr Edward Heath's face red at the cabaret for Sir Francis Chichester, he scored a resounding victory in the return bout. I did not meet him again for some time—he had previously received me in his room in the House of Commons. Our next encounter was at the 1973 Men Of The Year luncheon at the Savoy Hotel in London.

I had been asked to go to this lunch, and make some sort of speech, and in my innocence I accepted. I was absolutely astounded, when I arrived, to learn that I had been named as one of the Men of the Year—I think the title was Humourist of

43

the Year. In order to get things in their correct proportion from the very start of this story, I should like to list here the *real* Men of the Year, and to say right now that I was not worthy to be considered in the same company. In no particular order, they included the great sportsman and gentleman Jackie Stewart; another racing driver, David Purley, who gave up the chance of winning a Grand Prix in order to help a friend who was trapped in a burning car—unfortunately the rescue failed; Warrant Officer John Coldrick, a bomb disposal hero; John Harty, a fire service officer who released a lorry driver trapped in a submerged cab; George Leith, a lifeboat coxswain who superintended a rescue in a Force 12 storm; Flight Sergeant John Lomas, a helicopter winchman who had effected another notable North Sea rescue; Sergeant George Meredith, a police medallist who tackled a gunman; Lieutenant John O'Driscoll, another Army hero; Dougal Robertson, whose boat was sunk in the Pacific by killer whales; and Professor Michael Epstein of Bristol University and Professor D. Wright of Southampton University for outstanding work in cancer research.

So I went to the Savoy and had my first shock to learn that I was an unworthy title-holder. Major Norman Kark, the organiser, presented me to Mr Edward Heath, the Prime Minister, and there was the incident of this rather amusing photograph which you can see at the beginning of the book, with the Prime Minister being short-sighted about my glad hand and Ernie Wise hissing himself with laughter on my right. We had a good old cordial shake in the end, as you can see from the bottom of the page. We went in to lunch, and the batting order of the speeches was Major Kark, the Prime Minister, Jackie Stewart and myself. I was sitting next to the Lord Mayor of London, the official head of the function, about three places to the left of Mr Heath at the top table.

Mr Heath, naturally a very practised speaker at functions like this, started off with a great burst (which I greatly envied)

44

in the Establishment formula: 'My Lord Mayor, Your Excellency, My Lords, Gentlemen . . .' (There was an ambassador present, and foreign ambassadors take precedence over all but the Sovereign, male members of the Royal Family, the two archbishops and five politicians of very traditional office.) After this great fanfare of protocol the Prime Minister wickedly leaned over towards me and added: 'Prime Minister and Leader of the Opposition.' There were howls of laughter, of course. And I myself was very surprised because I didn't know Edward Heath had this edge of wit. Apparently I was more than surprised, because I dissolved into an enormous crimson blush. After all, when the Prime Minister of Great Britain leans over to a theatrical performer and addresses him as both Prime Minister *and* Leader of the Opposition, there's some excuse for embarrassment. Ted Heath saw it, and whipped in with what we call in the theatre a very apt ad lib. He said 'Oh, my word, look, he's actually blushing. He must be human after all!'

The laughter was mounting, and Mr Heath went on to congratulate the nation that if either he or Mr Wilson should fall under a bus there was a ready-made substitute who could be appointed without the expense of an election. He then made an appeal to me to 'get off his back.' I ought to spread the load with my impersonations. He implied that it was time that Jeremy Thorpe got some stick as well.

The Prime Minister was in very good form, and he went on to delivery a very witty—and, I should have thought, a highly politically pointed—crack about President Nixon and the Watergate tapes which were then the top subject of satirical comment.

'The last time I was here, Mr Chairman,' he said, 'you wrote to thank me for my remarks, and very kindly sent along a complete tape recording of everything I said. Not wishing to repeat myself—let alone contradict myself—I browsed through my tapes last night.' His timing here was professionally expert.

45

There was a pause of just the right brevity, and then: 'Very strange! I couldn't find the tape.'

The mirth exploded like thunder. He was going to be a difficult man to follow. Fortunately, the next speaker was Jackie Stewart, who with a very different style held the audience with his sincerity. Then the toastmaster called on me.

It ought to have been a 'magic moment.' It *was* a magic moment, for I'm honest enough to say that I cherish and collect these great occasions as keenly as a spinster looking at an album of pressed flowers from the bouquets of old sweethearts. Unfortunately, I'm shy. 'I can speak to a well-rehearsed script but even then, as my followers know, I can sometimes waffle. I certainly waffled here.

I had been so anxious about what I had to do that I had not been able to eat any of the lunch. I stood up, and I had this great fol-de-rol of titles to get rid of before I said anything sensible. 'Prime Minister . . .' I rolled out with great sonorous solemnity—but almost immediately I came a cropper over the ambassador. 'Your Allo-Allo-Excellency,' I stammered in sheer nerves. I thought I'd have another try, but the words came out the same. I threw the ambassador to the winds and got on with the lords and gentlemen. 'Unlike recording for television, we can't re-start with another take,' I commented. That got me the sympathy of the audience, and from then I was all right. I said I couldn't speak as eloquently as the Prime Minister because I wasn't particularly intellectually equipped for the task of public speaking, and also there had been a serious omission in my secondary school education: none of the teachers had ever taken me aside and said 'Look, Yarwood, in case you ever have lunch with the Prime Minister, this is how you play it . . .'

I warmed up with dotting in a few impressions. The theme of the lunch was Courage and Achievement, and I suggested that the best example of courage might be Brian Clough going

46

'Mr Thorpe, I put it to you that . . .'

to manage a football club at the bottom of the third division, and the best example of achievement was getting fifteen grand a year to do it. I did a little bit of Heath and a little bit of Wilson, and when I got to the point when I was doing Ted—which everyone was expecting—I noticed that the Lord Mayor, who was immediately on my right, was leaning forward and looking up so that he was masking me from Mr Heath. I said 'My Lord Mayor, would you mind please, there's one gentleman who particularly wants to see this!' It was all very light-hearted, and I summed up my own mood by commenting that when I first came into show business through entering a talent competition in a pub in Dukinfield, I never thought I should one day be having lunch with the Prime Minister and poking fun at him. I am very keenly aware that my life has brought me great privileges, and that this occasion was one of them, and it did turn out in the end to be the magic moment I had always considered it would be.

PEOPLE ARE GENEROUS

In passing, I'd like to add that my little stutter over 'Your Allo-Allo-Excellency' was typical of my experience in that it got the sympathy of the listeners. People don't bash you for errors, in fact I've always found that when you make a mistake it endears you more to the audience. This sometimes happens when I am recording a television show. If I fluff something and we've got to do it again, and I fluff it again, and the sweat is pouring off me as I panic, I often find that the audience is getting warmer towards me because they are sympathising with the situation. I say to them: 'Ladies and Gentlemen, we've got to do this little sketch again. I'd appreciate it if you'd pretend that you haven't heard the joke, because we need the laugh—you see, you're very important and we must have the laugh.' And we get a bigger laugh on the third take than we did on the first. I sometimes think it's worth fluffing it on purpose so that we can get a bigger laugh. But I'm dead serious over the importance I give to the audience. Even on television, the live audience is the most important thing to me.

This preliminary voyage round Yarwood would not be honest—and perhaps would not be such a help to others—if I did not candidly report a ghastly failure at the beginning of my career. So I had better grit my teeth and get on with it.

YARWOOD IN RETREAT

I was 22 years old, and I had been in show business only a few months. My typical engagements had been playing the working

48

men's clubs in Manchester, with an occasional spot of glamour like appearing at the Whisky à Gogo. An agent came in to the Whisky à Gogo and said he could get me a marvellous engagement at a London club. I was tremendously thrilled. The thought of London was so glamorous to me, and it was a practical step up in the business—I could probably get £2 extra in Manchester in future because I could be announced as 'Mike Yarwood—direct from London!' So I accepted the job with pleasure.

I set off for London as if I were beginning a trip round the world. I had been in London only once before, and that was for a social occasion. But when I arrived I was terrified. Everything was so remote and strange and unhomely. When I got to the club for the Sunday afternoon band call, my panic increased. It didn't quite have the glamour of a sort of Piccadilly *Folies Bergère* which I had given it in my imagination. It was a small restaurant in the Edgware Road which ran a cabaret turn after the clients had been dancing to a trio. They were saving the lights when I arrived, and the place seemed very small and dark. It was certainly so intimate that they did not provide a microphone—and I had been rehearsing microphone technique madly for weeks.

I went through the band call and got the impression that nobody could understand what I was saying. In my unease, I wasn't sure that English was an accepted language at this club. As the evening began, I got gloomier and gloomier. My mother had arranged that I should stay with my uncle who lived in Swiss Cottage. I left the house in time that night, but I just did not go to the club. I went into a pub somewhere—I hardly drank anything—and mooned away the time. Then I went back to the house and pretended I had done the show.

I didn't keep up this pretence with my family for long, of course. I told my uncle, and eventually telephoned home. My mother very loyally said that it didn't matter, it was my own

49

life, and I should come home whenever I felt like it, but she would consult one or two of my good friends who had been grooming me, and listen to their advice.

In the meantime I had been telephoned by the agent in London. 'You had better come and see me,' he said. So I went. He said 'What the — — did you do? You didn't turn up. You were the only artist booked into the club, and you have got me into a lot of trouble.' I said 'I got stage fright. I didn't think they would understand my humour. I wasn't even sure that they could understand my language when I did Prime Minister Macmillan and the Steptoes and other impressions.' Even to advance this theory to a professional agent who had booked me in to a London Club knowing full well what he was doing is an indication of how green I was, rushing to believe the excuses of my own fantasies—but, I *was* raw, *very* raw. All I had was a bagful of hats, and according to what came out of the bag, something happened.

'What were you doing before you came into the business?' asked the agent. 'Well,' I said, 'I used to be a salesman.' 'I hope you did well,' he said, 'because I should go back to that if I were you, because you'll never be any good in this business if you walk away from a job. Anyway, you can walk away from me, because I've had you.' So I left his office, stumbling through the ashes of my short-lived career as a performer.

I was brooding about this in my uncle's house when I had a blistering telephone call from Roy Mayoh. I should explain that Roy Mayoh—and you haven't heard the last of him in my story—is the very busy television producer now known as Royston Mayoh who is famous for his productions of *This Is Your Life*, *Opportunity Knocks*, and a legion of comedy series like the David Nixon and Tommy Cooper shows. Roy at that time was a comedy writer and also a television cameraman. Out of the sheer goodness of his heart and his overflowing love for comedy, he had taken me up from nothing, groomed me,

'I personally package every holiday myself, Sir!'

bullied me, flattered me, rehearsed me at every hour of the day he could pinch from making his own livelihood—and he had, in fact (though I didn't know it at the time) refused my mother's private request that he should accompany me on the trip to London, because he thought it was time I stood up on my own feet without having him as a prop. I had repaid all this by walking out of my first London show, as he had now learned from my mother.

'Go back to that club!' roared Roy down the telephone line from Manchester. 'Finish the week, or you will never work in show business in your life. And if you don't, you can also forget me. Tell the club you'll work the rest of the week for nothing.'

'I can't do that,' I said. 'I'm frightened to work there when I'm paid for it.'

'Go back and see that club manager,' Roy ordered. 'Tell him you've let him down, and be honest why you did it. Tell him you'll work the rest of the week for nothing.'

Well, it was an ordeal going back. The club boss was a very nice man, I remember that he was a Greek and am sorry that I have never met him again after that week. He accepted what I said. He had had to hire a belly-dancer in a hurry since he had no act at all at the club. So he gave me my spot after the belly-dancer. He also gave me a good proportion of my contract fee at the end of the week. 'Nobody works here for nothing,' he said.

And the ordeal of the actual performance? I didn't even notice it after my customary sick-making nerves immediately before I went on. The act went like a bomb. It was fine, fine, fine and I really enjoyed myself.

So much so, that I was able to ride an embarrassing and even potentially dangerous moment on the cushion of an ad lib which could never have been more apt if it had been scripted.

In the area of topical allusion, this year was Prime Minister Macmillan's last as a headline-maker. And it was Christine

'Mike Yarwood, this is . . . your round!'

Keeler's first.

Harold Macmillan was one of my special impressions, and it was much more of a talking-point at that time that a cabaret artist should be impersonating a politician, for this was perhaps the main originality of my act. I had a fairly pointed sector of my script which was a routine of Harold Macmillan commenting on the Christine Keeler affair. If I still think the lines were funny, it is a tribute to Roy Mayoh who wrote most of them.

I was in the middle of this routine when I seemed to sense a deepened hush among the audience.

I glanced up and saw that a good-looking woman had just come into the club, escorted by what I immediately summed up as a very powerful man. The woman's face seemed familiar, and I took a longer look at it.

It was Miss Christine Keeler.

Nobody said a word as Miss Keeler and her escort walked to a reserved table. I watched her with my Macmillan face while she settled herself. Then I said to her, in my Macmillan drawl: 'Rather amazing you should come in. We were just talking about you.'

There was a gale of laughter, in which she joined—whether it was out of tact, poker-facedness or genuine amusement I didn't then know. I wondered if I should book myself a couple of escorts to see me home that night. But all went well, and I was told afterwards that she used to lap up all the current jokes about herself with appreciation.

FAME IS THE NAME OF THE GAME

Such is fame. Macmillan, Keeler, and, if I may say so, Yarwood are all names which make a different impact on the public for reasons which do not necessarily have anything to do with their worth. It's the current impact that determines the force of fame—or notoriety—and in my humble opinion there's no point in trying to analyse the mixed motivation that makes a certain name a current focus of interest. The only thing to do about it is to turn that public interest into a force for good, by using notoriety in causes that help others. I first started on this line by using my passion for football as a means of raising money for charity.

It began by my turning out as often as possible for a team called the TV Allstars. Don't let the name deceive you, they took on anybody they could get. David Hamilton, the announcer, used to run it and get us together at various places. We once actually played at Macclesfield, near where Sandra

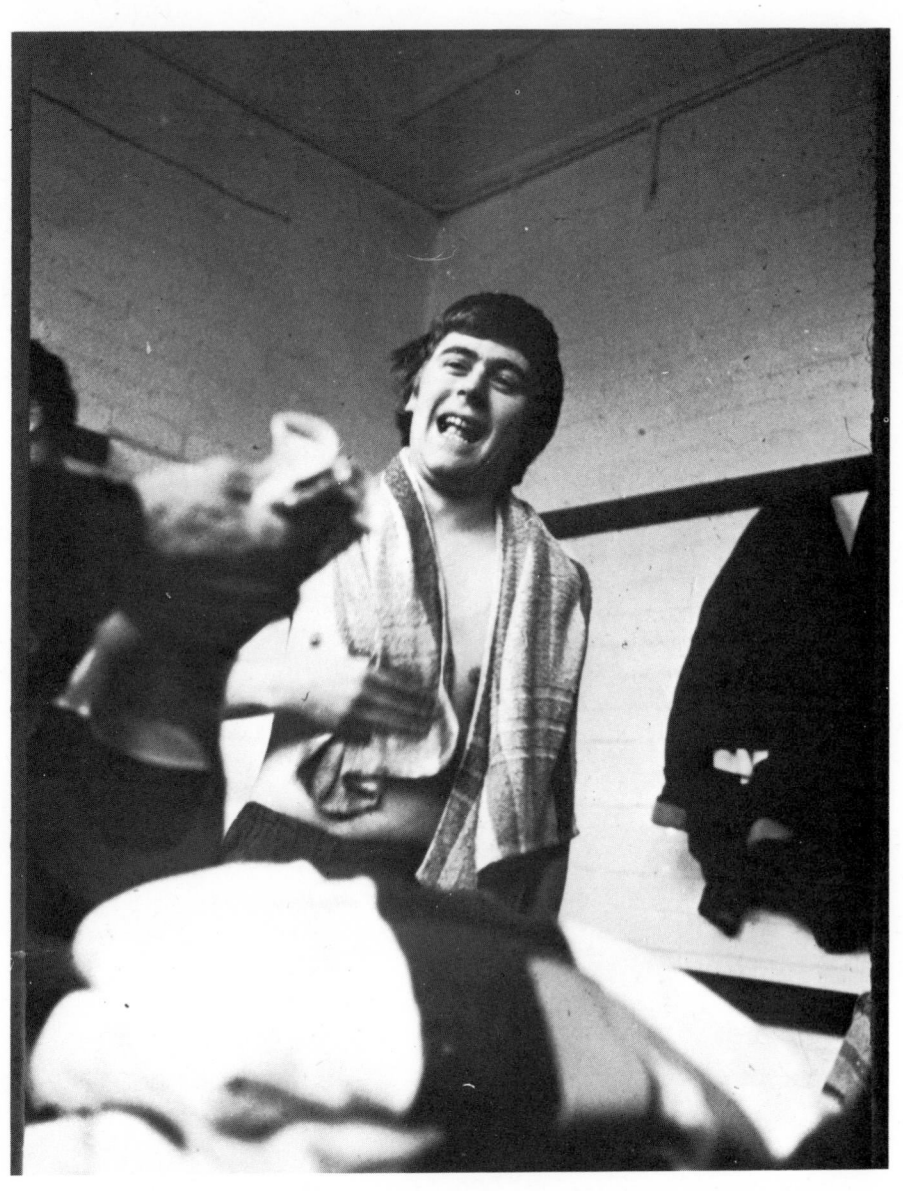

'Go on, Mike – do your Brian Clough!'

and I moved into a seventeenth century cottage after we were married. Jimmy Tarbuck played, Des O'Connor and others including your servant, and there was a gate of about 6000, which is some 5000 more than Macclesfield usually gets at a match.

This was all for charity. We still do it, it still goes on although I don't think I'm so fit as I was. I used to go all over with the team. And on summer seasons at Yarmouth or Bournemouth or Blackpool all the entertainers used to muck in. Somebody is always fixing a charity match, and they are always well supported.

In show business we consider this great fun, a charity football match. Better than opening fetes, in our opinion. Don't get me wrong, we do open fetes, but if I could offer some humble advice to charity organisers, they might think of something else which was possibly more profitable. Because entertainers get asked to open fetes at a maddening rate in the season of about four times a week. They can't do them all. They must turn some down. And in the course of the bargaining, or dodging, the very idea of opening fetes gets a bad image. Anybody will play in a charity match, but to get someone to open a fete is difficult. And that's surprising when you consider that a match involves you for a much longer time. It must be the fun factor that counts.

ARTHUR ASKEY ASKS A GOOD QUESTION

A remember Arthur Askey putting this point over rather well, but I fear too subtly for the people immediately involved. I was playing at a summer season in Yarmouth, and I had agreed to open a fete. The organisers, the hard-working charitable body of the Rotary, met me before the opening and very kindly offered to take me to lunch at the Carlton. I walked into the

'Hel-lo. I'm Den-nis Hea-ley . . . I . . . am.'

57

restaurant with my hosts, and Arthur Askey was sitting at the table next to the one reserved for us. He saw all the badges in the lapels of my hosts and understood the situation immediately.

'Hallo, Mike!' he said, very innocently if you didn't know the mischief brewing underneath. 'Are you opening a fete?'

'Yes,' I said.

His voice sank to a conspiratorial, but clearly audible tone.

'Tell me,' he said, almost pleading. 'How do you get one of these things?'

I said: 'I'm probably only doing it because you turned it down.'

I had seen the organisers brighten at Arthur's question. No doubt they were noting his name down for a future assault. But for everybody's sake I was glad that I had muted my own answer so that my hosts couldn't hear it.

I still open fetes. I personally consider that in show business the job is not just going on the stage and getting paid money to entertain people. You have a duty to do. If you're in a privileged position which, besides all the prestige, puts you where you can raise money for people worse off than average people, then I think you must recognise that it is part of your privilege and you must accept it, you must try never to turn it down (although it's not possible to go to all the fetes you're asked to open!). A lot of showbiz people don't want to know about this responsibility, and I think they've got their values wrong.

Some people actually make a charge for this sort of activity. In my book, this is not something for which you ask a fee. If it is for charity, then charity should be the only organisation which benefits.

The only variation on that which I permit is that I sometimes take a cut in favour of my own pet charities. I am a member of SOS—Stars' Organisation for Spastics, and of the Muscular Dystrophy association, and I am also involved with a local organisation, the Paediatric Welfare and Research Association, of Macclesfield. Sometimes, if people ask about a fee for a particular service, I do say: 'Look, I don't want a fee, because the cause is for charity. But I do have some charities of my own. If you can bear to give me a donation of your own choice towards my Spastics, or whatever, that is fine and you will make a bit for your charity and I will make a bit for mine.' I do know people who ask money even for opening an event for handicapped children, but this policy of eating into the profits of a charity do in order to make private bunce does not get by with me.

CALL BRIDGET YARWOOD

At this point in the saga, I have come to the conclusion that any reliable account of the real Mike Yarwood needs the stereoscopic aid of an outside witness. I am therefore putting my mother on the stand. At least she remembers incidents that I have forgotten, or sometimes never knew about, and which I therefore have to take on hearsay. As an expert witness, she has her worth. I don't promise that she is not biassed. But what can you expect? The truth of the matter is that I am also biassed towards her.

2. Yarwood - A Mum's Eye View

MICHAEL—as you will have to get used to hearing him referred to by me—Michael really began to get his teeth into this mimicking as soon as he could talk. I've always said that one of his best impressions was of me going up the wall, but he usually had the tact to reserve that one until I had come down the wall again. He would imitate someone in the family, or a friend or a neighbour—anyone who had any particular characteristic. He was not being naughty or cheeky or malicious, he just did it to amuse the family. And he made us laugh a lot. I had three brothers living around and about, and they each had a different brogue; one had travelled about a lot and picked up many shades of dialect, and my sisters would egg on Michael to do each brother individually, just to amuse the family. It was not just a capacity to imitate a voice, he had a gift of very detailed observation. My youngest brother, who liked a pint, had a habit of fidgeting around our kitchen until it was pub-time, and as soon as he knew they were open. 'Are ye coming out?' he would say eagerly to my husband Wilf—and Michael caught this identically. And so he would imitate his godmother fussing and tapping on the table, or an old lady who used to come in with dangling earrings—from very early on he seemed to be registering and recording voices and mannerisms.

MAKE-UP FROM THE CHIMNEY

When he was seven he gave us a re-run of his first grown-up film. At that time I was very keen on the cinema, but I didn't take the children. However, on a bank holiday afternoon Pop and I and some friends of mine took Michael and his elder sister Josephine to the pictures. The film was *Life with Father*, with William Powell playing a very heavy old-fashioned Victorian dad. We came back and began to make a cup of tea, and Michael disappeared. I thought he'd gone upstairs to the loo or something. He'd certainly gone upstairs, but to the bedroom fireplace, for a supply of soot to paint on a William Powell moustache. He came bouncing back into the room with his turn-down collar bent back to make a Victorian butterfly collar, and a ferocious frown fixed over the Powell moustache, and he gave us a version of *Life with Father* all over again. On this occasion, however, it took me a long time to laugh. He had made such a mess scraping the chimney that he was covered all over with soot. So the rest of him wasn't quite the immaculate William Powell appearance, and it wasn't really in keeping with his own nature, for he was always very fussy about how he looked.

Besides going to the films, we were keen radio listeners. At least, I used to listen but I never thought the boy was taking much notice. Until I was summoned one day to the convent where he went to school, he was only six at the time. The nuns were very strict and I think they kept an extra-beady eye on Michael because he was one of only four boys there and all the rest were girls. The Mother Superior took me walking in the gardens and complained that Michael was a great disturbance in the school, always playing about and fooling around and making the others laugh. 'And by the way,' she said, 'who is this Dick Barton and Snowy and Jock?' In those days, of course, the nuns never listened to the radio, though they're much more with it now. But apparently, although I had thought Michael wasn't taking much notice of the series at home, he was giving long sequences from the thriller in class, presenting not only Dick and Snowy and Jock but also the exciting build-up music, the *Devil's Gallop* or whatever it was called.

The Mother Superior suggested that his Daddy should smack his backside a bit more often than he did. This was a bit of a laugh to me, because my husband Wilf has never seriously chastised a child in his life. If anybody ever had to do it, it was me. But we weren't that sort of family, strict in some ways perhaps, but over-protective more than any other fault. I realised that later, and when the children left school I deliberately organised it that they went to work in Manchester, some miles from our home at Bredbury outside Stockport. I thought they should have some experience of city living.

I WON'T DANCE!

To get the family details straight, I should say that I was born in the First World War. I was born in Wales, but my father was in the Irish Guards, and after the war the family—there were ten of us children—went to Ireland. When I was 19 I came back to England as a nannie, to Marple Bridge in Cheshire. There I met Wilf, who has been a fitter in an engineering works all his

'School days! School days! Those dear old golden rule days!' Mike Yarwood, aged six, at the local infants' school. But where? Can you spot him?

(The back row, second from left!)

life, and we were married in 1936. Josephine was our first child, and 2½ years later Michael Edward Yarwood was born on the 14th of June 1941, having endured a large part of the Blitz before he arrived. We have lived almost all our married life in the house in Bredbury where Michael was born and which we still have.

I never visualised that Michael might go on the stage, because he didn't seem the type. On one side he was a very shy boy, and on the other his absorbing interest was in sport. He was very good at football and cricket and very taken up with all sport. I did see a possibility of my daughter Josephine taking up a theatrical career, and even had hopes for it. I must have been a frustrated ballet dancer myself, but anyway I certainly introduced Josephine to ballet lessons very early, and she also learned the piano. Josephine was very good, but we weren't too well off and we couldn't send her to the right places, so she just had to have lessons locally. Josephine became a nurse, and although she's married and has three children now, she is still very interested in the profession and has a part-time practice.

I did, for fun, once ask Michael if he would go to ballet lessons. He was only a tot, and I was pulling his leg, but he was horrified. 'I won't dance,' he said, and he started to cry when he thought I was serious. Later on, when he was in his teens I tried again to get him to dancing lessons, but it was no good. So any 'hoofing' he has had to do on the stage has been learned in his old age.

I myself have always been interested in anything theatrical. In the little town in Ireland where I was brought up, all the entertainment came by travelling shows—acting companies or variety shows at the town hall and circuses in the field. I used to go to them all. Then, from Cheshire, I always took the children to what shows I could. I would take Josephine to the ballet and we saw all the ballet companies and the great dancers who used to come to Manchester. With Michael, his preference was more for the pantomime and the music hall. We always went to a Christmas pantomime and often to the circus.

I loved to see the children responding to the magic of the pantomime. There were Jewell and Warriss in the panto, Billy Cotton and Anton Karas in variety. We all of us loved music. We didn't sing seriously, but music was a very fundamental part of our life. Strangely enough, when Michael was the guest on a *Desert Island Discs* programme recently, he chose practically all the records we have at home—Andy Williams, Perry Como, Charlie Chaplin's *Limelight* and all those lovely Neapolitan songs, we have kept the same taste. In Michael's car he has all my favourites on the stereo, not so much for me because I'm not in the car that much, but because he loves

65

them. They are all his favourites, too. He doesn't read music, which is a pity. Josephine took proper music lessons, but Michael never had the patience for the theory. But he would still get down on the piano, as I used to do—thump away, and we would have a lot of fun together.

He had this lovely gift of being able to improvise at family parties. I suppose it was all a part of his feeling for comedy which took really a long time to recognise, although he presented us with plenty of clues. When he was quite a little boy he went to play with the girl next door, and they started dressing up, which they found rather easier to do because the little girl's mother was out. Michael gold hold of a great picture hat, and some oddment to put round his neck, and he was down in the garden doing a terrific improvisation of Norman Evans

Mike Yarwood (right), aged seven years, with schoolchums. Twenty years and a hundred and fifty miles away from a Royal Command Performance.

conducting one of his 'Over The Garden Wall' conversations. A neighbour of mine, a friend called Mildred, watched it all and was absolutely spellbound as it went on and on. The end of the story was predictable. The little girl's mother came home and created fury because she found Michael wearing a hat that she had got for a wedding, and the end of the story was more like *Just William* than 'Over The Garden Wall'!

One of his favourite imitations was of Billy Bunter. He stuffed cushions up his blazer and perched glasses on the end of his nose, and got as much fun out of it as he gave to others. But his father particularly remembers one of Michael's first reactions to television. There was an old news reel of the 1900s shown, about the suffragettes. Because of the changed speed of the films they used to take in those days, the result today is that everyone struts around at a false pace like turkeys. Michael saw this film, and in a trice he was upstairs, raiding some cupboard. And he came down, clad in the best he could do for old-fashioned garb, an old fur round his neck and a long coat down to his ankles, and he copied this artificial walk all around the carpet. Wilf simply collapsed with laughing at him.

FOOTBALL CRAZY

The other great love of Michael's life was football, playing it and watching it, and the only team he ever watched was Stockport County, our local team. He has always been, from the very beginning, a stalwart supporter of County, and has suffered with them through the years. Even when he was very little his father started taking him to the matches. The first match he went to he lasted through the first half and enjoyed the band in the interval, but as soon as the band stopped he yelled to go home, because if there wasn't going to be any more music he wasn't too keen on stretching his neck any longer. But soon he learned the knack which small boys have to cultivate, of how to see a match well when most of the spectators are twice your size, and his father used to take him to away matches in Halifax and Bradford, or other grounds which weren't too far away.

Of course he played the game as well, and was very keen from the first. I remember we bought him the proper leather ball, which wanted quite a lot of preparation—a thing which none of the small boys seem to hanker after nowadays. One Christmas we prepared for his present a complete football strip in County's colours. He always used to make a big thing of Christmas, couldn't sleep for days beforehand while he went into fantasies about possible presents. And this occasion was certainly no exception. We had a bit of a grown-up party on Christmas Eve, with a few drinks and a bit of fun, and finally we went to bed about one o'clock. We were hardly dozing off when in stalks Michael, fully rigged in his football gear and as proud as punch of the colours, with: 'Look, what Father Christmas has brought me.' I felt like knocking him flat!

As another Christmas 'must' there always had to be annuals. I've still got them piled away now. All the *Charles Buchan's Football Annuals* I've saved for when I had grandsons, and Josephine's ballet books have been kept for my grand-daughters.

As Michael grew into his teens there began one annual characteristic struggle. This was on Good Friday, when for a long time we used to go to church for the three o'clock Stations of the Cross. But three o'clock was the time when County were playing. 'Do I have to go to church, Mum . . .?' – it was the usual struggle. But altogether he took a lot of religion, and he must have paid a lot of attention at some time, because one of his first impersonations, done without any great preliminary announcement, was of the parish priest delivering his sermon. The carved pulpit at church had ornamental holes in it, and Father Doyle had a habit of getting his foot through one of

68

these openings almost unconsciously in the middle of his address, and waggling it about. On one occasion when Michael was only seven or eight, he was suddenly standing on a chair without warning, with his foot lodged through the back of it, and he didn't only get the waggling right, he was very authentic on the words as well! Even at that age it was remarkable how successfully he changed his face for these character studies, although, of course his features were not so mobile as they are today.

He was fun to have as a child. He was imaginative and sensitive, and he could generally make you laugh. As for his sensitivity, it was sometimes a bit too much for his sister Josephine. He was about 12 when Josie took him one afternoon to the local pictures to see a Lassie film. He has always loved dogs, and he used to follow the Lassie films and be very affected by the sad bits. At tea-time Josie stormed back and said 'Don't ask me to take him to the pictures any more. I'm ashamed of him. He's cried and sobbed his way all through that picture.' The poor boy was still looking rather sad. 'Never mind, love,' I said, 'it's only a film, it's a story.' 'But . . .' he blubbered, and he told me all about the sad sequences in the film, and he had to start sobbing all over again.

OUT INTO THE WORLD

He was sensitive and he was shy, and yet he was always a leader. He was the one who organised the children's games and the football teams. He was the one who began to be the fun-making star of our home jollifications around the piano, although he didn't have the patience to learn the piano properly. But if there is any one mental picture of those happy boyhood days which stays in the memory of his father and myself, it is the memory of him running on to the ground for football at Stockport County, with a little red nose and a little red hat. He always wore a red peaked school cap. That was a picture that came back to Wilf only recently, at the County ground. For Michael has now been made an honorary vice-president of the club, and now he takes his father to see the matches from the directors' box. Wilf said the picture came back to him, the little red-capped schoolboy so full of enthusiasm who used to trot along to the popular side in all the fog and the rain.

The time came to hang up his red hat. Michael left school, and we didn't really know what to do with him. True to his nature, he gave us a good laugh about that milestone. We live in industrial Cheshire, and near us there is a big steel works, a foundry. The headmaster called the group of boys who were leaving—including Michael—and gave them a serious and possibly slightly pompous lecture about the new attitudes they must adopt, now that they were going out into the world. Michael came home and gave us an uproarious caricature of it. 'Going out into the world!' he said. 'Almost everybody but me was going to leave school and walk across the road to go to a job in the steel works. "Out into the world" is ten minutes away.'

It was certain that a steel foundry was not where Michael would end up, or even start. He was not only impractical with his hands, he was downright unwilling to use them. The only thing we could ever get him to do in the garden was have a snap taken there with the dog or the cat, it was no good asking him to cut the grass or anything. We recognised this, and his Pop said to him 'Whatever you do for work, you'd better not take your coat off if you can help it.' That was all right for indicating what he shouldn't do, but it still didn't show us what he should.

His schoolmasters weren't very forthcoming with suggestions. His final report said he was well-mannered and pleasant, very interested in sport, but not very hopeful academically. I don't think they were very perceptive in this. He was never in the top

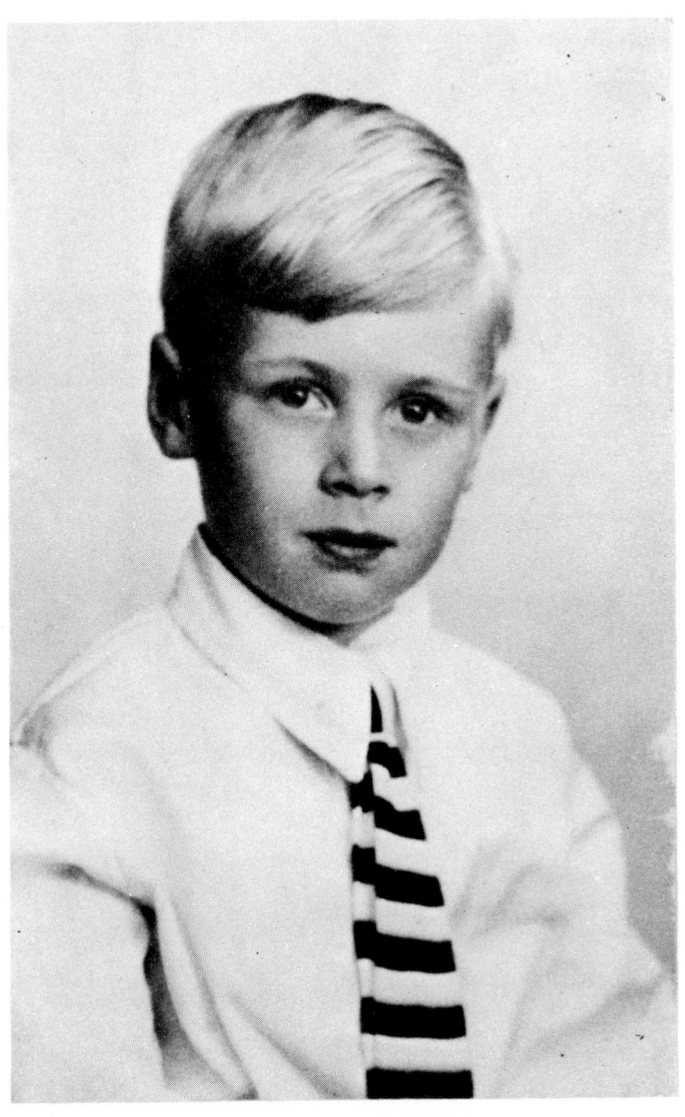

Mike Yarwood photographed on the day of his first Communion. Mike's Mum (Mrs Bridget Yarwood) recalls that, 'He looked so solemn for an eight year old!'

Master Mike Yarwood, aged nine, with older sister, Josephine.

half of the class over exams and marks, but he did have talent. He himself particularly wanted to be a journalist, but they solidly discouraged him in this. They said he hadn't the qualifications. And when he tried to get a job as a copy boy on the *Stockport Express* he had no school references that would back him up.

I know they were mistaken in this. I knew then that he could and would write for hours and hours. He would go to a County match and then come back and go up to his room, and settle down to write a full report on the match. He had a very good turn of phrase in sporting reporting, and I believe he was doing it then as well as many professionals. He also had a gift for what they call sub-editing. He would write very witty headline captions, for instance to every picture in the photograph album, and that perception and turn of phrase is really what he is using in his career today. I've still got all his writing in that back bedroom, and sometimes when his children come to see me, or my other grandchildren from Josephine, I get these things out and look at all the reporting accounts, and the jokes in the dog-eared snap albums—summing up friends, joking about pictures, pulling his father's leg—and I show the children these living relics of days not so long ago.

SIGN PLEASE

He also had one funny habit which, I have often thought since, might have provided a clue to the future. Whenever he doodled, he was always writing his signature. You can see versions of his signature on every scrap of paper. I used to say 'Michael, it's a sign of someone who's illiterate to be constantly signing your name.' Neither of us could see then how many times he has done it since he has been an entertainer. So perhaps he was sub-consciously preparing himself for all those autographs even then.

Anyway, here he was aged 15½ and in need of a job. Which meant that either his father or myself had to find it, because he was so shy then that he would never even go into a shop alone, let alone apply for a job. I did think that he ought to go to Manchester and get something of the experience of a big city. We were living about ten miles from Stockport, and I thought he should get out of our little district and let something from the town rub off on him. I even thought the travelling would be good for him, which is not exactly a widely held view nowadays when everybody pours scorn on the idea of commuting. So Michael was to catch an eight-thirty train every day. And he

73

did catch it, too, with remarkable diligence, even though he never got out of bed till the last moment. He would sweep into the kitchen and out again with a sup of tea in his mouth and a piece of toast in his hand—but he never lost that train. I started him in work by taking him to a mail-order firm in Manchester and 'selling' him on the strength of his school report. The headmaster hadn't said he was academically clever, but he did say that the boy was intelligent in expression, honest, punctual—and if his interests did lie somewhat more in the sporting field his character was such that he would be conscientious at anything he took on. Mike was enrolled as office junior.

A TIME OF TRIAL

Two years later he was politely asked to leave. He took the dismissal hard—he'd been doing impersonations of the boss at an ill-chosen time—but he was always over-sensitive about interpreting a change as a disgrace. And I didn't mind. To me it merely meant that he was coming up to senior status and they didn't want to pay a senior's wage. There was always another job to be found. (You could truthfully say that to the young generation of Michael's age, though it wouldn't have been possible when Wilf and I were at that age.) So he took a job with a small wholesale clothier, again in Manchester.

His ambition then, since he had been turned down from writing, was to be a professional footballer. He was serious enough about it to write off to a number of football clubs asking for a trial. Stockport County didn't even answer his letter, but I think he has since forgiven them for that. Oldham Athletic said they would give him a trial. He was scared stiff, which was not unusual, and wanted his father to go along with him, but this was impossible because of work. He played the trial. The club told him to go home, keep on training, and put some weight

On holiday in the early 1950s: (left to right) Mike,
Mike's Aunt Anna, Mum, and sister Josephine.
Formative years playing in the resorts of North Wales.

on. It wasn't a rejection, and the last piece of advice was very
sound, because he was such a slim fellow when he was young.
His father thinks he might well have made some headway if he
had gone in for football, but that is not how things turned out.
He has certainly maintained his conception of the glamour in
the game. He is still starry-eyed if he meets a footballer,
though nowadays it is more often the footballers who come
backstage to meet him after the show. But still, nowadays football is as much show business as Michael's line is, that is how it
appears to me.

With his sense of leadership which is always paradoxical in
his character he ran a scratch football team which he gave some
throwaway title to, like the Broadway Rovers or something
like that. But this enterprise was succeeded by another activity
He formed a group and called it the Drum Beats. Michael

always jokes now that they were so bad that they had to change their name every week in order to get a fresh engagement—because nobody ever wanted a return fixture. I don't deny they were bad. I know, because they used to practice in our front room and we could hardly stand the racket from the kitchen. But they did keep to their name, because Michael had some cards printed and I've still got the cards: THE DRUM BEATS, Mike Yarwood, and our telephone number.

That must have been the first time Michael used his professional name. They used to have a pianist and a boy with a guitar and Michael on the drums: not big drums, but something I think is called a high hat with cymbals and a bit of percussion. Once they had a booking at a pub near Stockport, and I nearly passed out picturing my son in this pub. Wilf and I used to take a drink in there occasionally, mind you, but I thought our boy was rather too young for this sort of thing. Anyway, they had a few engagements. I think Michael began to get the feel of an audience from that experience. And gradually I realised that he was beginning to do one certain thing on his own. He was actually singing, and he got the courage to do it by making it an imitation of Elvis Presley or Billy Fury.

He was also beginning to take a very perceptive interest in theatrical expression. As far as that concerned me, it meant Blackpool and television. The first holiday our family took after both children had left school was at Blackpool. Michael was at a bit of a loose end there, because Josephine had a boy friend, and a courting couple is never very sociable towards the odd man out. So Michael did the Blackpool shows, and one or two of them he went to over and over again. They were Al Read and also Ken Dodd, who in 1961 was just blossoming at that particular time. After that summer the children drifted off to take holidays on their own. And because I was the sort of person whose life was centred on her kids, Wilf and I used not to bother with set holidays since the children didn't want to come with us.

A young performer at the start of the road to success . . .

But when Michael was 19 I suggested to him that I might get a holiday flat in St Annes for a spell, and I asked whether, if I did that, he would care to come along, have a change, go out for a drink with his Pop, and generally make a holiday of it.

Michael, who had previously been off with a friend to places like the Isle of Man, said 'Yes'—to my great surprise but also to my relief, because I wouldn't have left him at home: he wouldn't eat a bite, he wouldn't put the kettle on the cooker, domestically he was pretty useless.

So we went to Blackpool. And he saw every show in the place, all the theatres and all the piers. I suddenly realised that this was more than just passing the time when Michael persuaded us, after seeing Bruce Forsyth at a matinée, to wait outside the theatre and see Bruce come out. It was a completely futile wait, because Bruce didn't come out. As Michael himself realised when it came to be his lot to play the North Pier Blackpool, it is fairly impractical to take a breather between shows because it is impossible to nip round the back óf anything, you have got to come out at the front into the crowds, and that is not generally what an actor wants at that time of day.

FASCINATION

But I was beginning to appreciate Michael's fascination with theatres and shows and comedians—and impressionists: the other Blackpool show to which he paid particular attention was Peter Goodwright. I could see this now in his absorption with television. There was a long period in his late teens when he would stay in every night, simply watching television and—of all things—eating sweets which he used to buy by the half-pound. (He didn't begin to smoke until quite late, and then the sweets disappeared—and also, temporarily, that fine weighty figure he was building up for Oldham Athletic, as if he ever remembered.)

It was not only theatre and comedy he would look at on the television. He would listen very keenly to politicians and debates. It was not entirely surprising, because Wilf and I had that interest in politics, but we were a different generation. Michael's interest also certainly seemed there, though I presumed that his knowledge was limited. And that's an assumption I'm not so sure of today, but we didn't know then because he didn't discuss things with us. He was in that withdrawn stage that many young men go through.

Looking back, it's easier to see the way in which he was going during this time of trial. But we couldn't see it, it never entered our head, even though he amused us so much within the family. We had parties when the children were allowed to stay up. I was a very 'Truby King' mother and I had very certain ideas of their having to go to bed in their age-group, but of course by this time a party was a party and fixed bed-times had gone by the board. It was in this period that Josephine had her 21st birthday party. She had two or three parties really, a family 21st and a teenager 21st and a lot of fun all round. Her party in our house would have fallen flat without Michael. He had everybody in stitches the whole night through and into the morning. He was at the piano for much of the night, doing all the flourishes, doing the Russ Conway tricks or the other styles of the day, just being very funny and making the party go. And, as he would have his Concert Chairman say in the marvellous act he does now, it was all good stuff and no rubbish.

It was when it came to Michael's 21st birthday that I as a mother realised with a blinding awareness that we had reached the crossroads of his career, although the situation was one which my son had been quietly wrestling with for some weeks before. If I tell the story in some detail it may give some picture of our family relationship, besides giving a reminder of how suddenly frustration can blow up into a crisis, and the crisis be cleared with speed and finality. It amuses me now to think that it all came to a head over a detached collar.

It was between Easter and midsummer 1962. The situation was that Michael had a girl friend who had really been rather wished on him as though by a marriage broker. He was not really happy at his work in Manchester, in part because although he was trained as a salesman-representative he was

79

not yet going out on the road for the simple reason that he hadn't passed his driving test. This probably affected his money, which was not too good, and in order to supplement it he had taken a Saturday job selling raincoats in a store in Market Street, Manchester. As far as the rest of his life was concerned, the group he had run was practically moribund, but in order to do a bit of entertaining he had developed his patter into something approaching a solo act. And he had, on a sort of old boys' network, been booked in on a quite unprofessional basis to do a turn the previous Sunday at the social club run by Mirrlees, the engineering company where my husband Wilf was working.

He was as fashion-conscious as any youngster. On the Friday night when he came home from the week at the clothing company and had to do his extra day at the raincoat shop, he produced a new shirt with a detached collar. The manager of the shop always wore a detached collar, and Michael thought it would be a good trendy idea to follow him.

Immediately I saw that collar I got a well-founded premonition of panic. I had seen my own father having hysterics through trying to keep the collar on the back-stud while he fastened the front. And knowing how hopeless Michael was with his hands, I feared the worst. So as we were finishing our evening meal I said: 'Michael, I suggest you go upstairs now and fix this collar and shirt for the morning, because you know the sort of panic you're in in the morning.' It was normal for him to fly down the stairs and gulp his tea and snatch his toast to take with him to the station, but I didn't really see this happening when there was a recalcitrant collar still springing straight off the back of his neck, and a disaster then would have spoiled his small but important record of never having been either late or absent from work since he started employment.

He agreed to do this, get his shirt and collar in order for the morning. He went upstairs, and very soon I knew the sparks were flying. The principal and unescapable reason was that there wasn't a backstud in the house and the shops were shut. I said I would get over that difficulty by sewing a tiny button on the back of the neckband, and letting him take it from there. So I put on this button and left him to it, and the fireworks increased. I thought 'Any moment now, he'll open the window and pitch the shirt out into the back,' because that's what I knew my father had done on occasions and there was the same spirit in me from time to time. What happened was more costly. I suddenly heard him go into the bathroom and rip the shirt into pieces and carry on with a fine old paddy of rage and frustration, an almost childish turn which I had never seen for years.

I thought to myself 'What do I do?' and I decided to do nothing. 'I'll let him get on with it,' I told myself, 'there's something inside that's got to come out.'

After a while he simmered down and went back to his room, and I called him. I said 'Sit down, love. What's it all about? What's happening?'

'Why are you in such a state?'

'Oh, Mum,' he said, 'everything's wrong.'

I thought it was the girl friend, and I mentioned her. We had a little talk about that, and he did say that he thought he was being pressured into taking it farther than he wanted. She was a very sweet girl, but there was influence from my family, and if the lead didn't come from him it was not really an ideal situation.

'That's no problem, love,' I told him. 'All you've got to do is to be honest about it. What else is the matter? Is it your job?

'I know you don't like your job, but that can be arranged. Get your holidays first.' (I was a very practical person.) 'Get your holidays first and then we can soon find something. Have a fortnight off, or longer if we can manage it, have a look around and you'll see something else you might like.'

81

He said 'That's not really what's getting me down. I have a lot of fun at work. I admit I'm not out on the road yet, but . . .'

'Well, what else is it for heaven's sake?' I asked.

He said 'It was last Sunday.'

I didn't know what he was talking about. He told me. The previous Sunday had been the day he had been asked to do his act at the Mirrlees Social Club. We had made it a bit of a family occasion. Wilf and I didn't go, but we baby-sat for my daughter Josephine and she took some friends along to the club with her. But Michael knew that when he did his act he was only playing to his immediate friends. The rest of the people sat round yapping without taking a blind bit of notice, and that had been what really affected Michael. It was about the first time he had done a turn in public. 'It flopped,' he said, 'and that's what it's really all about.'

'Oh, *that!*' I said. 'That's the least of your worries. Just find something that you like. It doesn't matter what it is, just feel your way around.'

'But *this* is what I want to do, Mum,' he said. 'This is it. This is what's frustrating me.'

'Well, love, you'll have to forget about that,' I said. 'You'd be hopeless at *that*.'

Looking back now at that casual brush-off by an uncomprehending mother of a son's carefully cherished ambition, I'm sometimes surprised that he didn't take an axe to me! Instead, he explained to me very simply and patiently that it was his ambition to go on the stage, as we called it.

And from then on, I at least took some notice. I gave due respect to his ideas. I thought the stage was a shocking place, a sort of lower shelf in Hell peopled by irresponsible Bohemians who would contaminate my Michael. But I did not try to scotch the idea or make any effort with women's tricks to ensure that it would never approach anything practical. Both his father and I thought that this ambition could not possibly

82

And Mike Yarwood remembers that he could have been asking Brian Clough for a job rather than impersonating him!

come to anything, because although we recognised his brilliant talent for impressions, we did not see how he could ever overcome his shyness. When it was almost an effort of will for him to go into a shop on his own to buy underwear, we thought 'How can he possibly make it in show business, walking on a stage to face hundreds of people?'

But we never rejected him, or scorned his ambition. I did try, out of consideration for him, to prepare him—not for failure, but certainly not instant success. 'It's so remote,' I told him, 'the idea that you can make it.' I had in mind that he would need years at drama school or other training, rather than plunge straight into the business. The truth was to be that one year after that unforgettable evening he was earning his living as an entertainer.

But even with that time-table, nothing notable happened for the first nine months, though Michael worked by himself in his free moments, developing an act. In March 1963 my husband Wilf came home from work one evening and told Michael that he was to appear in a talent contest in a pub at Dukinfield *that night*. So, although Michael had for long been saying that he ought to start in talent contests, it was his father who threw him in at the deep end finally. Michael got on the telephone to whip up a team of supporters, and they went out to the Albion at Dukinfield. He didn't win a prize, he came third, but the prize-money didn't stretch that far. The winners were Ken Goodwin and a singer called Eli Bond who is now singing as Don Bailey. But he got sufficient encouragement to enter the contest again the following week. This time he came second, and won twelve shillings and sixpence. But other pub owners were scouting for talent there, and the man who ran the Salvage Hotel at Collyhurst came up to Michael and offered him two nights the next week at thirty shillings a night. Michael was so astounded to be offered money for what he liked doing that he said he wasn't worth it, and suggested he should work for a pound a night. From then on the engagements began to flow in, and within a few weeks the day came when Michael came to me for his crucial consultation on his career.

JACKING IT IN

He told me that he had got his first opportunity of a full week's work at a club for £13 the week. He said 'Mother, do you think I could jack this job in and take a chance?' I said 'Most certainly. You can always pick up a nine-to-five job again.' I always made it clear to him that real success might never

The Queen Mother and two crown court-jesters
extraordinaire—Mr Mike Yarwood and Mr Ken Dodd.

happen, but I never used any influence to discourage him. I said 'You've nothing to lose. You're 22, and you're trained to be a rep, even if you're not going out on your own yet' (because he still hadn't passed his driving test). I said 'If it falls flat, you can always go back again.' But, of course, he hasn't been back.

At this point Michael was getting tremendous support from two very good friends he had made. Wilf Fielding, who was a few years older, was a businessman for eight hours every day and a show business devotee for the other sixteen—and he was active for most of those sixteen, I gathered from the late hours they used to keep after the club dates. Wilf Fielding always said he was most struck by Michael's confidence, youth and en-

85

thusiasm, though perhaps the confidence dissolved just before Mike's entry, and Wilf had to heave him on to the stage. Wilf was a most unselfish aide to Michael, and besides helping him to develop his act he used to chauffeur him around to all his engagements.

The other firm friend was Roy Mayoh, a charming young man who still gets in touch with my husband and myself from time to time, ringing us up to say he's seen Michael's show and it was lovely. Roy was then busy in Manchester writing comedy scripts for the BBC and working as a camerman for ABC Television, but he devoted enormous care to grooming Michael. He used to be stamping around getting Michael's delivery right, because he had the eye from working on the other side of the camera.

I think Roy was most impressed at first with the originality of Michael's work. Although his impersonations included the expected comedians, he was already introducing political figures and celebrities like Mr Macmillan and Lord Boothby into his act. Roy started by insisting on microphone drill for Michael. He would always be turning up at our house with a Ewbank carpet cleaner which he stood upright in the middle of the floor, and that was the microphone Michael had to play to.

ORDEAL BY EWBANK

I never seemed to get rid of that Ewbank for months, but it didn't work, it was only a dummy microphone. Roy would turn up at our house at all hours because he himself had irregular hours at the studio. The place was a shambles. We only live in a tiny semi, but the sitting room at the front was exclusively Michael's from the time he started his career all the way up to the time of his marriage. The telephone was there,

86

and all the rehearsing went on there. Roy would come, and put Michael through his act one way, and then another, try this and that, call me into the room and ask my advice. He called me in one time, and when I went in I saw that he had one trouser-leg hoisted very high, so that the turn-up was round his thigh. 'What do you think of this, Mrs Yarwood?' he asked. 'Would it look funny if Mike came on the stage doing something like that, just standing there and making no reference to it?' I said 'I don't think it's funny at all. Michael's not the clown type, he's not Ken Dodd.' 'Ah,' said Roy, 'I don't want him to look down and giggle at his bare leg. I want him to go right through the act as if he wasn't aware of it at all. Then it would be really funny. You see, Mike's trouble at the moment is that he puts on a funny hat for an impression, and then he can't leave it alone. He's always touching it and adjusting it. Now that destroys the impact, when he's always drawing attention to it. I'm trying to show him that he should have the courage of his comic convictions and rely on the original impact. If he could come on with one short leg and one long leg, and do his whole act and then walk off without letting on that he knew he was a yard of trousers short — then that would be fantastic.'

'Well, Roy,' I said, 'you know much more about show business than I do, but I sometimes wish you'd leave our poor kid alone, driving him on like this.'

'I'm not driving him on, I'm building him up,' laughed Roy, and of course he was right. Roy had this terrific enthusiasm for comedy, and naturally Michael was responding with enormous drive. Roy always praised him for the amount of work he would put in, rehearsing over and over again by himself an effect that Roy had suggested he should try for. Wilf Fielding recently reminded me of Michael's tremendous capacity for work, saying that he was never frightened of trying something new although he was a nervous person. Early in that first summer he got a return engagement at the College Club in Manchester,

87

'Well, Mike, I'm really proud of ye', said Baron 'Vic'
Feather of the City of Bradford, 'you'll not be out of a
job if you keep doing me!'

where he had appeared some five weeks before. At the band call
the manager said they had heard all this material before.
Michael and Wilf came home to Sunday dinner, and they sat
in the garden in the afternoon while Michael re-wrote the
whole script. And he went on that evening with a completely
new act. Incidentally, it was then that he began to bring in
Harold Wilson.

Roy came into the kitchen from the front room one day and
told us: 'He's got great potential, that boy. I'm not going to
stop until he makes the London Palladium.' We thought he
must be mad to say that, kidding poor Michael along. We
thought 'Michael's going to get hurt.' Because at that time we
knew—Michael being as honest as he is—that although he was
playing perhaps tuppenny-ha'penny clubs which shouldn't

have been too great an ordeal, as often as not he was being physically sick in the wings before he went on.

Roy didn't mind about that at all. He used to say 'It's because he's nervous that he has this great capability for concentration. The general idea of a comic is of some brash and cheeky chap who goes on stage and really has a ball for his own enjoyment. I sometimes wish Mike would loosen up, not worry before he goes on, not concentrate on being word-perfect. But I know that it is that single-mindedness that produces his tremendous discipline. When he's on stage he's not having fun — he's out there working, and for the moment I'm content with that.'

Wilf Fielding used to praise this concentration. 'He's got this marvellous attention to detail,' he said. 'He takes a mannerism and just fractionally exaggerates it, he's getting this fine detail uncannily, almost unconsciously, and his great merit over it all is that he's doing subjects that nobody has ever thought of up until now.'

STILL A LONG HAUL

Looking back now, I appreciate that it still had to be a long haul, even with all the help that Roy was giving him. Michael had the talent, but it takes years to put the professionalism in, and that smooth working has come only over the last few years. You can't become a star overnight unless you're a pop singer.

At some of his big club and cabaret engagements nowadays Michael stays on the stage sometimes for as long as an hour and a half. That's an exercise in endurance which calls for stamina. It has changed the rhythm of his life, of course. Afterwards he needs a lot of time to wind down. During the daytime he can be at his lowest ebb, but after midnight he's alive. That was a pattern which we ourselves took a lot of getting used to in the early days. When he first went to the clubs, Pop would be coming downstairs to go to work as Michael was going upstairs to bed. Then while he was in bed I would attend to all his phone calls. Father used to attend to his money and between us we'd handle most of his business until he got married. He has never been very practical about that side. He had a good accountant, but he never knew how much money he had.

He was always very considerate, sharing all the joys and trials of his career with us, ringing us up immediately after a big engagement to tell us how it went. It's a soft thing to say, but if a mother can't say it who can?—I've often said to Wilf 'We've been blest, absolutely blest, in our children,' and I know it.

He got his first breakthrough engagement when Roy introduced him to ABC Television and he was given a warm-up job to do an act in front of the audience before the transmission of a programme called *Comedy Bandbox*, to get them loosened up and in a good mood for the actual show. We knew that it was really a sort of audition, and we had high hopes from it. He rang me afterwards from the studios and said 'Sorry, Mother, nothing came of it.' I said 'Never mind, love, there'll be another time.' He said 'I'm only kidding, I've got a live spot, next week!' 'Oh, isn't that *marvellous*!' I said. He said 'We're going on now somewhere for a meal,' because he could never eat a bite before a show, 'and I expect there'll be some sort of celebration, so don't wait up for me.' But before we went to bed, I got the biggest piece of cardboard I could find, and I wrote 'CONGRATU-LATIONS!' on it, and put it on his pillow with 'Goodnight, God bless, Mom.' That was his first big break in getting onto the box.

Later, even when he had a big prestige engagement like a Royal Performance, he would telephone me while the show was still on, to tell me how it had gone. I could hear the show and the laughter coming through the speaker in the dressing room where he was phoning. I used to say how lovely it was that he would think of me at such a time. Pride, pride, I couldn't say how many times I've been overcome because I've been so proud of him.

I suppose today he is what is called a celebrity, and in a curious way has rounded off another full circle in his life. In the early days of the old *What's My Line?* programme we did not have a television set, though Michael always wanted one. He used to go across to an auntie's to watch this programme on a Sunday night. He used to grumble good-naturedly because everybody was always saying 'Shhh!' to him. 'You're not allowed to breathe there while the programme is on,' he used to say. He was always intensely interested to know who the weekly celebrity would be. Well, fairly recently, on the new *What's My Line?* he himself was the celebrity. He telephoned me afterwards and said there was really something marvellous about that, because these little highlights of life mean a lot to him. 'It took me back to the time when I used to go over to Auntie's,' he said. 'And to think that, some 16 years later, the celebrity is me!'

ENTER SANDY

In the autumn of 1968 Michael met a dancer called Sandra Burville, and very soon we knew he was serious. I reacted exactly as you would expect a fussy, over-protective mother to do. I thought 'I'm sure he's too good for her, and she must be interfering with his career.' So Michael said he would bring her for Christmas—he was really being put through the hoop, because he was trying to be loyal to both sides. I, being nasty, said she ought to be spending Christmas with her parents, who live in Brighton, and anyway she would have to stay in a hotel because I couldn't put her up, which wasn't being exactly helpful. They arrived, she driving Michael's Daimler. She gave me her big smile, which I've rarely seen her without since. She

Mr and Mrs, now!

knew what was going on, because it all came out, we don't say anything in our family that we don't say openly. She went back on Boxing Morning, and I said she was lovely. She was so sweet, very glamorous, and always wanting to help. And she has never changed. It was almost a year before they were married, and until the wedding she was a bit cautious of me. But she has realised now that I love her as much as I love Michael. She is so good for him, a perfect mother now to their two little daughters, and a most understanding wife in the domestically difficult world of show business.

It was a big wedding at the Church of St Thomas More in Swiss Cottage, London. The only sad thing about it was that my daughter Josephine couldn't go because her baby was a week overdue. They had put the date of the wedding back for her to try and catch it, but they couldn't alter it again because of

*On the Wedding day of Miss Sandra Burville and
Mr Michael Yarwood . . .*

Michael's professional engagements. There were lots of people from the entertainment world there, and the reception was very grand with a toastmaster and unending supplies of champers—but it was no serious sit-down knife-and-fork do like you'd get in a Northern wedding!

After his marriage I missed, of course the immediate telephone calls from a first night at the Palladium or the opening of a seaside season, because there was now a new focus in his life. But he is still unique in sensitivity and affection for his family and his parents. He is tolerant when he is being debunked—his Pop can send him up, call him a third-rate comic or much worse, and he loves it. When Michael first got established and used to buy mohair suits, his father called him Tinsel. 'Here comes Tinsel,' he used to say, and the boy would laugh as loud himself. The other day they were having a drink in a country pub, and Pop was smoking a cigar. 'Sometimes, Dad,' said Michael, 'I think I'll pack it all in.' 'Never do that,' said Wilf, 'I'm not going back to the old life.' And they fell about laughing.

My little semi that was his home for so long is crammed with mementoes and photographs and trophies. But Michael does take his toll of us, or rather of his father. He keeps on losing the pipes he uses for his Harold Wilson impersonation—for he normally only smokes cigarettes himself—and at the last moment he has to borrow a pipe from his father. So he leaves that one in the dressing room, too, and moves on. At the moment Pop is mourning a very nice Dunhill, the best pipe, he says, that he ever had! Those are the occasions when he is slower to agree that we are blest in our son!

Unfortunately I have seen Michael perform on the stage only twice in my life. I have become an increasingly bad traveller, and suffer from a sort of claustrophobia which makes me very uneasy in crowded places like the threatre: I cannot even attend church except to go in alone for a quiet prayer. But recently, in 1973, when Michael had a season at the ABC

Blackpool, he picked a quiet part of the theatre—first-house shows on Friday are usually pretty quiet—and took rooms for all the family in his hotel. And in the company of all my relatives I watched the whole of Michael's show. I thought he was marvellous. I said to myself 'I don't care now if I die tomorrow!'

But, of course, I do watch everything he does on television. And if there is someone at the door, or the telephone rings, I continue watching and won't get up! I yield to no one when Michael is on the screen.

On the sea-wall at Abergele in 1954. (Left to right) A friend, Mrs Bridget Yarwood (Mike's mum), and Mike himself, aged thirteen.

95

'Edward Heath, Esq.'

3. Stories of My Life...

WELL, FOLLOW THAT! as they say in show business. I knew it was fatal to share the bill with a child or an animal, but I thought it was all right with your mother! However, I'm not going to ridicule her, because she's dear to me. Nor censor her, because I believe in free speech. But you won't really believe I'm quite the angel she describes will you?

DAYDREAMS AND ACTION

The theatre always meant a great deal to me as a child, but only in a dream world which I never thought I should enter. My mother used to take us to the Theatre Royal in Stockport, or the Hippodrome on Ardwick Green, where we saw what I suppose was the last of the real music hall—Issy Bonn, Jewell and Warriss, Billy Cotton. And we went to the great specatcular pantomimes in the middle of Manchester. And even as a child it was so appealing to me, to see those crimson curtains part and the batteries of lights come on. When the orchestra started the overture I felt tremendous excitement, sitting tense on the edge of my seat. I recognised the urge. I knew that I'd love to have been up there on the stage. But I thought it all bore no relation to my real life. I was never a child performer, not one of those kids who spent much of their holidays going in for talent competitions. I knew all my life that what I should like to do was to be an entertainer. But I didn't really believe that would be any good at show business. I just looked at it from afar and thought 'Well, it would be nice, but it will never happen to me, I know that.'

But, because I was always fooling, I very occasionally allowed myself a taste of honey. I can remember the local kids urging me to give them a show when I was five or six. So I climbed on top of the roof of the air raid shelter in the garden and did my funny sketch. I remember lots of applause from my mates. Possibly it gave me the beginnings of an addiction. But I was really far more concerned with sport, particularly football, as my schoolteachers regretfully noted. I was avid both as a player and a supporter. My club was of course Stockport County, and I had been a regular fan of them since I was eight. I don't think I was developing into a football holligan on today's model, though I was once thrown backwards over the barrier at Edgeley Park by a stalwart policeman. It was soon after I left school, in 1958, when our Lillywhites of Stockport had beaten first division Luton Town 3-0 in the third round of the F.A. Cup. (Are you listening, Eric Morecambe?— Stockport 3, Luton 0!) With a few hundred others I went over the top to congratulate my heroes: and I zoomed back fast. And it doesn't seem long now since I was a kid, taking the bus ride to the ground on Saturday afternoons. I was always soccer daft. My Dad used to take me to Edgeley Park from the

98

moment I could see over the fence round the pitch. I remember I used to cry to go home after half time when the brass band stopped playing. I only enjoyed the band, because I could hardly see what was going on during the match. Now they have made me an honorary Vice President of the club, and I see it all from the directors' box. I won't say that I wasn't happier on the popular side.

So at school, sport got more emphasis than entertainment and it's possible that both got more emphasis than work. I did do one public entertainment at school—'Albert and the Lion', without uttering a sound. One of the masters was offstage reciting the piece through a microphone, and I mimed to it, going to the zoo and being swallowed up by the lion. I rather liked the applause I got for that. For the rest of the time I expressed myself by mimicking the teachers, for we didn't have a lot of school concerts. Possibly they thought there was enough entertainment provided by me during the terms. The teachers were well aware that I did impressions of them, and on my very last day I was nobbled by one of them and taken to the library. All of the staff were sitting there. 'Right,' said the headmaster. 'We know that you're doing us. Now let's see exactly what you do.' I was not keen to give this performance at all. But I was leaving school, I couldn't be expelled or given 100 lines. So I did my act. Everyone fell about laughing except one teacher at a time. He was always the teacher I was taking off at the moment. I have since found that life is often like that.

They didn't send me away from school with the grandest of references. Apart from wanting to be a professional footballer, which I didn't expect them to take seriously, I had a realistic ambition to be a journalist. I did not have a GCE in English, and the headmaster said 'You haven't got the qualifications, so don't pursue it. Be a salesman, or something like that, because you've got the gift of the gab.' It happened that English was about the only subject I was reasonable at, and privately I was

99

always writing. I just used to love writing descriptions and reports. I've got a slight chip on my shoulder about secondary modern education for not even seeing, let alone not bothering about, the only scholastic subject I was fair at. After this command performance on the last day at school a teacher said to me: 'If your observation of various subjects had been as good as your observation of the teachers you would have been a very good scholar.' But *observation* is almost the main requirement of a journalist, and I consider it was snide of him to turn the criticism against me without also including the school, which might have done something to notice and encourage this gift of observation.

WORKERS' PLAYTIME

The incredible thing is that since I have been in show business I have achieved two of my boyhood ambitions, and done that only because I was in show business. I have written my own column in a newspaper. When I have been on summer seasons in Blackpool and Bournemouth I have been engaged quite often to write my show-biz chat column, which has been more than a flash in the pan since it has had to go on for some months. And I have actually read my column in the newspaper printed exactly as I wrote it, which professional journalists tell me is a bit of a miracle, since there are usually a few sub-editors bursting to twist it into different English. I have also gone a little way towards professional football, at least to the extent that I have played in the same match with my old idol Tom Finney. I admit it was a charity match, and Tom had retired by then, but it still meant an awful lot to me. And I couldn't have reached either peak without the jumping-off platform of show business.

Anyway, Yarwood left school and went to work. I was given

a job in a mail order firm in Manchester. But I was moved from department to department for continually entertaining the staff and not getting on with the job. The boss there, the manager of the warehouse, had a particular walk which it took me some little time and skill to copy. He had steel tips on the ends of his shoes and it was quite tricky getting the sound right. Once I had it, I used to reproduce this walk going up and down the corridors, and put the wind up the workers who thought the boss was arriving. Eventually people got wise to this trick, and they would say 'It's not him, it must be that young Yarwood fellow.' The day came when there was a double bluff on this 'crying wolf' assumption, and the chaps continued larking around when the person who opened the door was not young Yarwood, but the boss himself. For some reason it fell to me to carry the can for this unfortunate episode. He got to know during the inquest that I was doing this walk of his and he he used it as a motive for another sudden death. 'We're not getting on very well, are we?' he said to me. 'I think we had better leave, don't you? I think we had better leave a week on Friday.'

I didn't take this suggestion well at all. I was not a terribly brash character, and the dismissal seemed like disgrace for me. I always had a deep fear of being sacked from a job.

Then I moved to a small family business in the wholesale clothing trade. The same sort of thing was going on there. I was really only kept on because I used to amuse the customers. I should have been an outside rep, but I kept failing my driving test. So I had to stay in the warehouse and sell to the customers who came in.

Outside working hours I was pursuing my most impractical ambition by writing off to all the northern clubs to ask for a trial as a professional footballer. I actually got a chance with Oldham Athletic, but Stockport County ignored me. Then I got involved with a group. I set out to play the drums. I only ever had one lesson. The moment the drum tutor said I would have to learn to read music I knew that the game was up. I have always been terribly impatient, and a long course of music study was just not on. As far as the people who booked us were concerned, a long course of our rock 'n' roll group was not on either. We had to keep changing the name of the group in order to get any return bookings. I really enjoyed playing those drums, but they gave me a terrible headaches. Curiously they did the same for my mother, and she only had to listen to rehearsals from the next room. I also have a suspicion that the same symptom was experienced by our audiences.

I packed in the drums, and was soon singing and playing guitar with the group. To vary the vocals I used to take turns, singing in the style of Elvis Presley or Cliff Richard or Adam Faith. On one occasion when we were appearing at a club, I had just done my best with one song and was preparing to sing another, when I heard a great shout of 'That's enough rubbish! Get off!!'—and the microphone was whipped away from me by an angry chairman who was pointing off stage in a manner that couldn't have been more dramatic if I had done something serious to his daughter. Years later I was asked to go back to the same club for a charity do. I found the same chairman was still there. This time he introduced me to the audience with a great build-up culminating in the usual fanfare of 'and here is the star' (which I certainly was not) '—Mike Yarwood!' I felt like turning round and telling him he had chucked me off the last time we met and I didn't feel much more kindly to him now. But it was for charity, and the audience hadn't come to see a punch-up over hurt pride, so I grinned and bore it.

Please note that I make no great claims for my singing voice, only that it's just about average for a comedian. Even if I could never achieve it, I always knew how I wanted to sing, and that was like Perry Como. In my youth I was a tremendous fan of his, always have been really, and when I sing now I try to take the best of his style. One of my youthful daydreams used to be how fantastic it would be to appear on his show—I don't mean as a singer but as an entertainer. You do dream of things like that. This fantasy had a rather remarkable sequel. Not long ago I was doing a show at the BBC Television Theatre. On the day before, they had shot the *Perry Como Special*. I walked along to my dressing room and there on the door was a card that read PERRY COMO. He had used it the previous day. And all my daydream came back to me. I thought: 'I'm actually using the same dressing room, working in the same studio, that Perry Como used only yesterday!' That brought it all back to me, all that boyish ambition. These are the times when you've got to pinch yourself and ask 'Has it really happened?' When I went out of my dressing room, the card on the door had changed, and it read, MIKE YARWOOD.

YEAR OF DECISION

All these reminiscences have brought me coasting through my teens to the year 1963, my year of decision. I started it in a Manchester warehouse. I ended it on television. And an awful lot had happened in between.

I have said that the boss of the wholesale clothing company was gallantly keeping me on because I at least entertained the customers who came in to make their purchases of stock. But I was naturally not being paid top money, because I wasn't doing the job I had been trained for—going out on the road as a rep and getting orders from clients. The reason for this was that I still hadn't passed my driving test. The boss's son, who was friendly with me, used to take me out in his car to get the feel of salesmanship, but that was a waste of manpower, and it was reflected in my wages-slip. I was in fact earning ten guineas a week from Monday to Friday. In order to make a little more, I

*Eamonn Andrews mediates when 'Harry Worth' meets
Harry Worth!*

got a Saturday job selling raincoats in a store in Market Street,
Manchester for an extra thirty bob for the day.

But at least I was cheerful. Or the people who worked with
me thought so. I was always loosing off an impression or two
which kept them and some of the customers amused.

One of my colleagues, Margaret Fairley, who worked in the
showroom, had formerly been a Tiller Girl, and her husband
was a musician in Manchester, so she knew something about
show business. She used to urge me: 'You really ought to take
this up professionally, you should have a serious go at this. Why

104

don't you try these talent competitions? Try to get an audition for television?' I did consider this, but didn't do anything about it immediately.

Then I met Wilf Fielding. Wilf is a few years older than I. He has his job in business, but he really depends on entertainment for the breath of life. In the years since we met he has run a double comedy act, managed groups, done production, and is now writing comedy. We met at the Whisky à Gogo club in Manchester. He was there with a party and I had come on a Christmas-season outing from my firm. We were introduced and we got on splendidly. He was interested in show business, and I told him I was thinking of going in for a talent contest. He asked me to be sure to let him know when I finally decided.

ENTER ROY MAYOH

We did more than keep in touch. We went about quite a lot together. And through him I met Roy Mayoh, whom even he didn't know when we started. Wilf's secretary, Linda Bailey, was going out with a Manchester television camerman and script-writer called Royston Mayoh, and we were introduced. I have never called them anything but Lynn and Roy, they are married now, and I really owe everything in my professional life to that meeting. It is amazing that things can happen to you that would never have occurred except by the pure chance of meeting somebody else. So much depends on luck in this business. Roy was just two-hundred-per-cent immersed in the entertainment business—he still is, he is a freelance television producer now. Roy took me up and spent hours and hours with me, perfecting an act—much of the time in his front room or mine, with a Ewbank cleaner stuck up in front of me for a dummy microphone.

In March of 1963, almost out of the blue, I decided to enter a talent competition in a pub called the Albion at Dukinfield. I telephoned Wilf in a hurry to come along and back me up. I did an act which started with some gags and went on to some impressions of Chic Murray and the Steptoes. I didn't win, I came third which was unplaced in that prize money. But I had enough encouragement to go in again, and the next week I came second and won twelve and six. Other publicans used to go to these shows to spot the talent, and a man came up to me and offered me a weekend engagement at the Salvage Hotel in Collyhurst, two nights at thirty bob a night.

I was staggered. I said 'I can't!' 'You can't?' he queried. I said 'I can't take thirty bob a night.' After all, I was earning ten guineas from the warehouse and another thirty bob for a Saturday's work selling raincoats, and it didn't seem right that I should take thirty bob for going on and doing what I had just done, which I had thoroughly enjoyed. So I tried to knock him down. 'Just give me a couple of quid,' I suggested. 'See how it goes.' He just smiled, and booked me, and after I had done the work he gave me thirty bob a night just the same.

Roy came along to this pub to see the show. After that, he went to work on me even harder. He really made me slave, and I enjoyed it. I was his discovery and he was very ambitious for me. He spotted potential and he helped me greatly along the way. He has never taken a penny off me in spite of all his sponsorship. The first full engagement he got me was at £13 a week, and he said 'Well, I can hardly take a percentage out of that, can I?' And that was the last he'd hear of commission.

Margaret Fairley, in the showroom at the warehouse, was very interested in the fact that I was at last trying a break-through. Her husband Bill was in the band at the Cabaret Club in Manchester, and he told us that the compere was leaving and I should apply. I asked Wilf to come along with me for the audition. The manager asked a lot of questions which, being shy, I continually left to Wilf Fielding to answer. I was a bit

'By jove, Missus, how tickled I am!'

nervous, if only for the fact that I was standing there in a borrowed suit. I hadn't got a decent suit, and Bill Fairley had lent me his. It was far too big for me, because I had a matchstick of a figure, but it was a very good suit. The manager cast his eyes on it. 'Have you got a tuxedo?' he asked me. I looked at Wilf. 'Yes, he's got a tuxedo,' said Wilf confidently. 'Here, what is this, an Arthur Worsley act?' said the manager to Wilf. 'I ask him all the questions, and you give all the answers.' However, he arranged for me to show my work. The audition was just a sort of one-night stand-in as compere. I was very thrilled to be there. The Cabaret Club was one of the top places in Manchester, a real night club—it did have a stripper but it wasn't basically a strip club. I didn't get the job. That was a real heartbreak for me. I wanted so badly to be compere there, a resident job, not travelling around. I was very sick with disappointment.

I suppose all that came of it was that I got my first tuxedo. Wilf bought it for me to Jacksons. I said 'I'll pay you for this as soon as I can,' but he wouldn't take it then, he was a very generous man. I myself don't think I ever paid for it, but Wilf says he did take a write-off sum for it after it had been pinched out of the back of the van in which he used to drive me around to my 'engagements'. But these are the sort of friends I had.

I got the occasional evening bookings, and still Roy worked on me. Finally he actually got me a whole week's engagement. We thought it was at the Prince's Theatre Club, Chorlton, which to us in Manchester had a prestige roughly equalling the London Palladium anywhere else. When we got there, Roy found that although you went in at the doors of Prince's, the actual engagement was for a place next door called the Ponderosa Club. They put on a cabaret there in an interval between the gambling, but the general atmosphere of the audience was a rather impatient expression of 'My gin and tonic's getting dangerously low and when do we get back to winning some money?' Roy did his best to cheer me up, but I did my then habitual routine of having to be sick just before I went on stage, and I was fearfully nervous as I made my entrance.

SHAKE, HANDS, HERE COMES YARWOOD

I started in a painful silence which only got worse when people began to mutter. I stuck to the act and went on. Suddenly there was a peal of uninhibited, absolutely joyful laughter. I recognised the carefree bay of Roy Mayoh, and stole a glance towards him. Wilf Fielding, next to him, was looking doubtfully towards him since it wasn't done for a 'manager' to laugh at his artist. But from the note of it, it didn't sound as if he was priming the pot with forced gaiety. It didn't matter. The laugh warmed up the audience, and, much more important, it gave me confidence. I finished the act without disgrace. Afterwards, I asked Roy what was the hell had amused him so much. He said 'It was your hands.' I had a routine then which I had worked up with Roy. They were very short gags using only my face, which was mobile enough even at that time, assisted by hand gestures. They were like cartoons: I would pull an incredibly long neck, twist my adam's apple into a knot, narrow my face to an extraordinary degree and press it in my hands, and the caption was 'Waiter, can I have another spoon, please?', the assumption being what I'd swallowed the last. What set Roy off was the cartoon when I did almost the opposite, with my neck concertina'd halfway to my pelvis and my eyeballs jerking down below the lower rims. My hands were supposed to be gripping the microphone stand, and the caption was 'Isn't this lift going too fast?' Roy saw faster than anyone that my hands were trembling so rapidly that they couldn't grasp the mike stand. As far as the audience were concerned it may even have improved the act, but Roy knew what the gesture should have been and laughed like a drain. However, it started the ball rolling and set me up for the night. Even if I finished the performance wringing wet with sweat.

Roy even got me a booking at the Yew Tree. This was an amazing pub in Wythenshawe run by Frank Tansey which was a mecca for hopeful variety artists. Sometimes there would be 25 acts crammed into a night. The pub held 800 people and it was impossible to get in after seven in the evening. Only a few weeks previously, Tansey had engaged a young comic and in the blink of an eye he was such a success that he had been booked for the Palladium: only he had changed his name to Jimmy Tarbuck. When Roy said he had actually got me a week's booking there it seemed unbelievable.

All this was happening within a very short time, certainly within six weeks of the talent contest at the Albion, Dukinfield.

The engagement at the Ponderosa caused me to think seriously about chancing my arm as a professional, and I took my annual holiday from the firm to prepare myself for the evenings and decide about the future. Previously, for the shorter club engagements, Wilf Fielding used to meet me from work and take me home for supper and a meal. I used to love the omelettes cooked by his wife Joan, who must rank as a very understanding woman in the light of the late hours we kept after keeping a club engagement. We were not getting home until three and four in the morning.

During my holiday I was reeling with this quite unexpected success. I think people were interested because I was using material that nobody else was touching. With Macmillan as Prime Minister and Harold Wilson coming up, though he was far less well known than he soon became, with Lord Boothby and Malcolm Muggeridge among my impersonations, I suppose I had an act that was different. I used to finish with a dialogue between the Steptoes which was an absolutely original feature then, and perhaps managers thought 'This is out of the ordinary run as far as mimics go,' and therefore I got a lot of work. At any rate, when a man came to me during my holiday from the firm and said 'You can play the Queen of Hearts and the College Club, doubling, you go on at one place and finish up at the other and we'll give you thirty quid a week'—well, I found it incredible. It seemed a bit better than twelve pounds for six full days a week. Then another offer came in for another thirty pounds a week . . . and I didn't go back to the warehouse. I rang up the boss, and he seemed quite pleased for my sake and possibly quite relieved for his own. He said 'You've made the right decision.' I profoundly hoped I had.

Almost immediately I got an engagement at the Whisky à Gogo, where the real drive towards professionalism had started. Ray Cameron was the compere there and he took a week off and put me in as a dep. The star was Cleo Laine and it was wonderful to work with her. The Whisky à Gogo was a great break for me because it was a classier night club, with a jazz group, and great prestige to work there. I was seen there by David Murray who became my first professional agent. He said 'I don't want to sign you exclusively, but I'm sure I can get you a lot of work. He did, perhaps because there weren't so many mimics around those days, and in fact I still do an odd show for him now.

I was still mixing my engagements with plenty of clubs different from the Whisky à Gogo. I still have the bills:

NEW LUXOR CLUB

Erskine Street, Hulme

Tonight:

STAG SHOW — MEN ONLY

Curry Hot-Pot Supper

All Draught Beer 1/– per pint

Until 9 p.m.

Please be early!

and:

COLLEGE THEATRE CLUB

COMEDY STAG NIGHT

MIKE YARWOOD

and

GIRLS! GIRLS! GIRLS!

My mother was visibly trembling, and so, quietly, was I. I'd never been in such places before. Some of the clubs in Manchester were pretty frightening. It would have been all right if they had only listened to you. The problem was getting them to listen and then reaching for the reaction as well. I used to do a lot of stag nights. Three times a week there was a skin show, with most of the comics believing that the only way to get laughs was to swear and be filthy. Some of the places were pretty terribly run. You would walk in and try to make your way through the shambles of a fight that was in full swing. The working men's clubs in Yorkshire were different and probably funnier, because soon after I started in show business they had these concert chairmen, one of whom I have now enshrined in my cabaret act.

I was never engaged for the permanent strip clubs, but for those which cleared out women clients for stag nights three times a week. Going into this sort of place for the first time was quite an experience. You would generally share your dressing room with the stripper, which I suppose didn't matter because she was going to strip anyway. I remember one stripper asking me to put the tassels on the cheeks of her bottom. She had glued the tassels on her breasts all right, but she couldn't quite manage behind. 'Just get it right for me, will you, love? Is the left-hand level with the right?' On stage it was not easy to follow a stripper for an all-male audience. The comics used to go as blue as they possibly could, but I didn't want to adjust my act. Roy Mayoh always used to say: 'Don't go down. Keep a nice standard. It would be wrong for your image to lower yourself just because it's stag night.' I think in most places the audience gradually began to appreciate it if you weren't blue. They admired you for having the guts to do a clean act. Or a comparatively clean act. In those days when I started I don't think I had very good taste. I was very raw. I remember old scripts now, and I think to myself, 'Oh, that was in very bad taste, I wouldn't do it now.' But they were rough audiences and you had to get laughs, as many comics, even big names, tend to do today in such circumstances. It's all part of insecurity, I suppose, fear that they won't get laughs.

When I doubled up club engagements in one night it was like going from a club with pub hours, and doing an early show, and then going on to a late night club with a two o'clock licence (though the Whisky à Gogo used to be open every night until dawn), with fairly continuous gambling and a late cabaret. I would be going on the stage at about half past midnight. The gambling never tempted me at all. I've never been near a table in my life. I don't even negotiate now, when it is a theatre show built round me, for a percentage of the take. It is open to me to start negotiations, but as I see it, it's gambling, and I don't like to gamble.

During all this time I was having to rely on good old Wilf Fielding as my literal guide as well as philosopher and friend, since he had to do all the driving—I still hadn't passed my test. He used to take me around in his van to all my assignments. He also found time—I don't know where he squeezed it from—to keep me up to the mark in improving the act. In modern theatrical terms, Roy was my producer and Wilf was my personal manager and roadie. But Roy had an uncertain schedule, and he would get telephoned reports from Wilf on how a certain line or piece of business went down—and if he couldn't get across to see me he would give his coaching through Wilf: 'Tell him to do this. He'd better leave out that. The Macmillan needs a bit of work on it in that sequence.' I would peg away at the work all night. This was the career I wanted, and I was going to spend all my time to perfect it. The praise from Roy that I most valued was that I was 'a hard grafter.'

AN EYE ON THE BOX

In his personal coaching, Roy was possibly in advance of his time. He had got me using the Ewbank-microphone with some

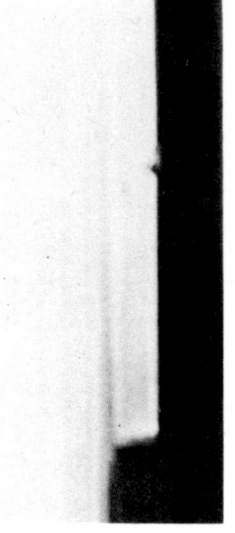

*'Harold—you ain't been knocking about with birds
again, 'ave you?'*

facility, and now he was concerned with training me for television. When I introduced the dialogue between Steptoe
Senior and Steptoe Junior—which was original in its period—I
had to change faces as well as voices between each line. Roy, as a
cameraman, was concerned with getting this the ultimate
eventual effect on the box. Because Wilfred Brambell was
small he would shoot from above, and because Harry Corbett
was tall he would shoot from below and accentuate his height.

Now, more than ten years later, when the technique is a
commonplace, I'm capitalising on Roy's early training which
was then done entirely speculatively from his own professionalism. For a television show nowadays, everything is worked out
at rehearsal. Jim Moir, my BBC producer, will always be
instructing me: 'Can you turn round a little that way for that

Harold Steptoe, Gent.

particular line . . .' Now that I am doing three-character dialogues, there is much more to think about. I have to concentrate on the character I am doing, and then on the change of character—it would be awful if I got the wrong one, or the right face and the wrong voice! But I also have to remember which camera I have got to favour for each character. What I like to do in television is to get the effect that there are three characters there, although the live audience can see that it is only me. I know which camera I am on, because I have rehearsed all week—first with imagination, or chalk-marks, when Jim says 'Camera Three's there, Two's there and One's there' (even if I can't see them until later in the week!). 'Vic Feather into One, Robin Day into Two, and Harold Wilson into Three.' In this way, with the camera angles plotted by the producer, we can get the effect that there are three different people present. And if I get lost, halfway through, we can stop and do it again. There is hardly any live television done now in light entertainment—though many people still think it is. But my point is that Roy was rehearsing me in this camera technique long before I had had even a television audition.

As part of my 'education' he was getting me occasionally into the ABC studios at Didsbury, to watch the real professionals working. He would say 'Jimmy James is working tonight. Be sure you come and watch him.' Although someone has been kind enough to write that I am in the line of the true music-hall tradition, I know to my regret that I am too young to have seen anything of the music hall in its prime. Even Max Miller I know only from gramophone records.

THAT SUIT'S FOR STANDING UP IN

I did mix and talk and reminisce and observe with the young professionals of my own generation. This occurred in the now blitzed (by 'redevelopment') Cromford Club in Manchester. The Cromford was where all the entertainers used to finish the night after their engagements in the clubs and theatres. Every name had worked there, and they all got the habit of dropping in after the show and chatting, talking shop—and, no doubt, gossiping. I am very proud that I was professionally booked there on a number of occasions before the club disappeared, in addition to all the time I spent there in more leisurely circumstances.

Wilf has driven me more miles than there are on the speedometer around Lancashire, with my property bag slung in the back of the van, containing the hats and caps, and Steptoe's raincoat and Steptoe's homburg, which had once belonged to Wilf's uncle. I remember the raincoat got tattier

116

'Just keep smiling, Ern—it hasn't fallen off yet!'

and tattier, and one night in mid-act I got my hands caught up in the sleeve lining as I was putting it on. I decided to play the situation for laughs in the Steptoe character, and Wilf said I got more comedy out of that situation than from the whole of my script. I have said that one tuxedo was stolen from the back of the van. In Liverpool, vandals even removed the rear windows, which created a curious turbulence so that we were asphyxiated with the exhaust long before we got home that morning. Painfully, under Roy's direction, I began to realise that stage clothes were important for the image. When I acquired a new dinner suit, I was careful to treat it kindly, always remembering Roy's thunderous rebuke: 'That suit's for standing up in, not sitting!'

The climax of this triumph of costume over comfort came one night when I had a triple engagement in Lancashire covering a seventy-mile circuit between Wigan, Westhoughton and Bolton. My principal embarrassment came from the company of Billy 'Uke' Scott, then a commanding voice in ABC Television's entertainment division, who had bravely decided to come on this round and see me in action. He had been introduced to me previously when Roy Mayoh brought him to the Ponderosa for my trembling debut. Roy had impressed on both Wilf and myself that my evening suit must not get creased, even though there was no time to change it between appearances. Accordingly, through all that rough ride, I sat up front like a comparative lord next to my chauffeur, and Billy Scott, the TV notable with a power of life and death, rolled helplessly around in a corner of the back of the van.

It was a psychological ordeal for Wilf, too, as my personal manager. But in addition to that he had to see me vomit too often, he saw me die at least once—at a highly paid do in the Adelphi Hotel, Liverpool, where by some quirk of the cabaret arrangements I had to change in the kitchen: that didn't put me off particularly, but something put the audience off. Plainly, my act just did not get across. I was so mortified that I said I couldn't take the fee, but Wilf, in his professional capacity, soon put a stop to such a mortification.

Wilf also had to suffer from afar the agony that accompanied my panic disappearance from the first night at the London Club, which I have mentioned earlier. I think I have said all I want to say about that salutary episode except to comment on the attitude of my mother. When I telephoned home and told her I couldn't handle the situation, she said one thing: 'Just get a train, love, and come home.' No recriminations, which I thought was marvellous. 'Blow 'em all,' she said. 'Just don't bother. But I will just make a call to Wilf.' Wilf, of course, got in touch with Roy, who gave me very sharp orders over the telephone. So I went back to offer to work for nothing, and found I could conquer stage fright after all. And what did my mother say when I finally came home? Not a hint of surprise or comment about my change of course. 'Now I know,' she said, 'that you really do want to get into show business.' Thanks Mum!

All Billy Scott's unfortunate bouncing in the back of Wilf's van did not deter him from offering me a television audition for ABC in Manchester. I found the occasion a frightening experience, with just the pianist, Billy Scott, and no audience. Doing an act cold has never appealed to me. But people seemed to be impressed, and Peter Dulay gave me a warm-up on a production called *Comedy Bandbox* which he was producing then. I did my act with lights and cameras, and the audience saw it on monitors, but it did not go out as part of the show which followed when it was presumed that the audience was sufficiently heartened. I knew that this was the real test. I also knew that Jimmy Tarbuck had done it only a few weeks before, and gone on to the Palladium. For once, I was not too tensely nervous. I enjoyed myself, and the audience reacted, and the producers registered their appreciation by booking me for a

Peter Noone (left) is surprised to find 'Tommy Cooper' on the show as well!

following *Comedy Bandbox*.

I was actually billed to appear on television. And a very faithful supporter of mine took the occasion to splash it. *The Stage* newspaper is kindly to actors. At the same time it is quite objectively critical of television. Loyalties were now crossed. Correspondents of *The Stage* had for some time been reporting on me in warm terms which I greatly appreciated. Now, faced with a crisis, they bravely burnt their bridges. 'Far be it from me to recommend the goggle-box,' wrote their prestigious informant, 'but if you happen to own a television set I suggest you tune into ABC's *Comedy Bandbox* on Saturday night December 21. You will see in my opinion the latest of the series of artists who have gravitated via this or another Ronnie Taylor production to London's top spots and seaside summer shows. Mike

Yarwood, scheduled for this Saturday, is an impressionist of outstanding quality . . .' In modesty I shall quote no more.

The show went out on network on a Saturday evening. Directed by Ronnie Baxter and compered by Ted Durante, the bill was topped by Ted Ray ('Gags Galore') and bottomed by Mike Yarwood ('Making a First Impression'). Roy Mayoh said 'Don't think about the cameras. Just stand there and we'll get you.' They seemed to get me. I had a happy Christmas, and the bookings came in. On the 31st of December 1963 I told myself that I had had a wonderful year.

Too good for humility, possibly. So I'll finish the chronicle of the year with this story. I was booked by Bernard Manning on a double engagement at the Embassy Club and the Palladium Theatre Club. I went on at the Embassy, and my act blossomed like a rose. I went so well that what had been intended for a twenty-minute act stretched into three quarters of an hour. I came off, intoxicated with applause, and glanced with shy happiness at Bernard Manning. But Bernard was a clubman with two establishments to run and a time-table to keep. 'Marvellous!' he said. 'Now get down to the Palladium Club before they start throwing bloody bottles!'

There's no business like show business.

I always say.

HOW TO SUCCEED IN CABARET:
SEE THREE FILMS A DAY

My forays into clubland were extending from Lancashire into Yorkshire and on to the North-East—Middlesborough, Sunderland, Newcastle, where club entertainment seemed often far more ornate (though not always better organised) than the Lancashire circuit. In these areas you could see some sense in the claim that the clubs had replaced the music halls. I took another engagement in London, at the Latin Quarter, which I did not greatly enjoy. Professionally, I was naturally more at ease than I had been at the start of the Caribbean adventure. But domestically I was not organised. I used to get terribly homesick, and longed to be back in the north. I had some digs in a bed-and-breakfast place off the Tottenham Court Road. The days were all so long that I used to go to three cinemas a day to kill time. I was not on stage until nine o'clock, and then I had a four-hour wait until the second show at one-thirty in the morning. I found that working in Soho at that time was a bit off-putting. In those days you didn't always get a very nice crowd. You could be heckled a lot.

As I gained experience I learned something about the delicate art of reacting to heckling. In general, there must be a pretty quick reaction. Preferably from the audience, because if they shush a drunk to keep quiet then you know that they want to hear what you have to say, and you have their sympathy to build on. If the audience don't intervene, and the heckling is a serious obstruction, then you've got to let them know you notice it, and squash it. I was being very severely heckled in a London West End club once, and I stopped to say outright: 'Madam, I've only got half an hour to earn my living tonight — you have all night.' That was a very strong one, with its crack at prostitution, and I would hever have used it outside Soho — and never unless I had been continually interrupted as I had been by this woman, who would not let me go.

There are stock answers which every stand-up comedian has to have in his repertoire, but they are often pretty broad: 'Last time I saw a mouth as big as that, Lester Pigott was sitting behind it.' But I prefer off-the-cuff ripostes if I can get them in. I was once being persistently interrupted by a man, and I finally stopped my act and told him: 'Look, sir, I don't mind working with you, but I would appreciate it if we could have rehearsed.' That was pointed enough to get a smile from

'Owzaboutthatthenguysangals??!!'

the rest of the audience, and delicate enough to have them appreciate my difficulties and get them on my side. It is their opposition that finally silences most hecklers. But it depends how much drink has been taken.

Because of my particular act, I get hecklers who are not so much disagreeing with me as with the characters of whom I am giving impressions—particularly the political figures. I was once doing Harold Wilson in a club in Southport, when a woman who had had a few drinks obviously mistook me for Harold Wilson himself. She gave a wild diatribe against me for not having allowed her make the profits out of rented property that she thought she had a right to. When it comes to delusions as deep as that, there is no point in making a big scene about it. What I did was to answer her back in the voice of Harold Wilson, and actually using one of Harold's lines which, in my studious researches, I had once heard him say to a heckler. I said: 'Madam, if you'll be quiet, I'll give you the facts. I can only give you the facts, I cannot give you the intellectual apparatus to appreciate them.' People sympathise with me and say 'How awful!' when this sort of interruption occurs. On the contrary, I think it can be a good thing, because if they are really taking you for the man you are caricaturing, the heckling helps the show along, so long as the remarks don't become indecent. I like to go to the big meetings of the political leaders, not only to study them, but to see how they deal with heckling. Sometimes the way they turn the arrows aside is a bit crude. I heard someone shout at Harold 'What about housing?' Quick as a flash he replied 'How many have *you* built?' When you analyse it, it is schoolboyish, but because of its speed it went down well at the meeting.

But even Harold can make a mistake. I was discussing this question of the balance between speaker and audience with Vic Feather, now Lord Feather, when he was general secretary of the TUC. We agreed that the man on the platform must be in command. You must never let the audience top you, and if they do manage to, you must top them again. Vic said that a very good rule to remember, for not leading with your chin, is *never to ask the audience a question*. Very true, because you can get some extremely embarrassing replies. As Harold Wilson realised when he made an election speech in Chatham, which was becoming an impoverished area during its run-down as a navy base. Said Harold: 'And why do I emphasise the importance of the Royal Navy?' And a beefy great matelot roared back: 'Because you're in Chatham.'

Whatever the success of my attempts to deal with the Soho hecklers, my engagement at the Latin Quarter was fruitful. London is the shop window of the profession, and a great place to be spotted. Colin Berlin and Ross Taylor came round to my dressing room and said they had seen my act, and would I like a summer season in Yarmouth. I said 'Great! I'm not doing one,' (meaning I'd never done one), and I signed to appear in the Larry Parnes/Tom Arnold *Big Star Show of 1964* at the Royal Aquarium, Great Yarmouth.

Soon after I had accepted the Great Yarmouth engagement I moved away from the status of a freelance entertainer relying for work on personal contacts and devoted friends, and I became a 'property'. Roy Mayoh had always joked that he would look after me until I got to the Palladium, and then hand me over. But now, within a year of our first meeting, he told me that I had reached the stage where I needed London representation and he was making the appropriate contacts. His life and all his enthusiasm was for comedy, not for percentages, and I never had a better friend, or could have had a better coach in those formative early days. I was telephoned by Dave Forrester, who asked if I would go and see him. I did so, and signed up with Forrester George Limited, theatrical agents, of Park Lane, London.

Dave has always been very good for me because of the easy

125

way in which we have got on. The trouble with young artists is that they can be very impatient, and they generally are. The great, impractical, dream incentive in my early days was that Jimmy Tarbuck had leap-frogged from the Yew Tree inn at Wythenshawe to the London Palladium almost in one bound — and why can't I become a name quickly too? I was patient with Dave, who used to counsel: 'Don't rush things. Take time. Take maybe eight or nine years.' He was always telling me how long it took stars like Morcambe and Wise to come up. He said 'Be patient, and I think we can make it with you.'

Nothing that Dave Forrester has ever said to me has not come true. He has never promised me anything that has not come off, perhaps because he has been cautious with his promises, though generous with his encouragement. He used to say: 'I might be able to have something very nice for you.' And I would say, 'Well, what is it, then?' 'No,' he would answer, 'I'm not telling you in case it doesn't happen.' He has been a very good agent for me, and I think I have played it all as quietly as he wanted. I have seen many good artists who had star potential, but have gone by the wayside because they have been impatient, often moving on to another agency which has not been good for them at all. Good management is very, very important in the entertainment business.

A BRISK LESSON FROM ROLF HARRIS

After a springtime in the clubs, I moved down to Yarmouth, where I had managed to find a flat above a restaurant near the theatre. I shall never forget the impact of the first thrill on that first summer season. The stars of the show were Billy Fury, Rolf Harris, Karl Denver and his Trio, and the Gamblers. Then came Yarwood, yet it seemed to me that my name was blazoned all over the town. Larry Parnes had covered the whole of the

Mike Yarwood at the 1973 Disc-Jockey Presentations with (left to right) – Pete Murray, Jimmy Savile, OBE, Tony Blackburn, Terry Wogan, and Jimmy Young.

front of the theatre with an enormous poster done in luminescent paint. What seemed fantastic was that although my name appeared at the bottom of the bill, it was enormous because of the size of the bill itself, and you could see it practically all over Yarmouth.

I was raw enough at the theatre game. I even had to ask the producer, Ross Taylor, to show me how to put the pancake make-up on. Then I began the hard graft. For much of the season I was working seven nights a week, because on Sundays they put on a pop concert which I compered. I had an all-in fee of £80 for the seven-day week. In the nightly show, besides my stand-up act, I was in various production numbers because the producer had all the artists running through the show. This was great training for me, because, having played the clubs on my own, I was a terribly badly behaved jumped-up bighead. Nobody was paying to see that show because my name was on the bill, and I ought to have known much better.

Gradually I learned. Sometimes through embarrassment. There was an occasion when Billy Fury was ill, and I took his part in some of the production sketches and numbers. Rolf Harris nursed me through, as it were, and he was always very professional. For the first item he very generously made an introduction for me before I was on stage: 'Ladies and gentlemen, there's a young man in the show whom you'll be seeing later on, but now we're going to do a bit of a song together . . .' and he called my name and gestured with his hand to the Opposite Prompt side, where I was supposed to come on. I thought it would be a great joke if I came on the other side instead, so while he was looking blankly at the OP side, I came on Prompt Side. The consequence was that he looked rather silly. And as for what he was feeling, I could tell it by the look in his eyes as we went through our number. Of course I was wrong. I thought the idea might have been funny, but, being inexperienced, I didn't check with Rolf first. If I had said earlier, 'Hey, it might be funny if you wave me on from one side and I come on from the other,' he probably would have said 'Yes, we'll do it,' and played the situation up. When I look back now, I still blush at horrible things like that. Anyway, Rolf told me what he thought of my amateurism when we came off. He was furious, he cleaned me, and I deserved it.

Since compering the pop shows went on only for eight weeks of the summer season, I worked another Sunday in Bournemouth, where Dave Forrester had asked me if I'd like to appear in a *Sunday Night at the Pavilion*. I still hadn't a licence, and had to get someone to drive me. It was a bad journey. I wouldn't dream of doing it nowadays, but then I would go anywhere to get into another theatre. The bill included Rawicz and

Landauer, the Four Pennies, and Ruby Murray. Sunday concerts used to be a bore at one time because of the old ban on make-up and costume. The odd theatre manager could still be old-fashioned and ask what props you were using. At that time I was using the Harold Wilson Gannex and the old Steptoe raincoat, and I used to say that these were the garments I wore offstage anyway, and get away with it.

At Yarmouth I stepped for the first time into the atmosphere of the crimson and the gilt which had fascinated me from the other side of the footlights years ago when I was a boy. It was not only glamorous, it was further excellent training, too. A lot of my contemporaries who came up in the clubs insist that it is a hell of a good grounding. In my opinion, it wasn't so good as they say, because you never learned finesse in a club. You didn't learn timing, because you had to fight the noise of the audience. Let's face it, if you weren't a star that they had paid extra money to see, they weren't particularly inclined to sit and listen to you. According to the mood of the night, they might not bother even if you were a star. I can illustrate that with a lovely story about one famous comedian. He was playing a club and nobody would listen to him, so he walked off. He said 'If you don't want to listen to me, I certainly don't want to listen to you.' The manager was furious. He said 'You've broken your contract, and you will never play this club again. 'Can I have that in writing?' demanded the comic.

CHRISTMAS WITH DODDY

At Yarmouth Dave Forrester brought Dick Hurran down to have a look at me, to see what I would be like for the *Ken Dodd Show* which was going into the Royal Court Theatre in Liverpool for the Christmas season. Dick came down and said 'Fine, we'll use him.' I filled in with short engagements that autumn,

'What a plumptious day!'

getting the keenest kick out of a televised show called *Club Night* from the Palace Theatre Club, Offerton, only three miles from where I lived in Bredbury. Donald Peers was in the chair, I worked with him later, and I always found him charming. It was great for me that I was doing my first BBC television show in my own home town. That really gave me a tremendous lift. Because there was a general election on, I was said to be gagged, but a lot of these gagging stories are rather exaggerated and in any case I didn't feel the pinch for characters to impersonate. I threw the situation away as neatly as I could be saying that Sir Alec Douglas Home and the fourteenth Harold Wilson had been given television series of their own to make up for it.

Then I opened in Liverpool with the *Ken Dodd Show*. Naturally I remember it warmly, because I stole the reviews: 'The lad from Knotty Ash was not at his best. Brightest spot was provided by Stockport boy Mike Yarwood . . .' and all that. It didn't do the size of my head any good. At that time I went through a very cocky period. I can't think I was very nice in those days. I remember Dick Hurran saying of somebody else who was about as big-headed as I was at the same time: 'He's got a mohair suit, twenty minutes of somebody else's act—and he thinks he's a star.' And that's the way I was: well, I had a mohair suit, anyway. I grew out of it eventually.

During this year I acquired a publicity agent, George Bartram. Perhaps I can clear one misunderstanding by saying that there is no way in which a press agent can get you, or buy you, a good write-up. Critics write what they want to write. What a press agent can do is to be sure that you meet the Press, and that the Press are informed about you. George also bagged a bit of idle space by sending out circulars saying that I had been booked for the first journey through the Channel Tunnel, or the first commercial flight to the moon—which of course was true as far as it went, because he had logged my name with a local travel agent. And at Christmas time he would come up with extraordinary games which I was supposed to have devised to amuse children at parties:

> *With children in mind, let's ask young up-and-coming impressionist Mike Yarwood, who is spending his Christmas in the Ken Dodd Show at the Royal Court Theatre, Liverpool, for a game for the very young.*
>
> *'If ever I am called upon to entertain youngsters at Christmas parties I always suggest we play "Animal Noises".*
>
> *'It's a simple game. Each child can be told that he or she represents an animal. Then begin a story bringing in all the animals, and each child can make the appropriate animal noise.*
>
> *'Just one tip: If you are not an experienced story-teller it is as well to prepare the tale beforehand, to ensure that some children do not get too many turns.'*

These paragraphs were tolerantly accepted and printed by newspapers all over the country, from Oldham to Hemel Hempstead. In retrospect, the only appropriate animal noise I can think of is a loud raspberry.

But in the Spring George got a lot of publicity with a stronger story that I had written to 10 Downing Street to ask Harold Wilson for facilities to study him speaking in the House of Commons, and so perfect my impression of him, and that Harold had replied that he would be delighted to arrange a seat in the gallery.

It was some weeks before I could keep that date, which of course allowed time for the story to bubble up again when I finally fulfilled it. There was a small flock of reporters and photographers trailing me when I did it. I had to do pictures with a pipe and a Gannex outside the House of Commons, and I hated it because people passing by looked at me as if I were some sort of nut, dressed up as Harold Wilson outside Parliament. But there was a terrific Press coverage.

OUT OF THE BLUE: THE PALLADIUM

In the meantime, the BBC hazarded a television take-off for me in a series called *Let's Laugh* which never really got off the ground. I didn't stop playing the clubs, though perhaps the audiences listened more frequently. I was cheered by odd observations, as at the opening of the Towers Theatre Club in Warrington, when one of the Mayors who was present was laughing so much that his chain was back to front. At a club in Leeds I was doing my act when there was a police raid. An inspector very politely requested me to pass him the microphone and he announced it from the stage. After the raid I came back for the rest of my performance, beginning: 'So much for my impression of *Z-Cars*, now for Chic Murray.'

Dave Forrester had booked me in for the summer at the Central Pier for twenty weeks with Bob Monkhouse at the top of the bill. I was getting £60 a week, which I thought was a lot of money for a complete unknown, unmarried, living in a flat costing only £6. I was a bit naughty: I sent some home to Mum, but I wasn't always banking the rest, and spent a lot on clothes and trappings.

I was now dreaming the impossible dream that I might somehow be summoned to *Sunday Night at the London Palladium*. There was only the thinnest of chances, because the series was ending its long ten-year run. Week after week, at home during the day and in the clubs at night, I was hoping against hope that the call might come. It didn't. The series was due to end on Sunday the 13th of June 1965, and I opened in the Blackpool show on Saturday the 5th of June. On that very nerve-racking night a man came to see my in my dressing-room. He said 'I'm

133

Alec Fyne.' I said 'How do you do,' not knowing who Alec Fyne was. He said 'We want you to do Sunday Night at the Palladium a week tomorrow.'

I couldn't believe it. This really was the biggest thrill of my life. He asked me what I would do on the show, and I told him. He said 'Good, good, you'll do about $4\frac{1}{2}$ to 5 minutes.' And that is a testing announcement to a young comic. 'That gives me time for about one gag' is the immediate reaction.

I crept into the Palladium for rehearsal on that Sunday morning, very nervous. The first person I saw was George Cooper, the stage door keeper, in his office. George is a fantastic character. It doesn't matter how big or small your name is, George always makes you welcome. This nice, friendly man met me and gave me a key to my dressing-room, and made me feel so good with his warmth. The Palladium is the premier theatre in the world as far as I am concerned, and topping the bill there my supreme ambition, but it has not only a breathtaking atmosphere, but tremendous efficiency. George is a living sign of that efficiency, too. You can go downstairs in a panic and say 'George! I've come without cufflinks.' He'll open a drawer: cufflinks. That's the sort of comfortable man he is.

I went on the stage and was terrified. It was all so big. I hurried through the band call, almost apologetic for delaying the other artists whom I could vaguely see in the stalls, though of course there was no need. The stars of the show were Cliff Richard and the Shadows, and Norman Vaughan was the compere, and it was the last-ever appearance of the Beat The Clock feature. In the performance, which was live in those days, I seemed to go over quite well with the television critics, in my view because I still had this originality. I was a chap who actually went on the stage and impersonated politicians. I can always remember Norman Vaughan saying in his cosy way with the audience 'We've got a lovely show tonight, we've got Cliff Richard and the Shadows, we've got this and that, and we've got a fellow who's going to come on and do the *Prime Minister!*' And that arch approach wasn't a gag. He was saying that somebody was going to come on and do what hadn't been done before. So everybody sat up to notice. For me, the prestige of playing the Palladium was marvellous, but I think the act must have been awful, for a friend of mine taped it and I heard it quite recently. I was raw, and the timing was bad, and just the re-hearsing made me recall that I couldn't walk on and off the stage properly.

I celebrated the Palladium by having a birthday, which I could hardly avoid, and passing my driving test, which had been avoiding me for about six years. I went on film as the voice of an unseen Harold Wilson in the Boulting Brothers' feature film *Rotten to the Core*. I left the Blackpool show in early October to join the Bachelors for a seven-week season of a variety bill in Coventry. In the middle of rehearsals I went up to London again to appear in the *New Palladium Show*, the Sunday entertainment working to a re-jigged formula. I was with Shirley Bassey, The Seekers, Ivor Emmanuel and Mrs Mills. The compere was Jimmy Tarbuck, and in this and succeeding shows he used to give me a tremendous build-up before introducing me. He so complimentary to me that my mother wrote to Jimmy and thanked him, which is one of the nicely funny things my Mum does. Arthur Askey came on this show as a last-minute guest artist, and they did a sketch in which Arthur ad-libbed so much that it ran well over time. I was standing centre stage behind the tab, waiting to go on, when the floor manager came over to me and said 'Cut two minutes.' This was terrible for me, having been all week rehearsing this act (and with my tenseness, I'm rehearsing it by going over it in my mind until the very moment I'm on.) And now to be told, ten seconds before entry, 'Cut two minutes.' But I did it, and that was the test, it was good hard training for a comedian's lot. It is always assumed that a comic is easier to cut than a singer. I

135

'I've seen some o' big show business names. An' I'll tell you, I weren't impressed any!'

could slash my patter so long as I made a reasonably smooth papering over the cracks. After all, they could hardly ask Shirley Bassey to cut two minutes from a song.

I took the night train back to Coventry, ready for Monday morning rehearsals. I got off at the station with unmanageable loads of gear, suits loose on hangers and all, and disembarked at my hotel. By the time the taxi had disappeared I realised that the hotel was not fulfilling its promise to keep a night porter on duty. There was no answer at all to my ringing, and it was two in the morning. I left my gear draped all over the entrance, and walked to a police box across the road. There was a policeman inside and I explained my problem. He said 'Seen you tonight at the Palladium, haven't I?' I said 'Yes.' 'You in the show over at the theatre then?' 'Yes.' 'Well, we'll knock up the night watchman at the theatre.' So I collected my luggage, got into the theatre, and slept in a dressing room with the realisation that the life isn't all glamorous.

I did the autumn season in Coventry. My impersonations then included Macmillan, Heath, Wilson and Muggeridge as well as the comedians. I met Malcolm Muggeridge, and he asked me how I mimicked him. I said 'I just put a lot of big words together, but I don't really know what I'm talking about.' He looked at me confidentially. 'Neither do I, dear boy,' he said. I didn't mention that one of my Muggeridgisms was 'Edible tubers fragmented and subsequently immersed in seething emollient fluid, transmogrified into brittle morsels of an amber hue'—a rather roundabout description of chips! Malcolm told me that, although he had never seen me impersonate him he was well aware of my existence. He subscribed to a press-clipping agency, and whenever a newspaper mentioned my impersonation of him on the stage or television, they sent him the cutting. He worked out that, so far, I had cost him thirty bob.

From Coventry I went with the Bachelors to Bristol to do the

Puss in Boots pantomime. This was something of a fraught occasion. The script was of the previous year's Palladium pantomime—so were the costumes and settings, for that matter—which Frankie Vaughan had done with Jimmy Edwards and Mike and Bernie Winters. Freddie Davis and myself were given the Mike and Bernie parts, but the other way round, with me using Mike's lines. So I was feeding Freddie. We were a little unhappy there—we're good friends now—but we were both at the stage of our careers where we were trying to get away, and one was trying to top the other all the time. Few comics like working with other comics. Maybe it's a very jealous, individualistic profession, but it's rare that you like anybody else getting the laugh—that's what you want for yourself.

SEVENTH BEST BEER MAT

After Christmas I found myself receiving wide publicity in a crackpot newspaper competition that printed a bad photograph of me and offered readers £3000 to state in order whether my face expressed my sense of humour, shrewdness, charm, vitality, benevolence, lightheartedness, strength of character, thoughtfulness and frankness. I filled it in by naming my ten worst vices, but I didn't win. In various zany publicity projects over which I had no control, I have been nominated No. 4 pipeman of the year, No. 7 in the favourite heads which hair-dressers would most like to cut and style, and the seventh face (Enoch Powell was first) which people would most like to see on beer-mats. The idea wasn't to publicise me, but the British Hairdressers' Federation, or the British Beer-mat Collectors' Society, or whatever—the last being termed, I understand, tegestologists. When it was announced that I had booked for the first commercial Concorde flight, however, I did publicly

'Lord George-Brown' and his favourite Book-of-the-Month choice!

withdraw my name, because I hate flying and will only do so when necessary.

FACING HARRY WORTH

That year I did some more Palladiums and went down to join Harry Worth for the summer season at Bournemouth. I had been impersonating Harry Worth all my career but had never met him until then. He was exactly as I expected him to be. I arrived for the first rehearsal, and Harry came up to me and said 'Let's go and have lunch.' I said 'I believe there's a restaurant upstairs, in the Pavilion itself.' 'We'll find it,' said Harry, and he went off walking away, and chose a staircase and we climbed it. When we got to the top we found just a wall, it went nowhere. I thought 'This is my first impression of Harry, and the situation would have been funny in any case, but it's funnier because it is Harry.'

Harry was fabulous to work with, always so nice. But we made one mistake. We did a sketch where he came on and started telling a joke, and then I came on in hat and glasses identical to him, and said in the Worth voice: 'You're telling the joke all wrong . . .' That was the first time I learned that you must never do an impression when the original is there. It didn't work, the audience didn't take to it at all. I did try it again once in a bowler hat with Bernie Winters, and opposite Max Wall, on television, but it was disaster for me and I now know better than to contrast actual physical features.

There was an election that year, in which it was again said that I was gagged. Harold won, and I went to see Edward Heath. The meeting was arranged by Sir Harmar Nicholls, the Tory MP who was Mr Heath's adviser on entertainment and the arts. I knew his daughter, Sue, who was acting in Bournemouth that season. I sat through Question Time and then went to the room Ted had as Leader of the Opposition. Sir Harmar suggested that I should do my impersonation of Harold Wilson. Ted agreed, but a bit nervously, saying: 'Make sure the door is shut, or the Leader of the House may wonder what the Prime Minister is doing in my room.' I noticed again that Ted never uses anybody's name if he can help it, but always refers to them by their title.

For the Christmas season I went with the Bachelors into a spectacular at the Manchester Opera House, and on Christmas Day I was with Secombe and Friends on a television show. The Bachelors did not have the same agent as I, but from the time of our first show together at Coventry they had liked my act, and everywhere they went they asked for me. This lasted for years, until Scarborough 1970. They did a lot of tours and theatre work, which let me go to bed earlier than if I had solely been

'Ask Ted for a bottle of beer, Harold.'

playing the clubs, where often one doesn't go on stage until nearly midnight.

ADVICE FROM MAX BYGRAVES

During one week of that winter season the Bachelors had to go off on a song festival, and Max Bygraves took their place. Maybe I was still a bit cocky . . . Max used to introduce everyone in the finale, and as I came down he used to walk across the stage, and I thought he was masking me. So I went to the stage manager and said that because of this movement the audience couldn't see me when I was taking my call. Max came all the way up to my dressing room—the place I had was a Dickensian chamber right at the top—and said very warmly 'I'm terribly sorry about this, Mike.' I felt about as high as a louse. I thought 'Oh, God, I've upset him now.' But it was nothing of the sort. Several times after that he used to come up, have a chat, and give me little hints on presentation and stage appearance that I've always remembered. And he is the only person who has ever done that. I have found that in general you really have to learn all the tricks for yourself. Nobody comes up to you and tells you. The only way is to watch the people who can do it, watch the professionals.

After a spring Palladium appearance I received the accolade of what I still think is the best single line of appreciation from any critic: 'I enjoyed the mimicry of Mike Yarwood on the *Palladium Show*, mainly because he brought such a debunking line to his victims that you could almost hear the wind hissing out of their reputations.' The phrase must have caught the fancy of other critics, too, for it has been used several times since, but I still record that it was used by Robert Ottoway in March 1967. I was then preparing a series for BBC2 with Lulu and Ray Fell called *Three of a Kind*. The Beeb splashed it sufficiently to grab the whole front page of the *Radio Times*, but I never saw the shows. I had just started a summer season with Mike and Bernie Winters in Great Yarmouth, and, apart from the necessity to work, you just could not pick up BBC2 in Yarmouth at that time! Later that year we made another series under the same title which became the first light entertainment television show to be seen on colour in Great Britain. Colour is only as recent as that!

I was asked to go on to a Billy Cotton Music Hall, which I greatly enjoyed because I had never met him, and here was another variety hall hero of my youthful theatre-going days. Bill was straight and bluff, and pretty scornful of some of the songs his guests sang. A young pop star was rehearsing, and he was sitting by me in the studio chatting. 'What a lot of rubbish this is!' he said. 'They don't write songs like they used to.' And he started humming *Just One More Chance*. 'What a lovely tune,' he said. 'You wouldn't remember that. Why don't they sing something like that?' I did a sketch with Bill about eager impressionists arguing between them over who should do Churchill. Bill won, because he wrote the script! Everyone has one impression in him, and Bill's was Churchill.

I did a one-night stand inside Norwich Prison, followed by five weeks with the Bachelors at Newcastle, with the interruption of a Palladium show, and then I moved on with the Bachelors for the Christmas season in Liverpool. A memorable year was to follow.

ROYAL PERFORMANCES

I was made a Water Rat in February 1968, which I found a strangely moving experience. This highlight was followed by the Royal Gala for the Olympics Fund, which I have mentioned earlier with its climax of the Queen's personal little message for

143

me. The Royal Gala gave me some grand splash reviews, and as a result of it, or on the strength of it, Lew Grade decided to give me my own series on ATV: *Will The Real Mike Yarwood Stand Up?* The show title was really leading with one's chin, for it was only too easy for a critic to reply—will the real Mike Yarwood sit down—or shut up! I don't really think I was ready to front a show at this time.

I had gone off for the summer season with Mike and Bernie Winters to Blackpool, where I was still playing charity football. In one game, Showbiz XI v International XI, on behalf of the blind, we pulled in a gate of 5000 people who paid some £700. 'To the astonishment of many,' runs a contemporary sports report, the beginning of which I don't much care for, 'Mike Yarwood proved quite a competent player and banged in a good goal, and delighted the crowd with his deft flicks and touches. And it was Mike who made the last goal of the match for Ted Rogers.'

I came to London to work for eight weeks at the Palladium with Cliff Richard. It was a very exhausting time, because I was rehearsing all day for the ATV series, then doing two shows a night at the Palladium, and on Sundays travelling to Birmingham to record the television shows. In the middle of all this I appeared at the *Royal Variety Performance*.

I was not down to do this show, but Eric Morecambe had a heart attack, and I happened to be at the Palladium. Eric and Ernie were doing two spots in the show, and as stand-ins Frankie Howerd took one and I did the other. My greatest personal thrill was that I was in the No. 1 dressing room, because it's theatrically ethical that if you replace a performer you naturally go into his room. I wasn't the senior star in the show, but I was in the star's dressing room, which was nice. Little things like that mean a lot to me. When I was at the Talk of the Town, I said to Tommy, my road manager: 'You must get me a programme and take it home in case I never play the

Talk of the Town again. 'Don't be ridiculous,' said the theatre manager, 'you'll be back next year.' 'Ah,' I said, 'but you never know what's going to happen in this profession.' I do tend to covet prestige things in the business, it's just a little obsession I've got—you should see what I've got framed at home! Any-

Mike Yarwood as 'Harold Wilson' as 'Gary Glitter'.

way, there I was in the No. 1 dressing room—sharing it with Englebert Humperdinck and Des O'Connor and Frankie Howerd, but that was no hardship. I just felt nice being in that room which I had only visited before.

SOMEONE ELSE ON THE STAGE

The Royal Performance was attended by the Queen Mother, Prince Charles and Princess Anne, Princess Margaret and Lord Snowdon. Prince Charles left after the interval—to travel to a *QE2* launching celebration, no offence to Frankie Howerd, who was the 'Surprise' act climaxing the show. No one in the audience officially knew that Frankie was appearing, because he had rushed back from America (where everybody thought he was) after appearing as star of a play which ran only four nights: the cheer that greeted him when he came on to the Palladium stage was volcanic.

The royal party came on stage after the show, and said pleasant things. I answered vivaciously, because I felt extra-wonderful. There were stars in my eyes, if anyone paused to notice. For, in the company which was crammed—yes, crammed even on the huge Palladium stage—behind the front line of performers to whom the royals were talking . . . there was a someone. It was someone I was going to meet afterwards, talk over the highlights of the evening with, run down with after the excitement of the show. She was a girl named Sandra Burville. She was my girl. She is now named Sandra Yarwood. She is my girl.

Sandra was then working in the *Lady Be Good* company, playing the musical at the Saville Theatre. By the lucky coincidence that these dancers had been invited for the Palladium big night, it happened that we both did a Royal Performance together.

146

I was also seeing Sandra in the daytime. She headed the Mike Yarwood Girls who were dancing in the ATV series *Will The Real Mike Yarwood Stand Up*, which I was still in the middle of making.

For the first few weeks of rehearsal and recording, 'seeing' Sandra was literally almost all I was doing. I occasionally talked civilly to her on the set, but I could never shoot a line. I have never been good at chatting up girls. I was both out of practice and it was against my temperament.

Sandra is demure enough, very understanding, but very warm and very straight. She was attracted to me and intuitively knew that I was not running in neutral. It happened that she was a great friend of Dilys Watling, who was not just the 'principal girl' in my television series, but the only featured girl, doing a lot of comedy and singing. Sandra jokingly confided to Dilys that she had her eye on me. Dilys invited me to a dinner party at her Hampstead house—and before my very eyes I arrived to find that Sandra was also there. Sandra was just as surprised and delighted to find me. My shyness went in this friendly and intimate dinner party. I probably talked my head off to Sandra, but it was all simple stuff, no chatting up. We knew that we were getting on wonderfully, and so we started going out together.

But not, actually, going out very often. The television series was still being made. It meant rehearsing every weekday at Elstree, travelling to Birmingham and back every Sunday to shoot the actual programme. And every weeknight I had my double stint at the Palladium and Sandra was working at the Saville. At least, we were travelling all the time together. But we rarely saw each other after the show. I would go to my flat and collapse into my bed, and she would go to hers and collapse in hers—and we would just chat to each other on the telephone. When we did go out she used to pick me up at the Palladium in her little red Imp—I rarely used my car in London—and we would go and have some Chinese nosh somewhere.

What immediately appealed to me in Sandra was that she was gentle and kind, but I was also struck by her natural consideration, which gave her impeccable good manners. On the first time we ever went out together, after our dinner at Dilys's place, we went to the Lotus House in Edgware Road, London. We ordered all the trimmings, as one does with a Chinese meal. Possibly, as usually happens, we ordered too much, but in any case I'm not a big eater, and after the show plus the excitement of being with Sandra, I very soon stopped eating. So Sandra stopped eating, too. She told me much later that she was being faced by all these appetising sights and smells, she had a very healthy appetite after strenuous dancing, she could have gone almost straight through the meal in front of her—but that she thought it would have been ill-mannered to have carried on eating. That's devotion!

It still took an extra push to get engaged. We were out to dinner with Lionel Blair and his wife at a restaurant in the King's Road, Chelsea, and the conversation got round to marriage, and Sandra said she supposed it was a good thing to get settled down some time. I thought about that remark all night. Next day I tried to work back to the subject. But my reserve intervened. So I thought it might be easier if I approached the matter (playfully, so that I could retreat quickly if I saw that I was going to be rejected) in some of my voices. I tried the Dudley Moore, and the Steptoes and Muggeridge—all on the lines of 'Er . . . what you were saying last night, not a bad idea, perhaps you weren't too serious . . .' Finally Sandra said that if I had anything to say to her, and said it as Mike Yarwood, she might take some notice. So I said it, and she did take some notice. What a relief! Marriage itself is a simple operation compared with the ordeal of getting engaged.

It all took time. Before our engagement, I had finished the Palladium season and gone off to Coventry to play Simple

Simon to Jimmy Clitheroe's *Humpty Dumpty* in pantomime. Sandra, who is a great driver, much more of a dedicated motorist than I, used to come up to Coventry on Sundays to see me, since she was still working in London. I took her to my home for Christmas Day, but on the following morning she had to travel to Copenhagen, where she was appearing in a television show. My ATV series was in the can, but it did not begin its weekend run until New Year's Eve.

It was still a long time before we were married. Sandra went on dancing, among other shows in a Palladium season and a Bachelors tour, and then she left show business as resolutely as she does everything else. I suppose everyone has their ideal girl. Sandra fitted my ideal because of her complete feminity and the fact that she is not over-awed by the glamour of the business I am in. Now she is a perfect mother to Charlotte and Clare—and if those young ha'porths turn out to be anything approaching their lovely mother, I'll be blessed with a really superb family.

And so 1968 went out as, in my personal estimation, a most marvellous year—so wonderful, in fact, that when George Bartram announced to the Press that I was booked for the first trip to the moon, not only did I not deny it—I was really half-inclined to believe it, being halfway there already. In the coming months I did a lot of work, bought a house in Cheshire, played Bournemouth for fifteen weeks in the summer with Frankie Vaughan, exposed myself to more football, and booked in at the Savoy Hotel, London, to play cabaret there not only on the eve of my wedding but for weeks afterwards. We were married at the church of St Thomas More, Swiss Cottage, on the 8th of November 1969. We finally reached Cheshire for a delayed honeymoon, and—far too soon—I started commuting again, to Liverpool where Frankie Vaughan and I were doing the Christmas show at the Royal Court Theatre.

We started a baby, and I began to be selective about the

venue of my professional appearances. Fortunately, my summer season that year was at the Queen's in Blackpool with Winifred Atwell. That was the year of the World Cup, in which I took an absorbed interest, as also, of course, did Brian Clough. I added Cloughie to my tally of scalps, and first put him on the air in a television show with Lulu which actually went out on the day I started at Blackpool.

The Blackpool show ended on Saturday the 19th of September. On Saturday the 19th of September, Sandra went into labour at St Mary's Hospital, Manchester. How I got through most of that last performance I just don't know. I had a friend ringing the hospital every ten minutes from the dressing room — I couldn't face the tension myself. Just before the finale, the message came that I had a lovely 7 lb. 3 oz. daughter, and Sandra was fine. What a finale that was, after that! And I jumped into my car and was driven straight to Manchester for that first reunion, and that first meeting with a new life, that every father must recall as perhaps the most magical moment of all.

THE DOWNING STREET SAGA

As a minor also-ran to Sandra's pregnancy and the World Cup—well, *I'm* writing this book, so I make my own placing— we had a general election (he's gagged!) in which Harold lost, and from then on Ted obviously got more official television screen time. From a professional point of view I loved them both, but thought I ought to stretch myself a little more in presenting them, and try something which was really technically difficult. After Charlotte's birth the BBC negotiated with me a prestige television series, ('prestige' means you get your name in the title), to be called *Look—Mike Yarwood!* My comedienne was to be the talented Adrienne Posta. This series of ten shows started in May 1971, and I began it with what I still think was something of a tour de force, when I 'did' Robin Day as a ventriloquist with both Ted and Harold as his dummies, one on each knee.

To give Harold his due, he joined immediately in the fun. If I may grace the story with its full point, I'll briefly go back to 1969, when I got *Weekend* magazine's award as Entertainer of the Year. Possibly as a result of this, I was asked to keep the party amused at the *Sun* presentation of entertainment awards the next year. I had to wait a long time for my best critical notice of that performance, until Elkan Allen in the *Sunday Times*, previewing *Look—Mike Yarwood!*, wrote: 'It has taken exactly the year since the 1970 *Sun* Awards party for Mike Yarwood to get the major show he earned there. After the televised bit, this clever young impersonator provided a cabaret of such brilliance that one of the toughest seen-it-all audiences gave him a standing ovation. Harold Wilson, his chief target, was among the most enthusiastic.'

Harold, I must say, mounted his counter-attack with his usual tactical brilliance—military jargon for cashing in on existing publicity and turning it to his own advantage. The first programme of my new BBC series was to be shown on the 14th of May, and hints of the ventriloquist act were in the newspapers on the previous Sunday. On the intervening Tuesday the Variety Club gave a lunch at the Dorchester Hotel to celebrate Harry Secombe's 25 years in show business. Harold Wilson gave a speech in praise of Harry Secombe. I wasn't there, so I have to quote from the Press: 'But it was Harold Wilson who really had them "in the aisles" with his crack that if his own speech seemed sub-standard when compared with those by show business stars, he was at a disadvantage. He had, he said, written his own speech on the back of a menu, "being forced to use such time as I've had left from writing scripts for Mike Yarwood." This brought a roar from all

151

the show-business personalities present—among them Arthur Askey, Tommy Cooper, Charlie Drake, Clive Dunn, Bruce Forsyth, Rolf Harris, Dickie Henderson, Vera Lynn, Kenneth More, Danny La Rue and many more—because the climax to Mike Yarwood's act is an impression of the ex-Prime Minister.'

I duly bounced back with my ventriloquist's dummy presentation, and followed it next week with a 'foursome' impersonation—Mike Yarwood doing Harold Wilson doing Frank Sinatra singing *I Did It My Way*, with critical comments

'We're not coming to terms with that organ cadenza, are we Mr Heath?'

by Ted Heath. And there I stopped the permutations. I thought the relationship between myself and Downing Street was possibly getting a little cannibalstic.

FLAKED OUT

While the *Look—Mike Yarwood!* series was still running I went into the Futurist Theatre in Scarborough for a summer season with the Bachelors. But exhaustion caught up with me, and within a few weeks I had to retire for a fortnight. I came back to the show, however, and additionally recorded a six-weeks BBC radio programme called *Yarwood Weekly*, which ran alongside the longer television series. But exhaustion struck again, and I had to pull out of a short season with Val Doonican at the Palladium, in order to get myself fit for pantomime—at Coventry again with David Nixon and Basil Brush in *Cinderella*.

Basil Brush came with me to the next season's summer show at the ABC, Great Yarmouth, with Freddie and the Dreamers. Meanwhile I was busy on another BBC series of *Look—Mike Yarwood!* which ran concurrently with my summer show into the autumn, and was succeeded by another radio series.

BACK-STABBING

In the autumn I was invited to appear at the *Royal Variety Performance*.

Maybe in 1972 I was watching the royal show with a keener eye, less bemused by the glamour, but it confirmed one impression I've always had of show business, which is that, egocentric as actors and their handlers may need to be to stay in the lark at all, it isn't really necessary to be quite so bitchy as they sometimes are. At the daytime rehearsal of the Royal

Performance there was the usual savage circus. Artists were muttering, and agents and managers were jostling around—so-and-so doesn't want to be in that particular spot, see what you can do . . . temperament . . . curses . . . the producer has a word with Bernard Delfont . . . utter mutiny over the final walk-down when everybody universally (except the last artist) declares he shouldn't have been brought down so early but kept until much later.

I personally thought I could well do a bit of yapping myself. I was in what is professionally regarded as a lousy spot on the programme. I was virtually on first. There was a speciality act, and then Dickie Henderson came on as compere—it was his fiftieth birthday, and we celebrated it with him—and then me. I said to Dave Forrester, my agent, 'Surely I shouldn't go on in this spot, even for your sake? This is bad prestige, this is where the jugglers used to go.' 'Never mind,' said Dave. 'You'll get the first bite of the apple.' I was upset about it, but I've always been one for a quiet life. I didn't want to give Bernard Delfont problems, he was getting aggravation enough from other people, so I thought 'I'll be nice.' And I created no havoc at all.

Having fought my own little fight inside myself on that point, I was then asked by the BBC to cut out a gag in my script because it clashed with a line that had been written in to a script of *Till Death Us Do Part*, which was being given a show in the performance. It is feeble to go into details about it, but it was a complicated dialogue between Bernard Delfont and Vic Feather which I was doing, where there was confusion between a booking for Jack Jones the trade union leader, being confused with Jack Jones the singer. Johnny Speight had made the same reference in his script. I told the BBC that *they* could take theirs out—it was a much less involved reference to Jack Jones and the Red Flag, with no reference to Bernard Delfont at all, and in the personality stakes I happened to know that Mr Delfont was very tickled with my gag. But no, no, no, no, no. The BBC

154

couldn't take it out of the entry which was their pride and joy, although we had the relationship that I was under contract to the BBC as well at the same time. So—quiet life Yarwood again—I said I would take it out. And this time Dave Forrester went mad. He told me I should never have consented.

The pay off: the show started with an act which everybody dutifully talked through, Los Diablos del Bombo, banging steel balls on the stage. Dickie Henderson came on and did six minutes. I went on for ten, and I was in the pub across the road while all the rest were still vomiting in the sink. And the BBC, who recorded the show for their television programme, slashed my act by cutting into a routine, lopping off the sequence and losing continuity. So much for being the nice guy.

A curious remark by the Queen Mother, who came with Princess Anne and Princess Margaret. She told me 'It's frightening how you appear to become Harold Wilson!' I occasionally spend a sleepless moment wondering just what she meant by that.

JANNOCK

From the intrigues of the Palladium I went back north to the Batley Variety Club, which I had had to leave for a couple of nights to do the royal show. I was glad to return. I knew the people surrounding me there, although more obviously in the old-ale than the champers belt when it came to class, when it came to character were jannock. But, much more important than any bruised artistic temperament, I wanted to be in the north for the birth of my second child. Clare was born on the 29th? of November 1972, and for once I stayed home for Christmas with my family.

I was establishing a fairly fixed rhythm through the year now, and I kept it in 1973: clubs in the winter; prepare a BBC

155

television series in the spring for early summer; seaside summer show—this time topping the bill at the ABC, Blackpool; and autumn cabaret and club work—topped in this particular year by two much-prized awards, as a Man of the Year, and the Variety Club of Great Britain's BBC TV Personality of the Year. I was lucky to be given a Christmas Day television show which pulled in $22\frac{1}{2}$ million viewers for the BBC. I began 1974 at the Talk of the Town in London, and went on for the summer to Bournemouth.

I live quietly with Sandra and Charlotte and Clare. That is the pattern of life I choose, rather than a fevered 'theatrical' life-style. I like my friends to remain the ordinary people—bus conductor, solicitor or dentist—that they were when we first became friends and had a gill together.

I don't claim that I'm not theatrical, because I'm always working, mentally at least, and I do use my lay friends as sounding boards, to try out aspects of new impressions on them. I hope they forgive me. We have a few laughs.

I have never had any objections from any of my 'victims' resenting their being impersonated. Occasionally I get objections from their fans, whose dignity is more easily offended than the sense of humour of their idols. Des O'Connor confirmed this with me when discussing his 'ordeal by Morecambe and Wise.' Eric and Ernie get letters from his fans saying 'Why do you make jokes about his singing?' But Des says 'I don't mind. I don't think I'm a good singer, anyway. I'm glad of the mention.'

The complaints I more frequently get are political. If correspondents convince me that a particular routine or joke is in bad taste, then I withdrew that sequence and I not only apologise to my correspondents, I thank them. But far more often the objection is to the political implications of a piece of dialogue. Sometimes in these cases I have to conclude that the complainants have no sense of humour at all. If I say something about Heath or Wilson, it usually comes out of the mouth of Wilson or Heath, though technically via Yarwood. I imagine the things that they would say about each other, but in a humorous way. The dialogue would not be funny—it would, strangely enough, be crude political insult, which some comedians to attempt—if it were spoken with a straight face by Yarwood. I try to make dialogue which sounds authentic but is at the same time comic, and therefore it has to be a bit larger than life. This is the art of the caricaturist, the controlled exaggeration of a significant detail. Look in any good newspaper, and you'll see that the artists caricature Heath and Wilson very well in cartoons, but in very different ways. A politician can end up in a cartoon as a knight in armour, an Egyptian mummy, a madame in a brothel—or even a horse. And on many occasions the 'victim' writes humbly to the artist begging to be sent the original drawing (free) so that it can be framed. I think my political subjects have much the same reaction to me. Harold Wilson, when we met in Blackpool, was very agreeable and gave me the impression that I had been a sort of public relations officer for him. He told me that some of my sketches had been as good as party political broadcasts *for him*. It is amazing how you only see what you want to see. I have never done a two-way sketch *for* anybody, but have always tried to balance the dialogue. Cliff Michelmore put it to me in a televised interview in *An Hour With Mike Yarwood* that the outstanding achievement I had brought off was to give politicians a sense of humour. In so far as this is true, I believe it is the real and only way in which I have acted as public relations officer for them.

But they are in danger if, when they do appear on the box as themselves, they fall short of the public image of them as men of humour which I have created. If they call each other names, the public notices if they do it stridently and without humour. I know that some of the humour I inject into their dialogues is pretty simple stuff, but I also use satirical lines to deflate their reputations which, I think, suggest the virtue of humility to every politician. For the simple knockabout, the following passage could come from any comedy duologue, say between a ventriloquist and his dummy:

> TED: I have just seen a poster in Parliament Square. It says Harold Wilson is a bounder.
> HAROLD: Don't believe everything you read.
> TED: I didn't read it, I wrote it.

But the satirical is a missile which digs deep before it explodes. I had Harold Wilson finish an angry argument about his responsibility as Prime Minister with this pronouncement from is gravelly throat: 'Talk of a housing shortage is only a cheap political scandal invented by those who are without houses.' That is the sort of indignant double-talk which many politicians *almost* utter, and that is a part of my caricature. In my view, as long as caricature is well done and makes an ongoing point—or even an acceptable humorous comment—it is valid.

The only mimicry I hate to see is bad mimicry. I cringe when people say 'Oh, there's somebody doing your Harold Wilson or your Ted Heath.' They aren't mine, I don't own them. I may have been the first to do them, but singers always sing the same song. People ask 'Does it annoy you to see somebody doing an impression of one of your subjects?' and I say 'Only if it's done badly.' I am all praise if people have done their homework, and studied the original instead of watching me. I myself can often quickly spot the failure to do this when the impressionist gives his character a catch phrase which the original never used but which I invented. For instance, I make Max Bygraves come out and begin: 'Here's a funny story . . .' Max has never used it, I created it. I have given Hughie Green the phrase 'I mean that most sincerely, friends.' I've never heard Hughie Green say

Mike Yarwood's Harold Wilson!

that, although it's the sort of phrase he might use. So when I see impressionists coughing up 'Here's a funny story' and 'I mean that most sincerely, friends' I know they've not been watching Max or Hughie, they've been watching me. I should be flattered, but it's a lazy way and it also saves the trouble of other people making the judgement on what characters are worth doing.

I try to be a good mimic. By constant observation, by a script with an edge as keen as I can get, by hard rehearsal, and by constantly setting myself the technical challenge of multiple voices, I try to present entertainment that does not insult the intelligence.

This is all I want to do. I don't see my presentation as a stepping stone to something different. This is what I do, and this is what people come to see. I'm a mimic. An impressionist always used to be somebody like a speciality act that never topped the bill. But it has happened to me. Thanks to *YOU*!

I do thank you.

Good-bye!

t4

REPAIR & RENOVATE

walls&ceilings

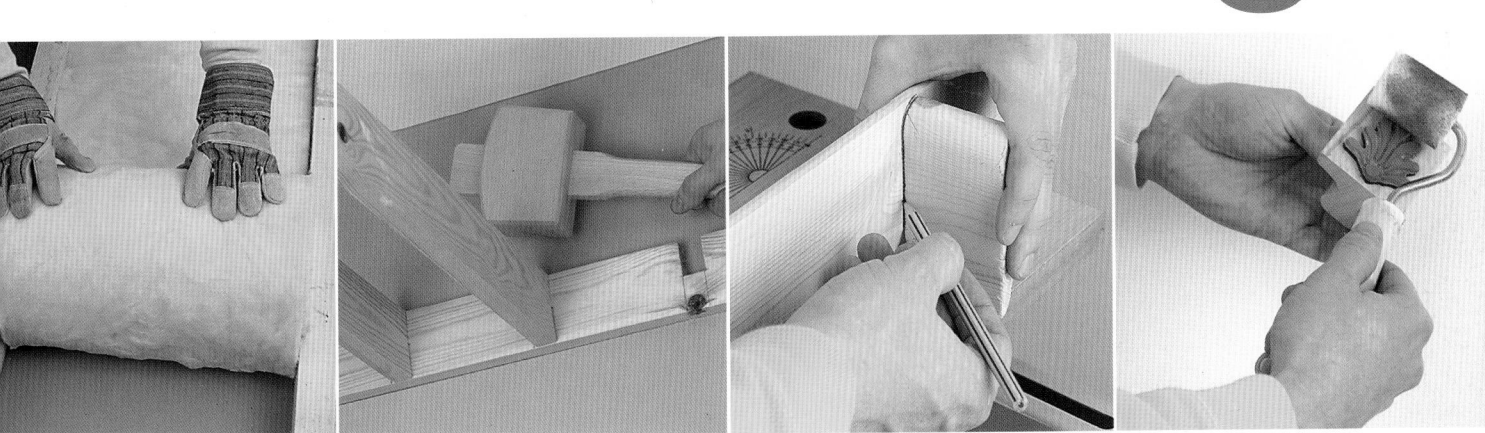

Julian Cassell & Peter Parham

MURDOCH
B O O K S

walls & ceilings **contents**

6 introduction

10 anatomy of walls & ceilings

12 house construction

14 ceiling & floor construction

16 external walls

18 internal walls

20 planning

22 options for change

24 tools & equipment

26 construction materials – 1

28 construction materials – 2

30 how to start

32 dealing with professionals

34 altering the structure of a wall

36 safety at work

38 recognizing problems – 1

40 recognizing problems – 2

42 removing a loadbearing wall

44 removing a non-loadbearing wall

46 aligning floors

48 building a stud wall – 1

50 building a stud wall – 2

52 making an arch profile

54 making a serving hatch

56 soundproofing walls

58 building a block wall

60 installing wall ventilation

62 building a glass block wall

64 installing a fireplace

66 altering the structure of a ceiling

68 lowering a ceiling – 1

70 lowering a ceiling – 2

72 building a suspended ceiling

74 soundproofing a ceiling

76 insulating a ceiling

78 building a loft hatch

80 constructing a slatted ceiling

694.6
1385341

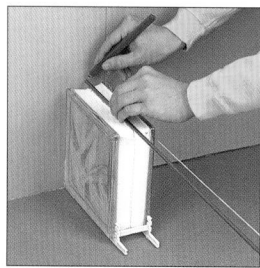 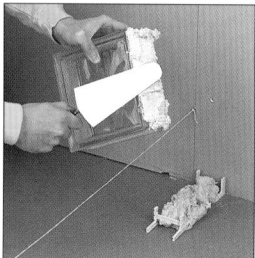
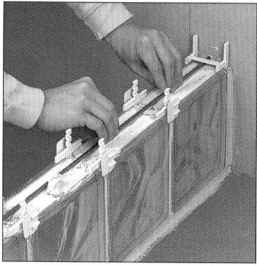 

*Glass block walls make stunning room features
and are remarkably easy to construct, see page 62*

82 **cladding & lining**

84   dry lining walls

86   plastering a wall

88   panelling walls – 1

90   panelling walls – 2

92   fitting coving

94   adding plaster features

96   fitting skirting boards

98   fitting decorative rails

100   applying decorative wall
       panelling

102 **decorative finishes**

104   choosing finishes

106   choosing materials

108   ceiling & wall preparation

110   painting techniques

112   paint effects

114   wallpapering techniques

116   tiling techniques

118   creating a textured
       ceiling finish

120 **repair & restoration**

122   making minor repairs

124   improving ceilings

126   patching a ceiling

128   making hollow wall repairs

130   making solid wall repairs

132   repairing corners

134   repairing wooden features

136   **glossary**

139   **index**

143   **list of suppliers**

144   **acknowledgements**

*Decorative panelling is simple to apply and helps
to protect wall surfaces, see page 100*

introduction

Home improvement is fast becoming a national pastime with more and more people tackling jobs that would previously have been left to the services of professional tradespeople. Taking on a job yourself can be cheaper and more rewarding than hiring a professional – ensuring that the finished effect is how you envisaged and falls within a budget that does not incur additional labour costs.

repair & renovation issues

This revolution has been fuelled by a booming DIY retail sector, which tries to convince us that no job is too difficult and any practically-minded person can set about full scale home renovation. Although it is true to say that there is indeed huge scope for applying oneself to home improvement tasks, it is always important to know your limitations right from the outset. It is best to approach DIY as a learning curve, building up your experience and knowledge before tackling jobs of greater difficulty. This book concerns itself with renovation and repairs in your home, which are directly related to two of the major structural elements in all houses – the walls and the ceilings.

Repair issues can be neatly separated from those of renovation – the former is concerned primarily with making good existing features, and the latter is related to adjusting the appearance of certain areas in your home. Renovation therefore clearly leans more heavily on the creative side of your abilities, whereas repairs generally tend to be dependent on your ability to apply yourself practically to restoring a particular finish or structure.

Most people are able to recognize when a particular area of their home needs adapting or changing, but realizing or envisaging what that change should be exactly can often be a more difficult process. Therefore, inspiration for change needs to be balanced with the potential options available, which in turn relate firmly to budget, personal choice, your ability to tackle the work and how much professional advice or input may be required for the task. It is best to try and tackle each of these areas in turn.

The smallest of renovation or home improvement tasks will always cost some money and therefore it is impossible to begin work without deciding on a budget. This prime area for concern is covered in more detail in Chapter 2, but right from the initial stages, budgetary constraints will be the major governing factor in deciding on the extent of work.

Personal choice is clearly of the utmost importance when you come to repairing and renovating your house. Work out your ideal situation, and then compromise according to the wishes of other people who will be affected, and the relative value of your house. Although most of the variable sales points in a house relate to fixtures such as bathroom and kitchen fittings, decisions on wall or ceiling structure will certainly affect the look of your house and therefore the appearance to a potential buyer. So decide whether your plans are to renovate purely to cater for your needs, or whether you

LEFT *Building a serving hatch between two rooms adds an attractive and practical design feature, while also allowing more light into what may otherwise be a dark area of your home.*

RIGHT *Where structural considerations allow, a glass block wall offers a striking and stylish alternative to more traditional wall design, allowing a wash of light into a room.*

are aiming to provide a general level of improvement
that will also appeal to others.

Next comes the question of your ability to tackle
home improvement tasks. This book takes into account
a wide variety of options and techniques covering all
aspects of ceiling and wall renovation. However, some
techniques are quite clearly more demanding than others,
and therefore it is important to evaluate your capabilities.
It is always advisable to have a source for some
professional advice when needs dictate, even if it is just
to provide a guiding hand rather than full scale employment.
The areas of plumbing and electrics are specific examples
where professional help will almost certainly be required,
especially when such services need rerouting or
customizing to adapt to your new room layout. There
is also a clear safety issue here as it is never advisable
to tackle any such work unless you have the relevant
qualifications and experience in these areas. Safety is
therefore one area where there is no room for compromise
when renovating your home.

difficulty rating

The following symbols are designed to give an
indication of difficulty level relating to particular tasks
and projects in this book. Clearly what are simple
jobs to one person may be difficult to another, and
vice versa. These guidelines are primarily based on
the ability of an individual in relation to the experience
required, and degree of technical ability.

*Straightforward
and requiring
limited technical skills*

*Straightforward
but requiring
a reasonable skill level*

*Technically
quite difficult,
and could involve
a number of skills*

*High
skill level
required, and involves a
number of techniques*

wall & ceiling consideration

By their very nature, walls and ceilings are the largest surface areas in your home, and so they can be the defining factor in general appearance. Much of this finished look will be due to the decorative finishes applied, but the actual layout and design of your home will supply the framework for these finishes and therefore the effect that is produced. In addition to personal tastes, sympathetic consideration should be given towards the basic architecture, period and style of your home.

For example, however much fun the idea of installing suspended ceilings in a period cottage may sound to you, it may not hold such an irresistible desire for someone else – thus you not only lose the natural features in your home, you may also inhibit your chance to sell at a later date. So there is a fine line to be observed between taste and personal flare, and it is always best to take time when considering your ideas before seeking to implement them. Most people have considered changing walls or their features in some way, but ceilings have always tended to

be a neglected area when it comes to home improvement. They are often dismissed at the planning stage, and are simply considered as an area that will literally 'get a coat of paint', once the constructional nature of the project is complete. Therefore this book does tend to emphasize that not all home improvement options relate to wall position and coverings, and there are indeed a multitude of options for ceiling renovation which relate both to the efficiency of its structure, and the decorative or design aspects which it can portray. Ceilings must therefore be considered as an integral part of the look of your home and shouldn't be sidelined as an area that will simply follow a trend – rather, see them as a surface that can add to and complement the general room and home design.

Safety issues are obviously a vital issue, particularly as the structural make-up of homes can vary so widely because of age and style. It is important to fully understand the structure of your home before embarking on renovation work, and issues of ceiling and wall structure are covered in considerable detail in the early chapters of this book.

Repair and renovation projects may therefore be as large or small in scale as you wish, and anybody can tackle

different DIY tasks around the home according to their own capabilities. This book helps to break down many of the myths or complications surrounding ceiling and wall renovation and repair, and aims to provide clear guidelines on producing looks and finishes which you may not have realized you were capable of achieving. For the best results, try to follow the order of this book as it takes you through a correct order of work, right from the 'Anatomy of Walls and Ceilings' in chapter 1, through the planning stages of chapter 2 and on to the following projects. Each of the projects relate specifically to the different areas and options relating to walls and ceilings.

Above all, you should enjoy working on renovation and repair projects in your home, for if they are completed successfully you will be enhancing the appearance and living space of your home, while also adding to its value.

RIGHT *Strong colours will always emphasise the texture and design of wall and ceiling structures.*

BELOW LEFT *Panelling has enjoyed a revival in popularity and may be used to clad both walls and ceilings.*

using this book

The layout of this book has been designed to provide project instruction in as comprehensive yet straightforward a manner as possible. The illustration below provides a general guideline to the different elements incorporated into this design. Full colour photos and diagrams combined with explanatory text, laid out in a clear, step-by-step order, provide easy-to-follow instructions. Boxes of text aimed at drawing your attention to safety issues, general tips and alternative options accompany each project.

colour-coordinated tabs help you quickly find your place again when moving between chapters

at the beginning of each job a list of tools is provided

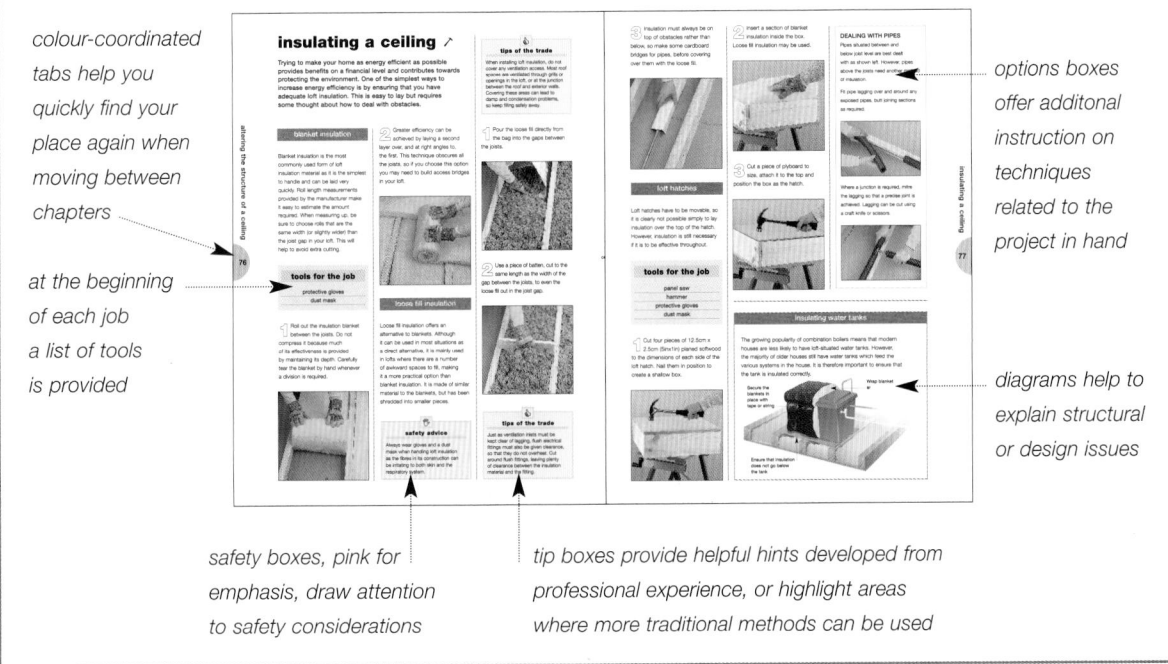

options boxes offer additonal instruction on techniques related to the project in hand

diagrams help to explain structural or design issues

safety boxes, pink for emphasis, draw attention to safety considerations

tip boxes provide helpful hints developed from professional experience, or highlight areas where more traditional methods can be used

anatomy of walls & ceilings

Many factors affect the anatomy or make-up of the walls and ceilings in your home. Some differences relate to age, with issues that were once common building practice or regulation now being out-of-date or superseded by improved design and modern materials. Architectural preference can also make a significant difference, which means that even buildings of the same age can have entirely different wall or ceiling structures. So before embarking on a renovation project, it is important to try and recognize the different types of house structure, so that you can make informed decisions on the extent and type of work that will be required. This chapter considers the most common varieties of wall and ceiling anatomy and how they are constructed.

11

Open plan living can be extended to split-level designs, where the 'open' theme continues over more than one floor level.

house construction

Ceilings and walls are, quite obviously, major components in house structure. So before embarking on any alterations, it's important to examine the make-up of your house in its entirety. This will help you to recognize some of the main design features and form a greater understanding of the structure of your home and its particular characteristics.

Most modern houses are referred to either as brick-built or timber-framed. However, there are wide variations on this theme, and older buildings can comprise a number of different structures and features. Understanding the principles of house construction can help with recognizing some of your home's characteristics.

It's important to remember that, regardless of house design, the role of walls can be isolated to one key feature – whether they are loadbearing or non-loadbearing. Non-loadbearing walls act as a partition and do not bear any of the house weight, whereas loadbearing walls play an integral part in supplying general support and bearing the weight of floors. This theme is common to all house structures and is the starting point for deciding on any alterations.

understanding timber & block

The majority of houses combine wood, blocks or bricks in their construction and any of these components can have a loadbearing role to play. In other words, a wall that is timber-framed is as capable of being loadbearing as a wall that is made from block or bricks. Similarly, a wall made of brick or blocks does not, necessarily, have to be loadbearing.

The common misconception that a timber-frame wall has less of a loadbearing capability than one made from solid block or brick must therefore be totally dispelled. Instead of judging walls by the material they are made from, it is more useful to think of walls in terms of the role they play within the total house structure (see the illustration on page 13).

brick-built houses

Modern brick-built houses are based on a cavity wall construction, with an outer layer of brick or block and a secondary, inner layer of brick or block. The cavity between the two walls is usually around 50mm (2in) wide. These houses should not be confused with older brick-built properties where the characteristics are more likely to be those specified under 'solid wall construction' (right).

To ensure structural strength, the cavity between the outer and inner brick walls is spanned by special ties. If the internal wall is loadbearing, it will

be made from block or brick. If it is non-loadbearing, the internal wall may again be built with blocks, or less heavyweight stud partitioning (timber frames) may be used.

timber-framed houses

As the name suggests, the main structural elements of these houses are built using timber frames, though they are also built on a cavity structure comprised of two walls. The internal, wooden wall framework is erected first and the outer wall is then built from brick, block or wood cladding. As with brick-built houses, the exterior walls are generally loadbearing. However, because the internal walls are made from wood, it can sometimes be difficult to determine whether these walls are loadbearing or not.

solid wall construction

This type of construction features in older houses, where there is no cavity and therefore not a two-layer system. Walls in these houses tend to be thicker, often with the stone or brick make-up extending from the outer to the inner face of the wall. Internal walls are either made of similar materials to the external walls or they may be constructed from timber partitioning, demonstrating lath and plaster characteristics (see page 19). Loadbearing walls in these houses nearly always comprise the same stone or brick structure as the external walls.

supports

Entrances in loadbearing walls, such as windows and doors, reduce the strength of the wall. For this reason, additional support will be needed over the window or door, in order to take the structural weight of the wall above.

(Non-loadbearing walls, because of their less structural role, do not always need this additional support.) These extra supports are referred to as lintels, and may be of wood, stone, concrete or metal. The type of material is dependent on the age of the house and the size of the opening. Modern techniques tend to favour rolled-steel joists (RSJs) for large openings, whereas reinforced concrete lintels or galvanized pressed-steel lintels are generally used for doors and windows. Exterior cavity walls may combine lintel types with concrete on the outer wall and wood on the interior.

house structure

To understand the role and function of ceilings and walls, it can be useful to put them in the context of an entire structure. This cross section of a house shows the integration of walls and ceilings, and highlights those areas of the house that bear weight or help to support the weight of the building.

A non-loadbearing wall acts as a partition between rooms and has no role in weight support in the house as a whole. *See page 18-19*

Non loadbearing walls may themselves need extra support to take their weight when they run in the same direction as the floor joists. Adding an extra joist in this area is therefore vital

All windows will have a lintel of some nature to support the wall above

The exterior walls of most modern houses are of a cavity construction in that they comprise an outer and inner wall. These are linked together with wall ties which span the cavity. *See page 16-17*

Ceilings (roof level) are generally constructed from wooden joists which are covered in plasterboard to supply the ceiling structure for the room below. *See page 15*

Opening up two rooms to make one will require an RSJ if a loadbearing wall is being knocked through. *See page 42*

Doorways or entrances in non-loadbearing walls do not necessarily require a lintel because the wall does not have a weight-supporting role.

Floor levels between rooms may require aligning if a wall has been removed. *See page 46-47*

A loadbearing wall, as its name suggests, is an integral part of the structure of a house, supplying general support as well as taking the weight of floors. *See page 18-19*

Floors and ceilings between levels are generally constructed from wooden joists whose weight is supported by the exterior walls and internal loadbearing walls. *See page 14-15*

Doors and entrances of interior loadbearing walls will always have a lintel above them to provide support for the wall above

Underfloor construction varies according to foundations. The floor surface will normally comprise a concrete screed, wooden floorboards or building boards

ceiling & floor construction

The structure of a house dictates that the ceiling of one room will generally combine to make up the floor of the room above. Since alterations to one room can thereby affect the structure of another, it is vital to consider both ceiling and floor anatomy when planning changes. All the structures shown here have wooden joists which make up the framework of the ceiling. Quite a few modern homes, however, incorporate solid concrete ceilings — so there will be some variation on the themes outlined below. As with most designs, trends vary with time and the basic ceiling structure will be very dependent on the age of the building.

lath and plaster ceilings

An old design, lath and plaster ceilings are now avoided in modern techniques of construction. However, they are still commonly found in older houses and may well feature in a house that is intended for renovation.

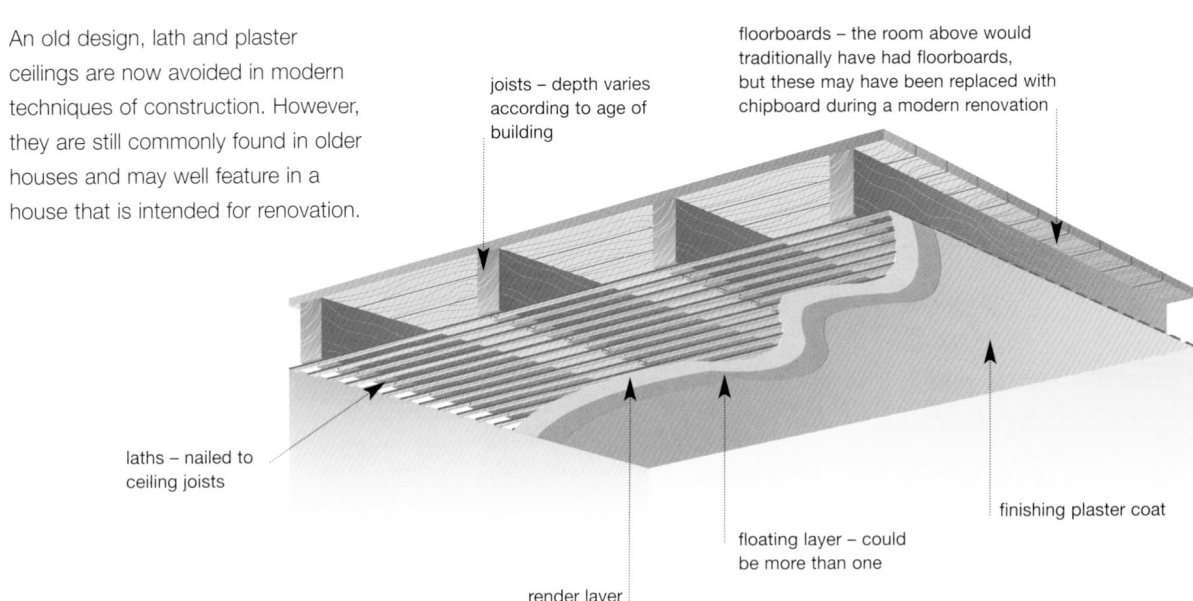

joists – depth varies according to age of building

floorboards – the room above would traditionally have had floorboards, but these may have been replaced with chipboard during a modern renovation

laths – nailed to ceiling joists

floating layer – could be more than one

finishing plaster coat

render layer

plasterboard and plaster ceilings

The invention of plasterboard made lath construction an out-of-date and time consuming method for building ceilings. Therefore, most modern ceilings have a plasterboard base, which is either plastered as shown here, or dry lined as shown on page 15.

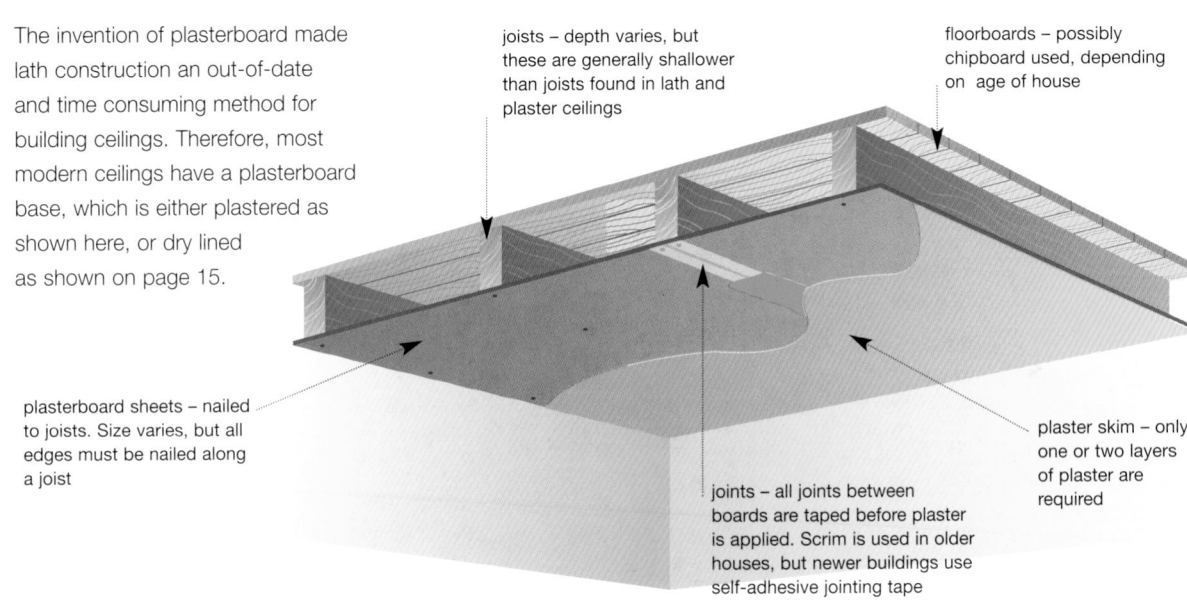

joists – depth varies, but these are generally shallower than joists found in lath and plaster ceilings

floorboards – possibly chipboard used, depending on age of house

plasterboard sheets – nailed to joists. Size varies, but all edges must be nailed along a joist

joints – all joints between boards are taped before plaster is applied. Scrim is used in older houses, but newer buildings use self-adhesive jointing tape

plaster skim – only one or two layers of plaster are required

dry lined ceilings

Similar to plastered plasterboard ceilings, dry lined ceilings are finished using a slightly different technique. Dry lining tape over the tapered edges seals the join and produces a smooth surface ready for decoration. This is probably the easiest ceiling structure for a home improvement enthusiast to tackle.

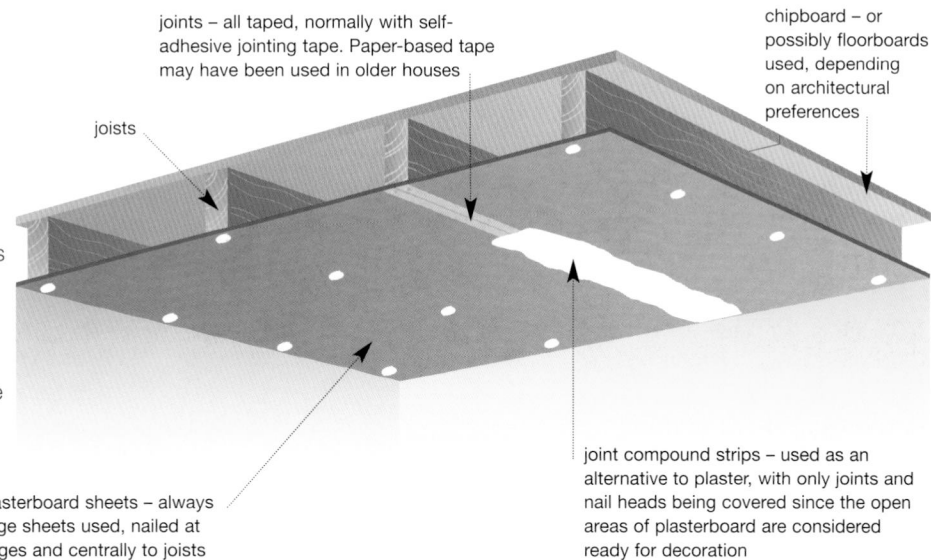

joints – all taped, normally with self-adhesive jointing tape. Paper-based tape may have been used in older houses

joists

chipboard – or possibly floorboards used, depending on architectural preferences

plasterboard sheets – always large sheets used, nailed at edges and centrally to joists

joint compound strips – used as an alternative to plaster, with only joints and nail heads being covered since the open areas of plasterboard are considered ready for decoration

wooden ceilings

Not all ceilings have a plasterboard or plaster-based finish, and wood is a common alternative to this type of finish. In fact, wood is often used as a cladding mechanism for finishing the ceiling, with tongue and groove boards being a popular surface choice.

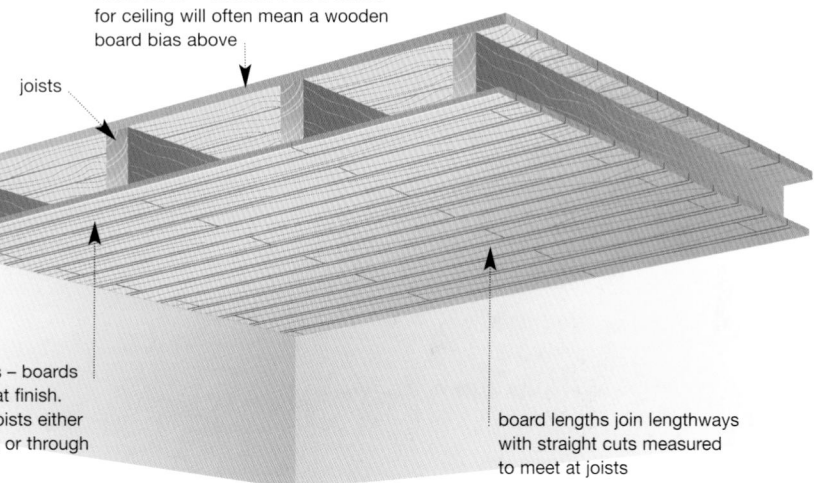

floorboards – wooden board choice for ceiling will often mean a wooden board bias above

joists

tongue and groove boards – boards interlocked to create a neat finish. The boards are nailed to joists either 'invisibly' through tongues or through the board face

board lengths join lengthways with straight cuts measured to meet at joists

top floor ceilings

The ceiling between the top floor of a house and the loft space is often slightly different in make-up to the other ceilings in the house. The overall structure will depend on the age of the building and may therefore look like any of those already shown. The main difference will be the presence of an insulating layer between ceiling and loft, and a basic chipboard floor may be fitted on the upper layer.

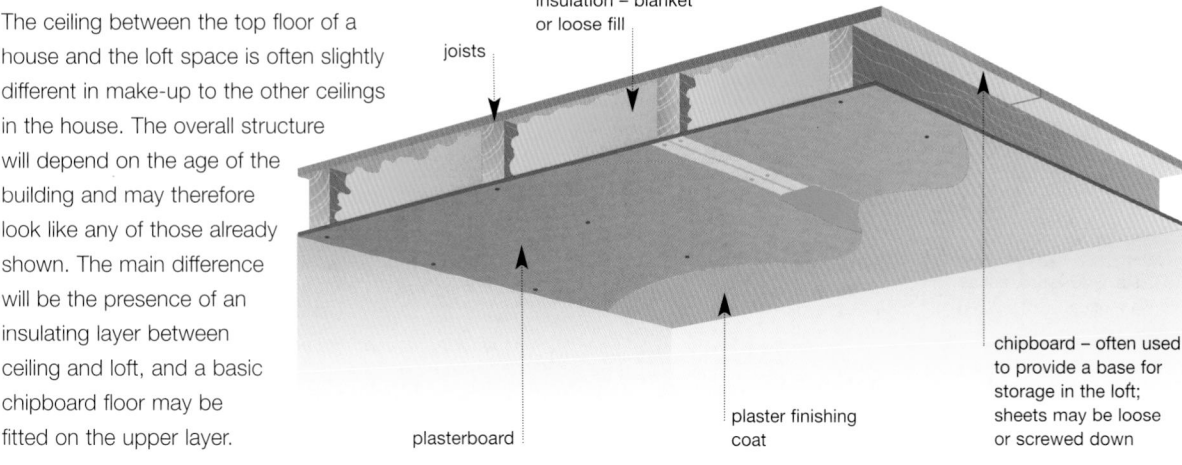

insulation – blanket or loose fill

joists

chipboard – often used to provide a base for storage in the loft; sheets may be loose or screwed down

plasterboard

plaster finishing coat

external walls

Wall purpose and structure can be categorized as to whether the wall is internal or external. Much like ceilings, the age of the property can affect the type of structure considerably, as can architectural or design considerations. This is particularly the case for external walls, which are visible as a finished product, whereas interior walls are constructed to provide a flat surface which will then be further decorated. That said, external walls can generally be identified by two simple categories — whether they are of a solid or cavity structure.

solid walls

Solid external walls, or those with no cavity, tend to be found in older buildings. Depth and make-up is varied, but most show similar characteristics to the examples outlined below.

cavity walls

Nearly all modern houses have external walls which are constructed with a cavity. This means that the external wall effectively consists of two layers, with a void or cavity between the layers for insulation.

There are many possible combinations for how these two layers are constructed but the examples on the following page demonstrate the most common variations that occur.

brick/block solid wall

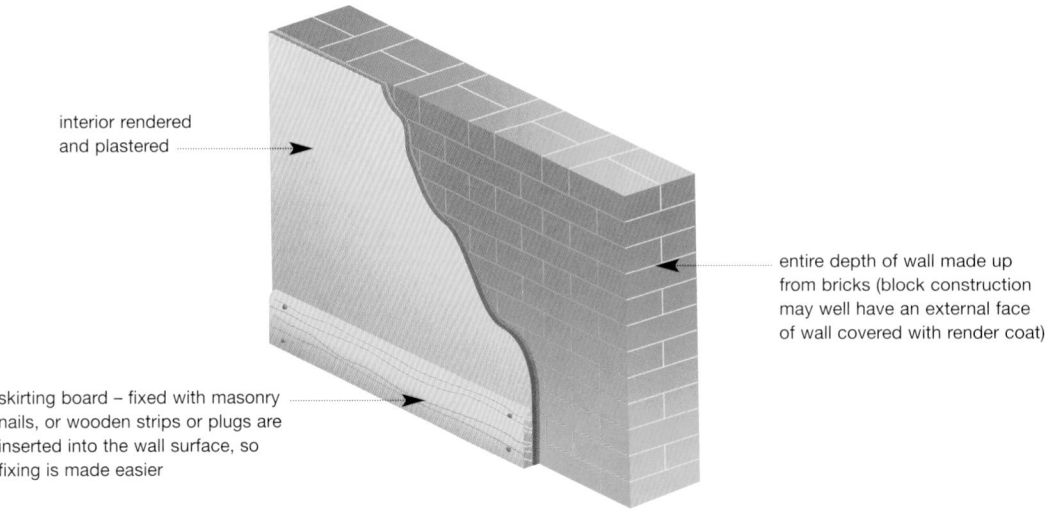

interior rendered and plastered

entire depth of wall made up from bricks (block construction may well have an external face of wall covered with render coat)

skirting board – fixed with masonry nails, or wooden strips or plugs are inserted into the wall surface, so fixing is made easier

natural stone solid wall

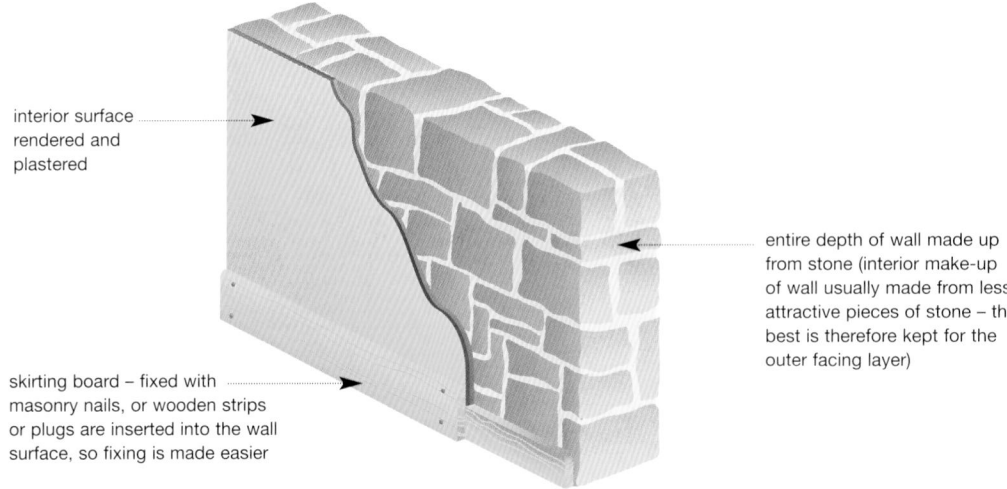

interior surface rendered and plastered

entire depth of wall made up from stone (interior make-up of wall usually made from less attractive pieces of stone – the best is therefore kept for the outer facing layer)

skirting board – fixed with masonry nails, or wooden strips or plugs are inserted into the wall surface, so fixing is made easier

brick/block cavity with render & plaster

This type of cavity wall employs solid wall construction materials to provide a brick outer layer for the finished exterior of the house, and a block inner layer which requires further rendering and plastering before decoration can be applied.

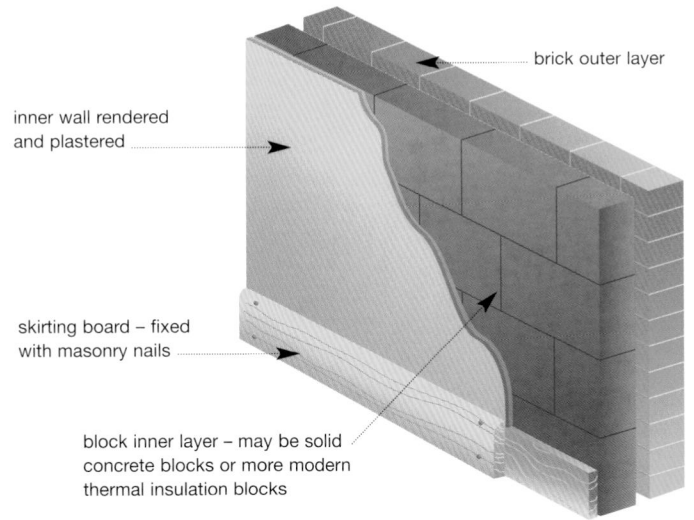

inner wall rendered and plastered

brick outer layer

skirting board – fixed with masonry nails

block inner layer – may be solid concrete blocks or more modern thermal insulation blocks

brick/timber cavity

This is a popular form of construction in modern houses, where the exterior wall layer is made from a solid facing material such as brick, and the interior layer takes the form of a wooden framework.

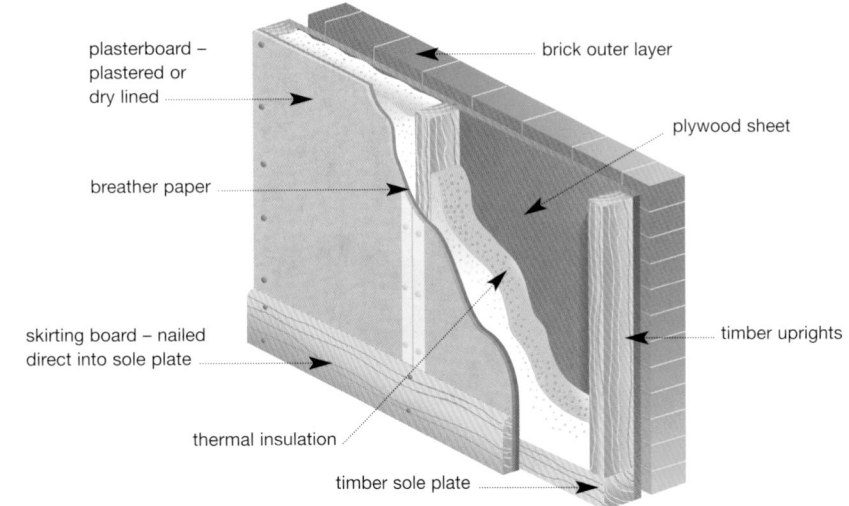

plasterboard – plastered or dry lined

brick outer layer

breather paper

plywood sheet

skirting board – nailed direct into sole plate

timber uprights

thermal insulation

timber sole plate

brick/block cavity – dry lined

This example shows that block walls can be combined with dry lining techniques for finishing purposes. Outer and inner wall construction is similar to that shown for the first example of cavity walls, but the internal finishing is clearly different.

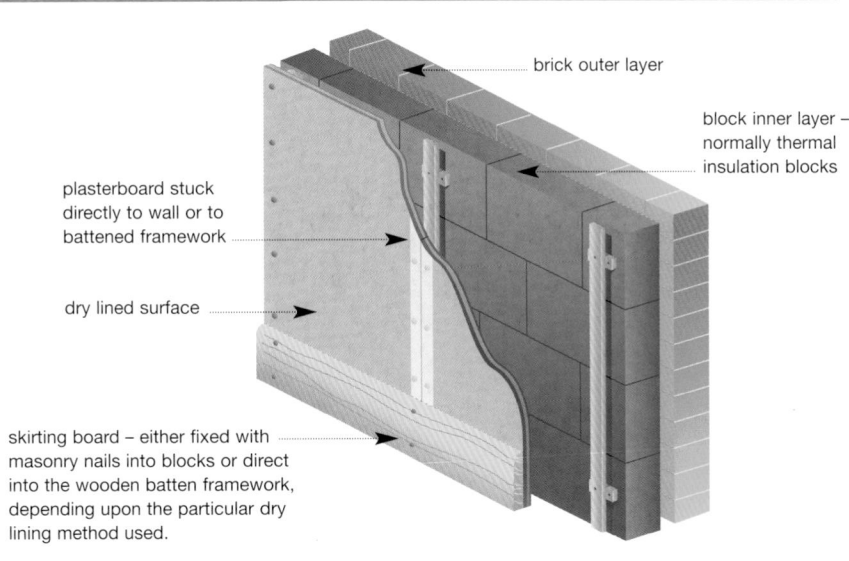

brick outer layer

block inner layer – normally thermal insulation blocks

plasterboard stuck directly to wall or to battened framework

dry lined surface

skirting board – either fixed with masonry nails into blocks or direct into the wooden batten framework, depending upon the particular dry lining method used.

internal walls

Internal walls are usually constructed as a single layer and therefore do not have the same depth as external walls. Many characteristics are similar, but there tends to be a wide variety of structure in terms of the internal make-up of the wall itself. Much is dependent on whether the wall is loadbearing or non-loadbearing, and therefore what structural requirements it has in relation to the rest of the building.

solid construction

As the name suggests, these walls are made from solid materials, blocks or bricks. The main structural differences depend on how the outer faces of the wall are finished.

hollow construction

Hollow wall construction is very common in modern houses, with most homes containing some form of 'hollow' wall. However, this does not necessarily mean that the wall is non-loadbearing, and it is important to check such issues out before commencing work. The examples on the page opposite illustrate the most common types of internal hollow wall.

block

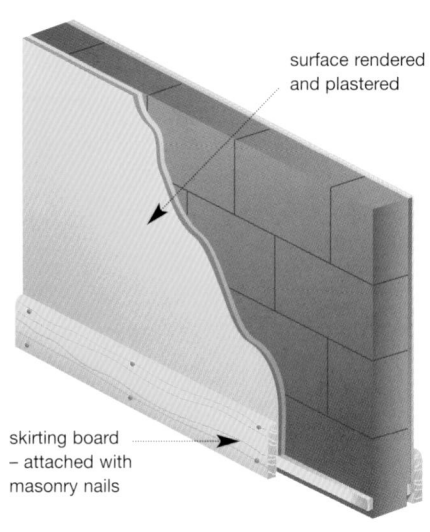

surface rendered and plastered

skirting board – attached with masonry nails

brick

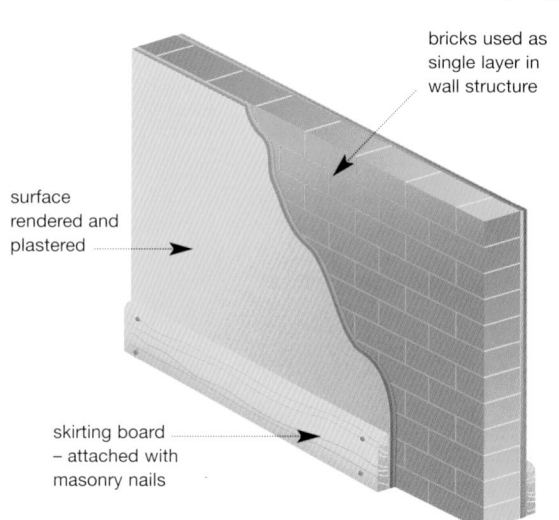

bricks used as single layer in wall structure

surface rendered and plastered

skirting board – attached with masonry nails

block/dry lined

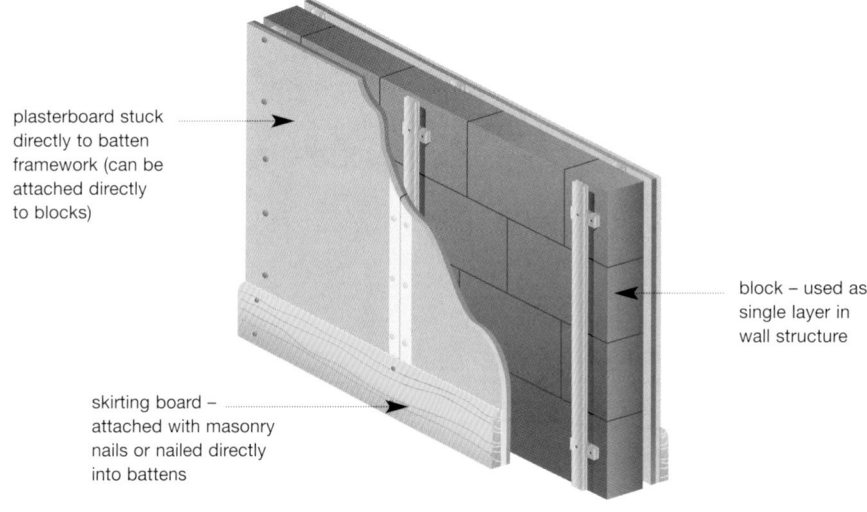

plasterboard stuck directly to batten framework (can be attached directly to blocks)

block – used as single layer in wall structure

skirting board – attached with masonry nails or nailed directly into battens

plasterboard/stud partition

Probably the most commonly occurring of all modern internal hollow walls. Easy to build and adaptable to most circumstances.

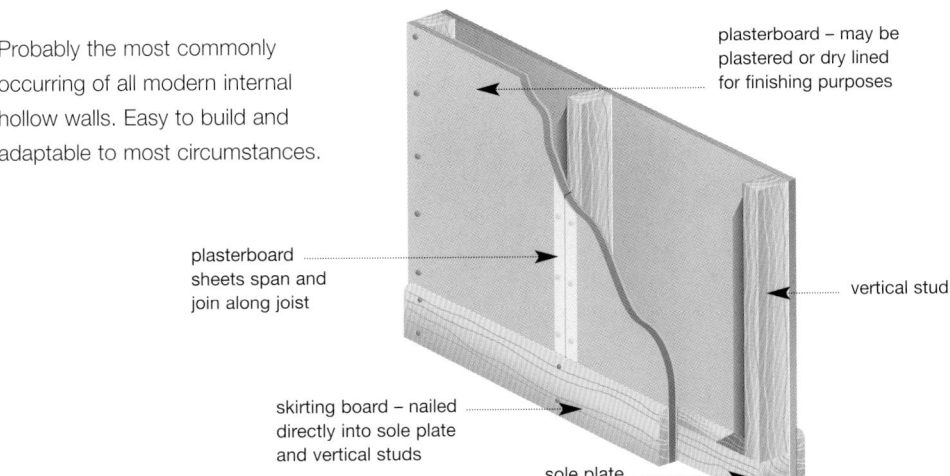

plasterboard – may be plastered or dry lined for finishing purposes

plasterboard sheets span and join along joist

vertical stud

skirting board – nailed directly into sole plate and vertical studs

sole plate

dry partition wall

A lightweight and simply built wall. Its make-up still provides a rigid finished product.

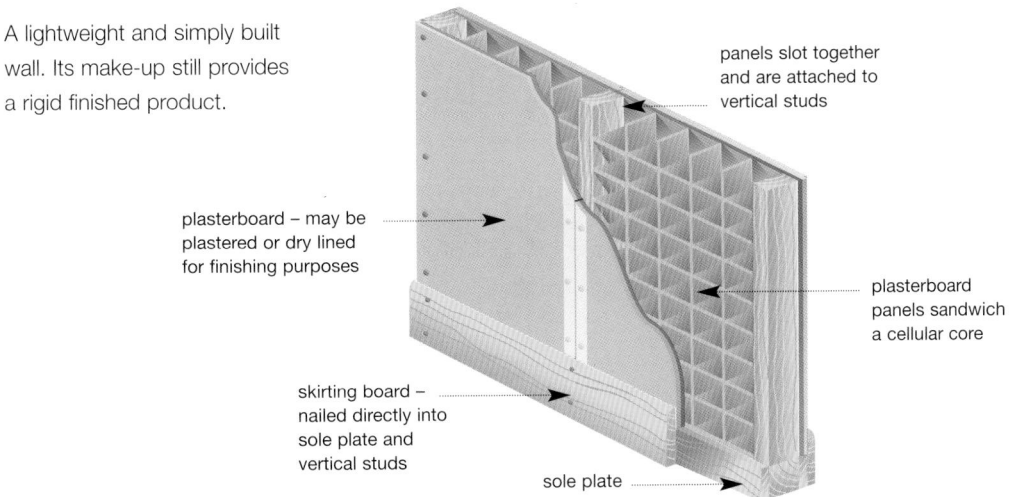

panels slot together and are attached to vertical studs

plasterboard – may be plastered or dry lined for finishing purposes

plasterboard panels sandwich a cellular core

skirting board – nailed directly into sole plate and vertical studs

sole plate

lath and plaster partition

As with ceiling structures, lath and plaster dates back to older houses before the advent of plasterboard.

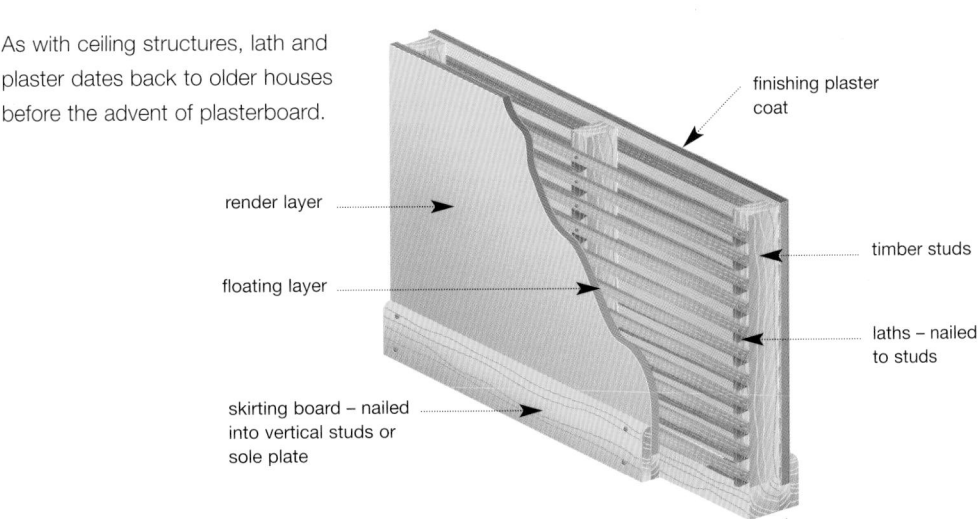

finishing plaster coat

render layer

floating layer

timber studs

laths – nailed to studs

skirting board – nailed into vertical studs or sole plate

planning

Careful planning is crucial for any type of repair or renovation because there are so many issues that need close consideration. In addition to gauging tool and material requirements, it is also important to establish whether planning permission will be necessary, whether you are capable of carrying out all the work yourself, and what the total cost and time frame will be. The extent and nature of a project will be highly dependent on at least some, if not all, of these considerations. This chapter provides some basic guidelines in all of these areas and helps to provide a framework for decision making and setting about a renovation project.

The careful use of mirrors, as shown here, can create the illusion of space for your bathroom.

options for change

The first stage of planning should focus on what currently exists in the home, and what you would like to change. This can be considered as the inspirational stage, though any potential ideas must be checked against the compatibility of your existing house structure. Design inspiration can take many forms, and you may be able to picture your requirements quite easily. Alternatively, you may need to find ideas in magazines or from other people's homes.

open plan

Knocking two rooms into one, or widening entrances between rooms, is a way of creating a more open plan layout. Whilst providing a lighter, more spacious atmosphere, consideration needs to be given to the feasibility of removing whole or partial walls, especially if they are loadbearing. However, this sort of renovation can dramatically change the look of your home and totally transform a cramped, rather gloomy atmosphere into a design of far greater appeal. In an age where space is at a premium, every opportunity should be taken to make the best use of all areas.

RGHT *Open plan dining and living areas create a very relaxed and comfortable feel to your home, which is appropriate to modern design and space utilization.*

en-suite options

Putting up a wall to form an en-suite bathroom is a very popular renovation carried out in many homes. The construction considerations are straightforward, but remember to account for the expense of actually installing the bathroom and the cost of plumbing that will be incurred. Not only may you have to extend supply pipes, but also deal with any new drainage requirements. The end result is invariably worth the effort, adding greater convenience and comfort to your lifestyle. This is especially the case for larger families, where the addition of an extra bathroom will ease the demand on the main bathroom.

LEFT *Although en-suite bathrooms may sometimes feel slightly cramped, mirrors may be used to counter this impression by creating an illusion of space.*

split-level exposure

Ceiling design need not always be restricted to a flat and two-dimensional appearance. Look at options to build split-level ceilings or, on a top floor, look at the possibility of exposing roof rafters to create a more open, airy atmosphere. Both these options require some quite extensive work, but the results can add much greater interest to the ceiling structure as a whole.

ornate ceilings

It is not always necessary to go to great efforts structurally in order to improve the appearance of a ceiling. For example, simply adding decoration to the existing ceiling, such as cornice or ceiling roses, can make a dramatic improvement. These features can be fitted relatively easily and provide an instant effect that 'lifts' the entire decorative scheme of a room.

ABOVE *Open plan living can be extended to split-level designs, where the overall 'open' theme is continued over more than one floor level.*

LEFT *The ornate mouldings that make up this ceiling appearance add great decorative appeal to this entrance hall – an area often neglected in many households.*

BELOW *In this bathroom, the tongue and groove theme has been used on both the walls and ceiling, providing an unusual but well-balanced decorative scheme.*

wall options

Just as ornate fittings can be added to ceilings, simple decorative features can also be applied to wall surfaces, helping to 'break up' a flat, monotonous surface. Different types of wooden cladding can be used, together with various other decorative techniques such as special paint effects or natural wood systems. Manufacturers are increasingly catering for this market, producing a range of proprietary products which provide a traditional look while still being easy to use.

23

tools & equipment

The range of tools and equipment necessary for completing DIY tasks can be vast and expensive. Yet many of the basic tools are in fact multi-purpose, and make up what might be called a 'household tool kit'. Once this strong base of essential tools has been established, you can go on to purchase more specialized tools as and when they are required. Although it is not necessary to spend a fortune on equipment, it is generally a good rule to buy the best tools that you can afford. Top quality tools tend to last longer and give better results, time and again.

household tools

This general household tool kit contains the essential tools for carrying out any number of small jobs and tasks around the home. Although the kit will not cope with every situation you encounter, it provides a good starting point to which you can add more specific tool requirements.

claw hammer

sanding block

wire brush

slot-head screwdrivers

cross-head screwdrivers

insulated sleeves

nail punch

pipe, joist and cable detector

craft knife

combination pliers

bradawl

carpenter's pencil

side cutters

long-nose pliers

half-round rasp

general purpose chisels

cordless drill/driver

oil stone

plier wrench

sealant dispenser

stepladder

wooden mallet

tape measure

clamp

mini hacksaw

mini level

scraper

mitre block

panel saw

power tools

Power tools are designed to make jobs easier and less time consuming. For most enthusiasts, mid-range tools are ideal, as the very expensive equipment is designed for everyday work, and the very cheap equipment for the occasional DIY person. Even so, the cost of power tools has dropped considerably, and it is possible to buy quality products relatively cheaply. For some tasks, it can even be worth buying very cheap tools for limited use before discarding.

power drill

router

jigsaw

electric sander

construction tools

brick jointer

external corner trowel

internal corner trowel

pointing trowel

gauging trowel

brick trowel

plastic bucket

In order to carry out alterations to walls and ceilings, the household tool kit needs to be supplemented with construction tools for heavy duty tasks. Try to concentrate on specific needs when purchasing such tools, as it can be tempting to fall for gimmicky options or cheap alternatives that will be of minimal use in the long term. Instead, stick to good quality, tried and tested tools which should last for several years of DIY projects. If you are unsure of the best product, consult your retailer.

shovel

sledge-hammer

plastering trowel

hawk

wood plane

dry wall saw

board and door lifter

wrecking bar

power stirrer

mitresaw

combination square

plumb line

chalk line

hacksaw

caulking blade

water level

spirit level

bolster chisel

cold chisel

club hammer

taping/coating knife

workbench

HIRING TOOLS

For isolated tasks that require particularly heavy duty equipment, or tools that are very expensive to buy, hiring is often the best option. This area has become a growing sector of the DIY market, and hire shops are increasingly catering for home repair enthusiasts, as well as traditional trade customers.

construction materials – 1

The materials used in house construction are clearly wide and varied, and depend on the age of the building and its design. However, there are many items which are common to the majority of building work, with many examples shown here. The items outlined below are the modern structural components which can be used for renovation projects – the items used to fit all these components together and 'finish' them prior to decoration are outlined on pages 28–9.

planning

26

building boards and accessories

plasterboard – manufactured in various thicknesses and varieties. Used as a base for plaster or dry lined finishes.

medium density fibreboard – better known as mdf, used as a general purpose building board. Manufactured in various thicknesses and varieties.

ply – all-purpose building board constructed from compressed wooden veneers. Manufactured in various thicknesses and varieties offering different properties.

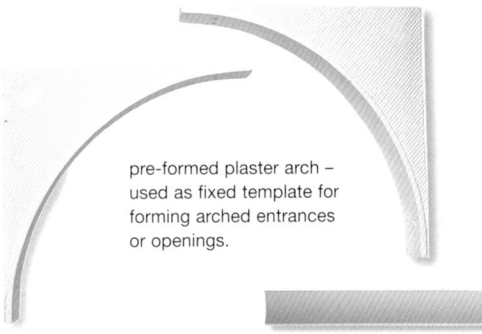

pre-formed plaster arch – used as fixed template for forming arched entrances or openings.

coving – used as decorative embellishment around wall/ceiling junction. More ornate forms are referred to as cornice.

brackets and bars

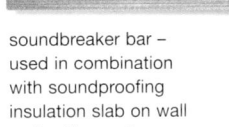

soundbreaker bar – used in combination with soundproofing insulation slab on wall and ceiling surfaces.

wall profile – used as bracket to tie in new block walls with existing ones.

wall profile tie – clips to wall profile and is inserted between block courses for extra strength.

joist hangers – all these are used for supporting ends of joists at the wall junction.

angle bead – metal former used to create precise external corners when plastering.

bricks and blocks

brick – manufactured in different colours, finishes and general make-up, displaying varying properties and characteristics.

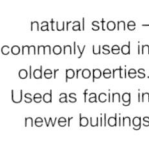

natural stone – commonly used in older properties. Used as facing in newer buildings

thermal insulation block – used mainly for internal layer of cavity walls. Sometimes manufactured in greater lengths than standard block size.

glass block – decorative wall construction material. Non-loadbearing.

concrete block – used for internal layer of cavity walls and internal loadbearing or non-loadbearing walls. Sometimes manufactured with reconstructed stone facing and used for external walls. Also sometimes used as external wall and then rendered.

wood and mouldings

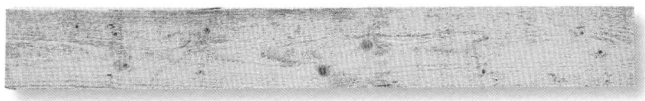

sawn softwood 10cm x 5cm (4in x 2in) –
multi-purpose building material

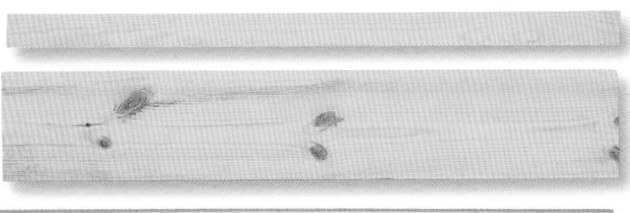

prepared softwood 5cm x 2.5cm (2in x 1in)
– used for frameworks for cladding or plasterboarding.

prepared softwood 12.5cm x 2.5cm (5in
x 1in) – common floorboard size and
other multi-purpose building uses

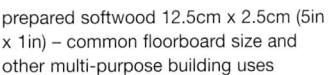

tongue and groove boarding – used as cladding for
wall surfaces or on ceilings. Deeper or more heavy
duty boards sometimes used for floorboarding.

panel moulding – decorative feature added to
flush doors or to create a panelled wall effect.

rail moulding – decorative rail used around perimeter
of a room. Available in all sizes and many designs.

architrave – decorative trim around doorways.
Available in all sizes and many designs.

skirting board – decorative and
protective trim at floor/wall junction.
Available in all sizes and many designs.

insulation materials

suspended ceiling system

soundproofing insulation slab –
supplied usually in 120cm x
60cm (4ft x 2ft) sections. Used
in walls, ceilings and floors for
sound insulation.

mineral wool – supplied
in roll or blanket and
used for thermal
insulation in
lofts or stud walls.

loose fill insulation –
alternative to the
mineral wool option.

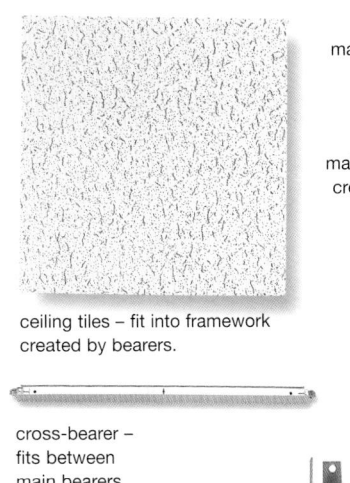

ceiling tiles – fit into framework
created by bearers.

cross-bearer –
fits between
main bearers.

angle section –
makes outer frame
of suspended
ceiling.

main bearer –
creates main
frame of
system.

angle brackets –
used to attach
supporting wire
to ceiling.

wire – holds
framework in place,
extending from main
bearers to ceiling.

construction materials – 2

In addition to major structural items for building projects, it is obviously necessary to have correct materials for fixing components and for reaching a suitable finish. The materials listed here should cover the majority of tasks involved in ceiling and wall constructional work, although it must be understood that there are sometimes slight variations in material design or make-up between different manufacturers, so always check with the retailer if in doubt.

mechanical fixings

screw-in frame tie – used around the frame of blocked-up entrance to tie in new section of wall. Supplied with wall plug.

wall plugs – come in a range of sizes, shapes and designs and are manufactured for use in all types of wall surface. They are positioned inside pre-drilled holes before screw insertion.

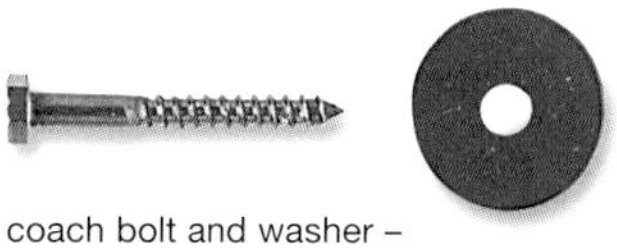

coach bolt and washer – alternative heavy duty screw fixing.

round wire nail – used for carpentry work. Larger sizes ideal for use in stud wall construction.

frame fixing – screw and wall plug supplied as one. Used for heavy duty wood or masonry fixings.

proprietary design wood screw – specially designed shank makes screw insertion easier.

masonry nail – used for fixing into masonry.

clout nail – general purpose use.

concrete anchor screw – can be used in masonry without the need for a wall plug.

drywall screw – used for fixing plasterboard to soundbreaker bars or into wooden studs.

lost-head wire nail – used in all manner of carpentry jobs.

panel pin – used for fine fixing purposes.

standard screw – can be used in combination with wood or masonry.

brass screw – generally used in situations where the screwhead will be visible, and so is chosen for its decorative finish.

plasterboard nail – used for fixing plasterboard to stud work. Sometimes has a rough shank to improve grip when in position.

fillers and sealants

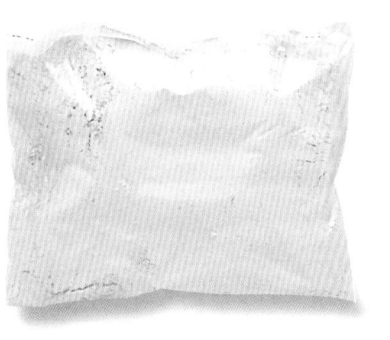

sealant or filler tubes – many sealants or flexible fillers are supplied in a tubed form. Sealant gun required to expel material from tube.

jointing compound – supplied ready mixed. Used for filling over taped joints and nail heads when dry lining.

all-purpose filler – multi-purpose filler, mixed with water to create 'paste' for filling holes in most surfaces.

bonding and finishing materials

bonding coat – water added and used as heavy duty filler prior to plastering.

undercoat plaster – water added and used as undercoat to multi-finish plaster.

cement – added to water with sand to create mortar for building purposes. Other general uses.

one-coat plaster – water added and used as general purpose plaster.

textured coating – added to water to form textured coating for ceilings or walls.

building sand – added to cement and water to create mortar for building purposes. Other connected uses.

multi-finish plaster – water added and used as top coat finishing plaster.

fine sand – used for some mortar requirements and general purpose use.

adhesives

plasticizer – additive to mortar to improve mortar mixture ease of use.

tapes

corner jointing tape – used when dry lining on internal or external corners.

jointing tape – covers joins between plasterboard sheets.

masking tape – used to mask surfaces before decoration or to temporarily hold lightweight objects in position.

self-adhesive jointing tape – used to cover joins between plasterboard sheets. Easy to apply.

insulating tape – multi-purpose pvc tape.

sound/heat insulation tape – used around ceiling/wall junctions and/or door and window surrounds.

pva – multi-purpose adhesive used in concentrated or dilute forms.

wood glue – used for bonding wooden surfaces.

how to start

Before commencing any project, it is important to plan your overall approach to the job and a specific order of work. Simple repairs or minor renovations tend not to raise too many problems, but inadequate planning on larger scale projects can produce very real difficulties. Even if the physical work itself is organized, issues such as building regulations and planning permission may need to be addressed.

planning permission

Before any construction project can begin, some consideration must be given to whether the particular work will need planning permission. The majority of projects inside the home do not need planning approval, and so this is not an issue for most works that you are likely to carry out. However, there are some circumstances which you should be aware of before beginning renovations.

restrictions

Most restrictions are applied to houses that are listed buildings and/or are in conservation areas, national parks, or areas of outstanding natural beauty. If your property fits into any of these categories, always call the local authority planning department before commencing any plans.

However, even in these cases, formal permission is rarely required for internal alterations, minor improvements, and general repairs and maintenance. Projects that definitely require planning permission are generally those in which an area of the house has a 'change of use', normally when business purposes are proposed. For example, if you wish to divide off a section of your home for business use, or you want to create a separate bedsit or flat. So generally speaking, in addition to the restrictions mentioned here, as long as the external appearance of the building is not changed, internal work may be carried out relatively free from too many planning obstacles. However, if you are in any doubt about what is permissible, it is best to contact your local authority.

External work can often be subject to strict building restrictions. Always check with an appropriate body before embarking on work that may require authorization.

building regulations

While most internal renovation is unlikely to require actual planning permission, all construction work should adhere to building regulations. So whenever you plan to carry out any construction work, contact the Building Control Officer at your local council, who·can provide any necessary guidelines for potential work.

making a scale drawing

It is always sensible to make a scale drawing of a proposed construction job, in order to get a firm idea of material quantities. This does not have to be up to architectural standards, but it should provide enough detail to give you a good idea of the effect a project will have, and how it will change the existing look of your home. Graph paper always makes any technical drawing easier, and allows for more accurate measurement. It can often be helpful to add furniture to the diagram, so that you can gauge the effect of the alteration on the overall layout of the room – this can be especially important when dividing an existing room into two separate areas, as the amount of space is obviously reduced.

timescales

Always consider the timescale required to complete a project, as this can influence the most convenient time to commence the job. For example, while some projects can be completed in a weekend, other jobs will take longer, causing disruption to the household for several days. Most projects in this book are designed to be completed within a weekend, although the actual finishing may take longer, as

Many DIY tasks will cause some inevitable disruption to the household. Bear this in mind when planning a job, and aim to commence work at a time convenient to all of those involved.

Making a scale drawing can help you to visualize the effect of any work on the surrounding environment. Adding furntiture to the diagram will also help.

you return to the job for final decorating. As soon as you begin to combine a number of projects, or work on large areas, completing jobs can become more difficult. This is especially true of projects that run between weekends or evenings, so it is advisable either to break them down into smaller sections which can be completed as part of an overall larger renovation, or take time away from day-to-day work in order to make headway into the particular task. Otherwise, pressure to finish the job and minimize disruption can lead to inadequate work with poor finishing. Never underestimate the time involved in a project, and consider it an important part of the planning procedure to decide on dates and times when the work can be done, and within what timescale it can be finished.

budgeting

The greatest expense in a construction project is usually the price of the labour itself, and therefore by reducing this input costs are reduced. If professional trades are required, this should be given priority in terms of your overall budgeting strategy. Aside from this, material costs can be calculated relatively easily so long as accurate measurements are taken. Remember that bulk buying of particular materials should mean financial discounts, and it is always worth shopping around for the best deals. This is especially the case with common items such as general timber and plasterboard because the market is so competitive, and suppliers can vary their prices from week to week. If your planning is comprehensive, you have a better chance of remaining within your budget. However, it is always worth building in a slight surplus requirement to your figures so that if work does take longer – or require more materials – you are able to complete the project without delay.

dealing with professionals

Prior to any construction work, it is important to establish what work you are capable of fulfilling, and to what extent you will require professional help. Small renovations or repairs are unlikely to require a great deal of assistance, but when tackling any major renovation, it is almost certain that the services of plumbers, electricians or general builders may be required. In these cases, try to identify the kind of assistance you require, and understand how to get the best service out of them.

architects and surveyors

In some circumstances, it may be necessary to draw on the services of architects and surveyors. Although not considered conventional 'tradespeople', they supply services which enable the practical side of major renovations to be planned and carried out in the correct manner. Architects only really need employing on larger projects where major design features have to be considered. However, on large projects, architects or surveyors can be employed in a kind of project management role, overseeing general work to ensure it meets building regulations (see page 30). Bear in mind that these services cost money and fees for monitoring work can add a further 10 per cent to the original price of drawing up plans. There may also be daily rate charges for site attendance.

Professional advice for major projects is always advisable, particularly for projects that may require planning permission. Bear these costs in mind when planning the work.

finding good tradespeople

Finding good, reliable tradespeople can be difficult – there is no point in hiring the best best bricklayer in the area if he never turns up for work. The best method is to use personal recommendations, as you can see or hear about the quality of the work from a genuine customer. The other alternative is to contact three or four advertised companies for separate quotes. However, although this may help to ensure a competitive price, it does not gurantee the quality of the work or the reliability of the tradesperson. Even companies that display particular trade association badges may be no more reliable than other advertisers, so check the credentials with the association itself, and then with an independent body. Always ask to have a look at a person's work, preferably through the property owner, and then perhaps with the builder or tradesperson.

estimates, quotations and prices

Before allowing any tradesperson to begin work in your home, it is essential to know how much the actual job is going to cost. Estimates, quotations and prices can be a minefield – and are frequently the source of customers' disgruntlement. The main factor to bear in mind at this stage is that if you receive an estimate or a quotation, this is exactly the case – they are only estimates or quotations and therefore the price you pay can inflate considerably. If at all possible, it is therefore best to get a specific price from the tradesperson, which should not fluctuate unless you decide to change the specifications for the work. In some circumstances, an estimate may be necessary, as you may not have made final decisions on specifications and need to see how the project develops. However, the closer you can get to deciding on a price before the work begins, the better position you will find yourself in when budgeting for the job and keeping track of payments.

Never make the mistake of paying any money 'up front' unless there are exceptional circumstances. (For example, if the tradesperson is supplying expensive materials, it is only fair that you should make an initial downpayment towards the cost of those materials.) However, generally

Keep the lines of communication open. Although the cost of work may rise slightly as the job progresses, this can be negotiated at each stage, helping you monitor the cost overall.

speaking there is no reason to pay until the job is complete and you are happy with the finished product. For long projects, it is fair to stage payments throughout the job, but always leave the largest payment until completion. Finally, treat builders or tradespeople who insist on cash-only payments with some suspicion. Although there are potential savings to be made in this line, it means you have no come-back in terms of defective work or problems at a later date. Such methods of payment could also suggest illegal transactions in the eyes of the relevant tax authorities.

extras

On making any final payment, seeing the word 'extras' or 'extra work carried out' can add a surprising amount to the figure you were expecting to pay. In many cases, these may be items that you authorized during the overall works. However, it is always best to get a price for extra work before it is done, so that shocks do not occur at the final stage of payment. Alternatively, arrange during the initial price agreement that any extra work has to be carried out on your authority and is charged at a specific hourly rate. This makes it much easier to keep a track of expenses and prevent unexpected surprises with the final bill.

avoiding disputes

Disputes can easily be avoided so long as you follow the recognized 'rules of engagement'. Over half the battle is won if you have chosen the right tradesperson. Further gains can be made by ensuring that the price you are quoted is written and detailed in terms of the work to be carried out. This therefore acts as an accurate referral document for all parties. Aside from this, the only problems which generally arise concern the standard of work compared to what was initially agreed. Most of these problems can be sorted out through discussion and compromise, and it is best to avoid legal wrangles unless absolutely necessary. If you are that unhappy with the work carried out, your only option may be to withhold payment and hand the matter over to a legal team of solicitors.

In following these simple guidelines, you should be well equipped for employing the services of people from various trades. Simply remember that, in all occupations, there are both good and bad operators and that the building business gets more than its fair share of criticism. However, if you do have a reliable tradesperson at your disposal, pay them on time and recommend them to friends – in looking after their interests, you will almost certainly be looking after your own.

Professional tradespeople will do a good job for a fair price. However, before agreeing on the terms and conditions of the contract, establish the length of time and expense of the project.

altering the structure of a wall

The type and extent of work required to alter a wall structure will largely depend on the existing structure. Before deciding on the exact changes you would like to make, it is important to identify the kind of wall you currently have, so that you can gauge the best procedures for transformation. As always, the key issue is whether the wall is loadbearing or non-loadbearing – only once this has been established can planning commence for alteration. This chapter covers a range of projects, some with more structural implications than others, but many of the outlined tasks deal with the more aesthetic intentions of altering the structure of walls within your home.

*Open plan dining and living areas
create a very relaxed and comfortable
feel to your home and surroundings.*

safety at work

Safety is always of paramount importance when considering any aspect of home improvement. Aside from general working tools, it is therefore necessary to build up a collection of safety equipment, so that you are adequately protected when carrying out any task around the home. When choosing safety equipment, never compromise on quality and ensure that the articles you purchase display the relevant safety standard markings.

first aid kit

By far the greatest number of injuries resulting from home improvement are very minor grazes and abrasions, and therefore it is essential to have a well stocked first aid kit in your home.

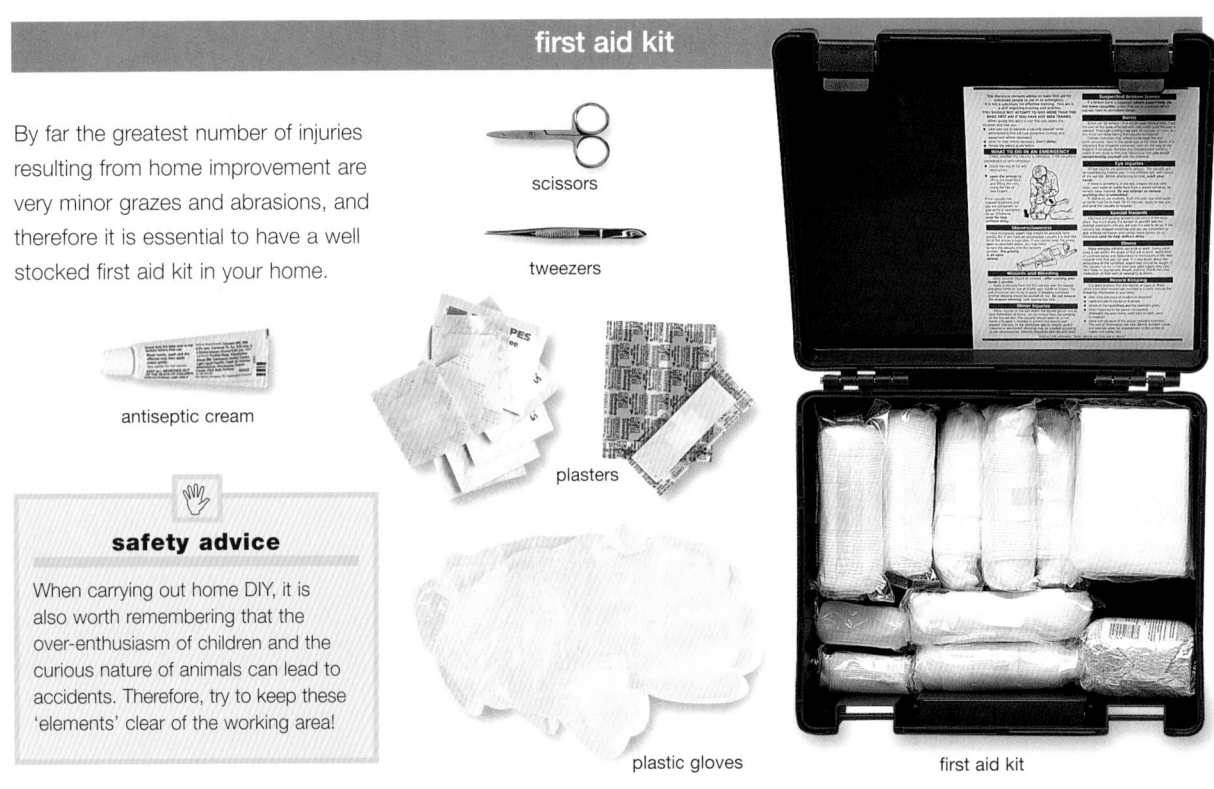

scissors

tweezers

antiseptic cream

plasters

safety advice

When carrying out home DIY, it is also worth remembering that the over-enthusiasm of children and the curious nature of animals can lead to accidents. Therefore, try to keep these 'elements' clear of the working area!

plastic gloves

first aid kit

safety equipment

A range of safety equipment is available for various DIY tasks. Some items are intended for particular jobs, but many pieces, such as work boots, goggles and protective gloves, should be worn in most situations.

dust mask

protective gloves

knee pads

hard hat

lead test kit

respirator mask

goggles

ear defenders

work boots

Gaining easy access to all areas of a room is an important part of the safety at work code. Never risk injury by overstretching or overreaching – instead use ladders or access platforms so that you can reach all the areas in a room with ease. This is especially the case for exterior work, where tower scaffolds or mechanical platforms may be a practical option. This kind of equipment can be hired and helps to provide a safe working environment, as well as save time when extensive, high level work is needed.

ladders

Ladders have always been the most commonly used and versatile of access equipment options. However, despite their simple construction and ease of use, there are a number of simple but important rules to obey when using them.

- Ensure that the distance between the base of the ladder and the wall is one quarter the distance between the base of the wall and top of the ladder.
- Ensure that the base of the ladder is on a level, non-slip surface.

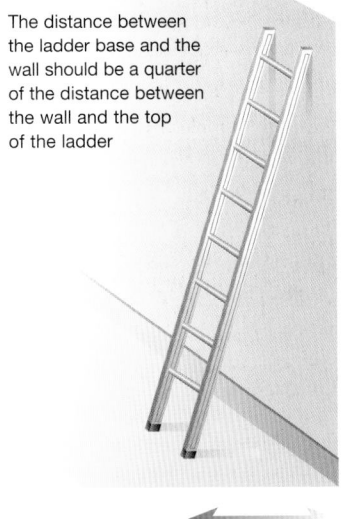

The distance between the ladder base and the wall should be a quarter of the distance between the wall and the top of the ladder

Careful ladder positioning is vital for the safety of its user.

- Ensure that the top of the ladder has total contact with the wall surface.
- Ensure that all rungs are secure and have not been damaged in any way.

Multi-purpose ladders are usually constructed from aluminium and can be used as step ladders, extra-long traditional ladders, and even as a working platform. However, such versatility means that you must check the user guidelines carefully, as joint locking systems can vary between different models.

GENERAL TOOL CARE

Accidents can often be caused by tools that have either been poorly maintained or are so old that they are no longer safe to use. Therefore careful tool maintenance will always ensure that you get the best out of them, as well as making sure they are safe to use. Below are a few points to consider regarding tool maintenance and safety.

- Chisels, planes and cutting equipment must always be kept as sharp as possible. More accidents are caused by blunt tools slipping on the surface than by sharp tools. An oilstone is ideal to keep tools such as chisels razor sharp.

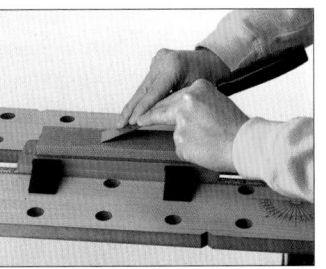

- Electric cables and wires on power tools can break or crack, so they should be inspected regularly to ensure they are in good condition. Power tools in general may also require periodic servicing. Power tool efficiency can also be hampered by the accessories you use with them. Therefore bits and blades should be renewed when necessary, as old ones can strain the workings of the power tool being used.

- Hammers can often slip right off the head of a nail when you are attempting to knock it in. To avoid this happening, sand the striking face of the hammer in order to both clean it and provide a fine key. It is surprising what a difference this simple procedure can make. This technique may be applied to all types of hammer and is useful for any hammering procedure.

a simple working platform

Adjustable trestles allow their height to be suited to the particular job at hand

Ensure the trestles are spaced every 1.5m (60in)

Position trestles at intervals below the scaffold planks

Ensure that all trestle feet are touching the ground

recognizing problems – 1

Cracks and faults in wall and ceiling surfaces can often look more problematic than they actually are. However, while the main concern may appear to be aesthetic, cracks should also be seen as signs of potential structural problems – such as movement – so it is important to try to determine their cause. Many cracks form for particular reasons and can easily be identified and categorized. The diagram below shows common areas where cracking occurs.

testing cracks and movement

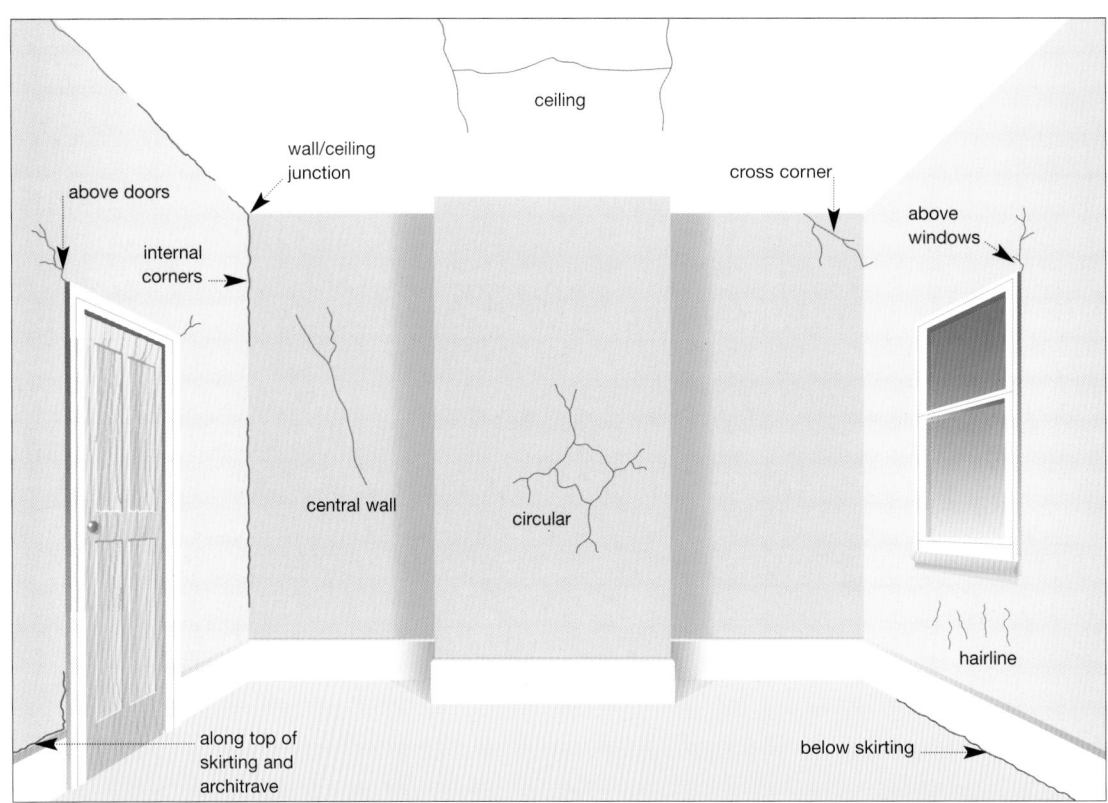

Determining the movement and development of cracks – if any – can obviously be difficult. Such movements tend to be slight and take time to develop, making it virtually impossible to monitor accurately. For this reason, proprietary crack monitoring systems can now be bought which enable accurate measuring of any movement. Although manufacturers' guidelines do vary, the general principles of use remain the same for most commercial brands.
If in doubt, contact the product manufacturer or a structural surveyor for further assistance.

1 Screw the detector in place, with the detection scale roughly positioned over the crack. Do not overtighten the screws at this stage.

2 Shift the scale on the detector so that it sits precisely in line with the crack. Tighten the screws when you are happy with the position.

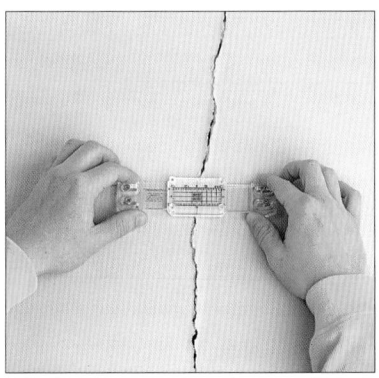

3 Remove the plastic lugs from the edge of the detector to free the two-plate mechanism. If movement does occur, the scale on one plate will move in relation to the other, thereby making it possible accurately to observe the extent and timespan of any movement. Detectors, of slightly varying designs, can also be used across corners or at ceiling and floor level.

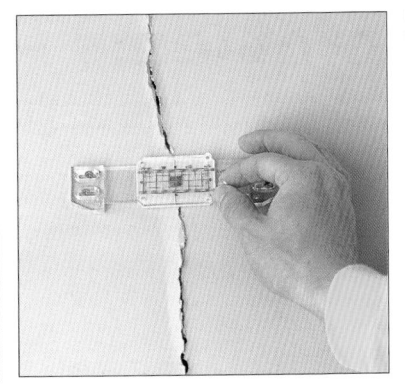

safety advice

Always seek professional advice about cracks that may represent structural problems. Detecting subsidence or structural faults is a skilled profession, and should never be underestimated. Failure to gauge the gravity of the situation could present long-term dangers to both the structure of the house and the health of its inhabitants.

type	causes of cracks & remedies
internal corners	These cracks are often a result of settlement in new homes and therefore can be filled and decorated. Persistent cracking should be monitored.
ceiling	Ceiling cracks which are very directional, in that they have a relatively straight course or turn at right angles, tend to result from slight board movement in the ceiling structure. These can be filled and decorated or, if they persist, lining can normally prevent them from reappearing.
cross corner	Cracks which extend across a corner from one wall to another can represent a subsidence problem, especially if lines of brick or blockwork can be picked out. In such cases, seek professional advice.
above windows	Cracks are often visible extending from the corners of windows up towards ceiling level. So long as they are relatively small, they generally represent slight settlement or movement. However, large cracks that show a vertical shift should be investigated further.
hairline	These cracks are common, multi-directional, and suggest slight movement of a plaster surface. Numbers tend to increase with the age of the building. Most are superficial and do not represent any cause for alarm. However, if new plaster surfaces display a number of persistent cracks, this could suggest that the plaster was poorly mixed or has not bonded correctly to the wall. In such cases, replastering may be necessary.
below skirting	Gaps below skirting tend to suggest that the skirting was poorly fitted. However, cracks that continue to develop could reflect floor problems or some subsidence. Those which continue to grow should be investigated by a professional.
circular	Cracks that form irregular, circular shapes tend to reflect areas of plaster blowing away from the wall background. This is common in old lath and plaster walls, where age has taken its toll and the plaster surface has become unstable in localized areas. The affected area can be removed and patch-plastered.
central wall cracks	These may occur for any number of reasons and should simply be monitored to check that they do not grow wider. Seek professional advice in extreme cases.
along top of skirting and architrave	Cracks occur in these places either because of age and slight building movement or because the materials are new and take a little time to settle to the atmospheric conditions of the particular room environment. Unless the cracks persist or grow after filling and redecoration, there is generally no cause for alarm.
above doors	See explanation for cracks around windows.
wall/ceiling junction	These cracks commonly occur during settlement in new houses, and as a result of age in older ones. Small cracks can be filled and redecorated, whereas larger types should be monitored to check that they do not expand, thus requiring structural repair.

recognizing problems – 2

In addition to movement, structural areas of the home can also be affected by the action of damp and insect or fungal infestation. Many such problems are easily redeemable, but others can have wider consequences and be extremely damaging to the building structure, especially if they are left untreated. These sorts of problems can take many forms and affect different areas of the home, but the diagram below outlines many of the key areas to look out for.

damp and infestation

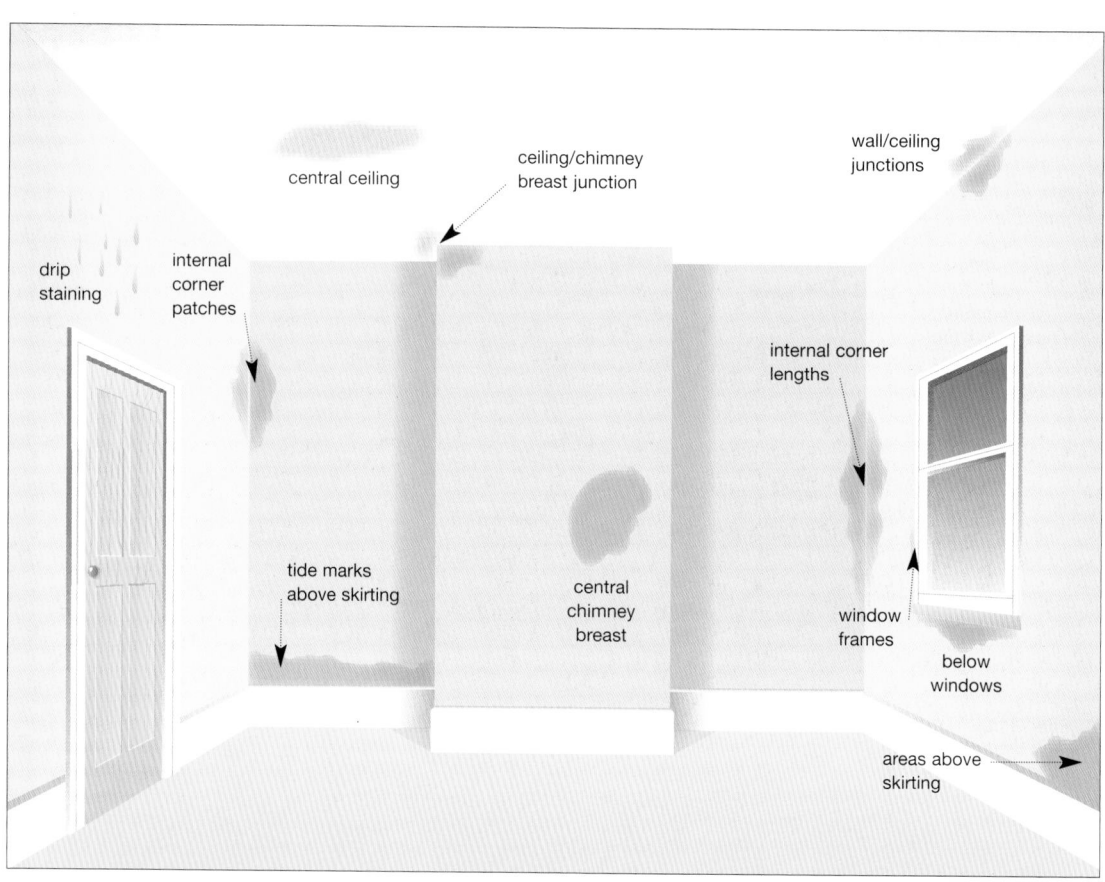

central ceiling

ceiling/chimney breast junction

wall/ceiling junctions

drip staining

internal corner patches

internal corner lengths

tide marks above skirting

central chimney breast

window frames

below windows

areas above skirting

other problems of infestation

Aside from those problems usually associated with damp, there are other potential problems that can be linked to insects and fungal attack.

dry rot

This is an exceptionally damaging form of decay which mainly affects timber but also spreads across masonry.

While identifying and counteracting the source will remedy the problem, dry rot attacks with actual fungicidal spores which spread the disease very quickly, making it difficult to eradicate. Dry rot does initially take hold in areas of damp and poor ventilation. It is identified by thin, white strands which spread along surfaces, rather like a spider's web. The effect breaks down building structure irreparably. Treatment should therefore be hasty, involving the cutting out and destroying of all infected areas. New timber and

materials should be treated to protect it against dry rot infection.

woodworm

These are basically the larvae of particular beetles, and so there are two methods for discovering if you have the problem. Either the appearance of the beetles provides evidence of their presence, or more commonly, the actual flight holes are visible, indicating their existence in the household woodwork. Action against woodworm must be swift as the parasite can quickly break down timber and spread throughout the entire house. Spray infected areas with the appropriate insecticide and also any unaffected woodwork that is nearby, to prevent further spreading. When replacing any timbers, always ensure that the new material has been preserved properly. If in any doubt, seek professional advice.

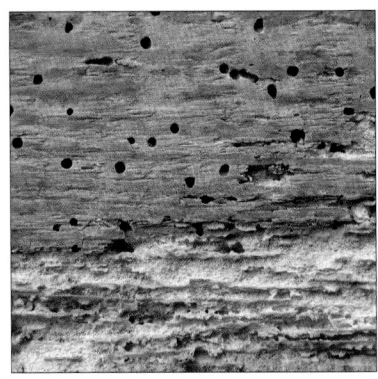

type	causes of damp & remedies
central ceiling	These patches tend to be a result of leaking pipes in the ceiling, or at top floor level they may be a roof leak dripping on to surfaces below. Consult a plumber for fixing pipework, and make any necessary tile repair work at roof level.
ceiling/chimney breast junction	Damp patches which develop in these areas may be a result of a gap in flashing around the chimney. Therefore inspect the area and effect a repair if required.
wall/ceiling junctions	At top floor level, this is often a result of a blocked gutter. Unblock the gutter to eliminate the resulting damp penetration. This sort of damp may also result from a lean-to building, where the flashing at the point where it joins the main building has deteriorated. Check the flashing and repair if necessary.
internal corner lengths	Elongated damp patches along internal corners often indicate a blocked or cracked downpipe on the exterior of the building. Dripping water therefore gradually penetrates, causing a persistent damp wall stain. Unblock or replace the downpipe as required.
window frames	Damp penetration is common around the edges of windows due to a build-up of condensation or because of a break in the seal around the edge of the window frame itself. Check that the window is sealed correctly and reapply silicone sealant if necessary. If the problem is more condensation-based, install better ventilation systems for the room or simply open windows more often.
below windows	Seals beneath windows may be damaged or the drip guard below the sill may be blocked. Check both areas and clear or re-seal as required.
areas above skirting	Large damp patches above skirting are often a result of the build-up of material, such as piles of soil, on the external side of the wall surface. This bridges the damp course and causes damp penetration. Simply remove the obstructive material, and ensure soil levels are kept below damp course level.
central chimney breast	These patches commonly develop in disused chimneys where the chimney and fireplace have been blocked off. The disused chimney void therefore has no ventilation, causing the moist damp air to penetrate through the chimney breast. To cure this problem, install an air vent in the chimney breast in order to improve air flow and circulation.
tide marks above skirting	If these are not a result of the damp course being bridged on the other side of the wall, then it may be straightforward rising damp. This is common in older houses with no damp course or in houses where the damp course is damaged and therefore allowing water penetration. Various damproofing injection systems are the most effective cure. These systems are always best carried out by professionals.
internal corner patches	Small damp patches in walls often result from patches of damaged pointing or render on the exterior of the building. Simple repair of the appropriate material should cure the problem.
drip staining	Visible stains from drips or running moisture on the walls tends to point in the direction of a condensation problem. This commonly occurs in kitchens and bathrooms. Simply install better ventilation systems and open windows more often.

removing a loadbearing wall ⁄⁄⁄⁄

Removing a loadbearing wall is not a project that should be tackled lightly, and professional advice and instruction should be sought before carrying out this procedure. Total wall removal is rare, and it is more common to knock through a loadbearing wall in order to open up the floor layout and convert two rooms into a single area with a more open plan design. The work involved is strongly based around supportive measures.

The most important factor when taking on work of this kind is to ensure that there is adequate support, both while the area of wall is being removed and when the work is complete. This latter point is crucial – an RSJ (rolled steel joist) or beam of some nature will be required to act as the permanent support. Its size and make-up can depend on two major factors, namely the structure of the wall you are wishing to remove and the span of the opening you need to make. Both these factors require serious calculation, and the beam type and construction should be decided in consultation with a structural engineer. Once the necessary safety precautions, procedures and planning have been finalized, the actual work itself is possible for most practically minded, home improvement enthusiasts. Work may therefore be divided into two stages. Firstly the opening has to be made, and secondly the supportive RSJ must be inserted.

making the opening

Preparation and planning is essential for this procedure, and because the nature of the work is relatively demanding in a physical sense, two people are much better than one in this instance. Also keep the working area clear of any obstacles as much as possible, as this will help to reduce the likelihood of accidents.

1 Mark out the size of the opening on the wall surface

2 Knock holes through the wall above the proposed opening

3 Insert needles through the holes

4 Support the needles by props on both sides of the wall

5 Use a stone cutter or club hammer and bolster chisel to cut around the edge of the opening

6 Remove the blocks or bricks by first loosening with a club hammer and bolster chisel and then levering out with a wrecking bar or lifting by hand

7 Continue to remove blocks until the entire area is clear

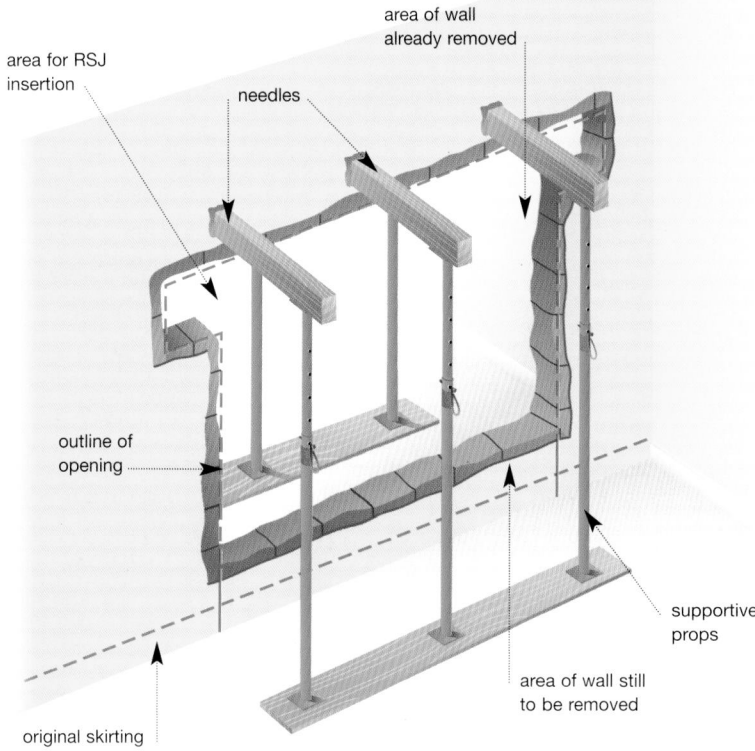

area for RSJ insertion

needles

area of wall already removed

outline of opening

supportive props

area of wall still to be removed

original skirting removed

Two people or more will definitely be required for this stage of the project as even the smallest lintels are surprisingly heavy. It is also a time-consuming process when setting the RSJ in position. Make sure that you check the level of the RSJ because problems will be difficult to rectify later.

patched-in holes where needles had been

RSJ

cut away edge of wall

RSJ supported by cut bricks and mortar. Sometimes structural engineers may specify the need for padstones for RSJ support.

1 At the top corners of the opening, take out bricks or blocks to accommodate the RSJ ends

2 Check and re-check measurements to ensure that the lintel will fit into the required space

3 Apply a bed of mortar to this area before lifting the RSJ into place

4 Check that the RSJ is level. Use cut bricks or blocks, wedged beneath the end of the RSJ, to rectify if necessary

5 Apply more mortar around the RSJ ends to ensure it will be held securely in place

6 Make good with plasterboard and/or render and plaster around the RSJ

7 Make good with plasterboard and/or render and plaster around the cut blocks or bricks which make up the sides of the opening

8 Remove needles and patch in holes

factors to consider

In addition to the practical considerations of how to support your wall, there are also a number of other issues that should be carefully addressed.

needle requirement

The number of needles that you will require for the support will depend on the width of the opening that you plan to create. The actual needle dimensions should not be less than 15cm x 10cm (6in x 4in), but you should consult a structural engineer in order to establish the exact needle requirements of your wall.

propping

Steel props can be hired at a relatively low cost, and their adjustable nature makes them ideal for these supporting purposes. Make sure that the bases of the props are positioned on scaffold planks so that the weight distribution is evened out. Most prop bases have nail holes so that they can be nailed into the scaffold planks to eliminate any risk of them moving.

RSJ support

In many cases the new RSJ may be accommodated in the existing wall structure with no extra support below it. However, in some cases it may be necessary to install extra concrete support or padstones. Consult a structural engineer for correct requirements in your circumstances.

safety equipment

This sort of work requires close attention to safety and all the necessary precautions must be taken. Wear protective gloves, goggles and a hard hat when taking down the wall. A dust mask may also be needed, especially when clearing away the rubble and dust caused by wall removal. As with any DIY task, the area must be kept as clear as possible from obstructions, and rubble should be removed regularly. (See page 36 for more practical health and safety advice.)

removing a non-loadbearing wall

Before embarking on this project it is vital to ensure that the wall is definitely non-loadbearing. Once this is established, removal requires little more than a simple methodical approach. However, it is important to bear in mind that there will undoubtedly be a certain amount of making good to do once the wall has gone, so try to minimize the amount of damage caused to the ceiling and other wall surfaces.

The techniques required for removing a non-loadbearing wall will largely depend on whether the wall is of a stud construction or built from solid bricks or blocks. Once this has been established, ensure that electrical sockets, switches and pipework have been removed and re-routed as necessary by an electrician or plumber.

tips of the trade

Never underestimate the amount of mess and dust that can be generated by projects such as wall removal. Plan the task to fit in conveniently with your busy household (such as at a weekend, when disruption will not be a problem) and take the time to remove all furniture and floorcoverings from the room(s) in which you will be working.

removing a stud wall

The lightweight construction of stud walls means that their removal tends to be a fairly straightforward job, so long as you follow an organized, basic order of work.

tools for the job

wrecking bar

joist detector

panel saw

1 Begin by removing any features on the wall surface such as picture rails, coving and skirting boards. A wrecking bar is the ideal tool to prise

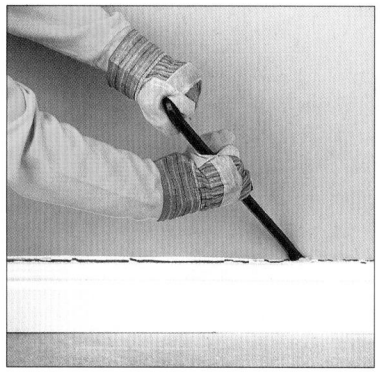

skirting away from the wall. Try not to damage the skirting as it can be saved and possibly re-used on another wall.

2 Locate a central stud in the wall, either by using a joist detector or by tapping along the wall surface with the head of the wrecking bar – areas between studs will sound hollow, whereas stud positions will make the noise of a dull thud. Dig into the wall

by the stud with the end of the bar and lever the plasterboard away from the stud framework.

3 When all the plasterboard has been removed, begin to take out the wooden studs by sawing through

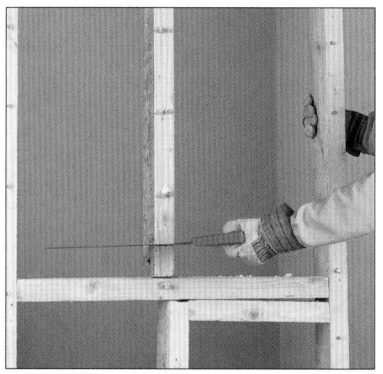

each one in a suitable place. Cut slightly above the joint/nogging cross section – if you cut too tight to the joint, the saw may catch the nails or screws in the studs.

4 To remove the floor plate, it is often easier to saw it into separate sections. This helps to reduce the strength of its bonding 'power' with the floor surface.

safety advice

When carrying out any sort of demolition job, wear gloves, goggles and a hard hat to protect yourself from any flying debris or sharp edges.

Use the wrecking bar to lever the sections of the plate away from the floor surface. A similar technique may be used for the ceiling plate and wall plates as required.

part removal of a solid block wall

Non-loadbearing block or brick walls may be totally or partially removed to create a larger room space. Partial removal can provide a more aesthetically pleasing finish because, instead of producing a completely open new room, it creates two areas with character and interest.

tools for the job

pencil or chalk line
wrecking bar
club hammer
bolster chisel
angle bead
hacksaw
plastering trowel
spirit level

Removal of blocks can be harder work than that of a simple stud wall, and you will need additional tools such as a club hammer and bolster to break down the joints. It is always best to start at the top and work down, removing single blocks if possible. When partially removing a wall, draw guidelines directly on to the wall surface using a chalk line or pencil and level. A stone cutter can be used to make an accurate cut down these guidelines, but in most cases it is easy enough to follow the line using the club hammer and bolster chisel.

1 Once the main area of wall has been removed, straighten up the block edges as much as possible, and remove any loose mortar.

2 Use a hacksaw (see page 133) to cut some angle bead to the required height of the wall edge and position it along the edge using bonding plaster to hold it in place. It may be necessary to use a spirit level in order to gain a truly vertical position for the bead. Position another angle bead on the adjacent edge. Hold the angle beads in position while the bonding plaster dries.

3 Mix and apply pva solution (5 parts water to 1 part pva) to the edges of the trimmed blocks. Work the solution into every crevice and allow to dry to a tacky consistency.

4 Then apply more bonding plaster along the entire wall edge. A perfect finish is not required at this stage, so just ensure a good coverage of the whole edge. Score the bonding plaster (see page 130) before allowing it to dry.

5 Mix and apply finishing plaster over the top of the bonding coat, creating a smooth, flat finish. Use the rigid frame of the angle beads on which to rest the edges of the plastering trowel so that the finish is flush. Apply plaster along the adjacent edges of the angle bead, feathering it with the original wall.

aligning floors ⚒

Once a wall has been removed – whether totally or partially – it can be common for the floors between what were once two rooms to vary slightly in level. This happens most often in older houses, where either there has been some slight subsidence, or an extension has been built with slightly different floor levels to that of the original house. The reasons for variation in levels is not that important, but making good the situation is vital in order to obtain a suitable floor join.

Even when floor levels are similar, it is likely that you may need to fill the gap left by the old wall. This is often the case when a block wall has been removed – either the blocks break off at ground level, producing a rough surface, or the blocks drop below the floor level, leaving a gap to fill between the two rooms. The techniques required for such tasks will be mainly dependent on whether the floors are concrete- or wood-based.

concrete floors

tools for the job

dusting brush
bolster chisel
club hammer
paint brush
gauging trowel
wooden batten
plastering trowel

After removing a stud wall, little reparation is normally required because the wall would have been built on top of an existing concrete screed. However, when removing a block wall, it can be common to find that the concrete screed was laid after the block wall was erected. This means the block removal either leaves a large hole along the line of what was the wall base, or the blocks are broken away leaving a rough, unfinished joint across the floor. In either situation, some repair work will be required.

1 Dust out as much debris and loose material as possible from the old block wall base. Ensure that none of the broken block edges protrude above the surrounding floor surface. Trim such protrusions using a bolster chisel and club hammer.

2 Mix up a pva solution (5 parts water to 1 part pva) and apply it generously along the entire broken block joint, allowing the solution to overlap the edges of the concrete screed on both sides of the joint.

3 Mix up some mortar (5 parts building sand to 1 part cement) and press it firmly into the joint. Use the edge of a gauging trowel to

'chop' the mortar in, thus ensuring it gets into every area along the length of the joint. Allow the mortar to protrude slightly above the surrounding concrete.

4 Cut a length of batten, slightly longer than the width of the joint, and position it across the joint. Slowly push it along the length of the joint, agitating the batten slightly from side to side so that it gradually removes the excess mortar, to create a flush join between the existing screed

and the new mortar. This process may need to be repeated two or three times to produce a finish that is totally smooth and flat.

5 Once dry, mix up some self-levelling compound and apply it along the joint, allowing a large overlap on to the surrounding screed. Gently spread the compound using a plastering trowel. Allow it to settle and dry, providing a perfectly smooth and level joint.

making a slope

Where floor levels vary slightly, a slope or step may need to be constructed. Slopes can be created by simply feathering the edges of the self-levelling compound to produce an even drop between the two levels. Alternatively, the floors can be evened by applying a greater depth of compound to the entire surface of the lower concrete screed level.

wooden floors

tools for the job

cordless drill/driver

claw hammer

wrecking bar

One of the key considerations when working on a wooden floor is whether the surface will be exposed – thus making aesthetic considerations important. If it is to be covered, a firm, level joint is the only major concern, but exposed floors need more care.

reparation of a covered floor

1 Attach lengths of 5cm x 2.5cm (2in x 1in) batten to the wooden joists on either side of the old wall joint. Ensure that the top edge of each length of batten sits directly flush with the top of the joist and therefore precisely below the wooden boarding.

2 Filling the gap will depend on its dimensions. Ideally, nail a new floorboard in position along the joint, allowing the nails to go through the board and into the battens that have been attached to the joists. Different gap dimensions may require you to cut a board such as chipboard to the appropriate size before nailing it in position along the gap.

reparation of an exposed floor

Most exposed floors are made up of traditional floorboards, so filling gaps may also entail adjusting the original board position.

1 Attach lengths of 5cm x 2.5cm (2in x1in) batten to the wooden joist on the floorboard side of the old wall joint. Use a wrecking bar to lift every other board carefully along the joint junction and to lift the chipboard flooring. (Alternatively you may find the boards need to be unscrewed and for this a wrecking bar is inappropriate.)

2 Use a claw hammer to remove any old nails that are protruding from the floor joists.

3 Cut boards to length and use them to infill across the floor surface, creating a neat finish.

building a stud wall – 1 ⟋⟋⟋

Stud walls are built in two main stages, and the following four pages explain each step. Before any work can begin, however, you must first establish the direction of the ceiling and floor joists – this will determine whether the head and sole plates are to run parallel or at right angles to them. Use a proprietary joist detector for this task. These simple tools contain sensor pads which trigger a light every time they pass over a joist.

When the wall runs parallel to the joists, it is best to position the sole plate directly above a joist and the head plate below a joist. On first floors, a further joist below floor level should be used to provide extra strength (see page 13).

When the wall is to run at right angles to the joists there is greater flexibility because fixings will be made on subsequent joists across the span of the room. So be prepared to find a compromise between your desired position for the wall and the most practical location for fixing.

making the frame

tools for the job

joist detector

hammer

chalk line

spirit level

pencil

panel saw

cordless drill

tape measure

board lifter (optional)

plumb line (optional)

Studs may either be 10cm x 5cm (4in x 2in) or 7.5cm x 5cm (3in x 2in) in dimension, and are generally made from sawn softwood. Traditionalists choose sturdy, thicker studs whereas most modern buildings will contain the smaller ones. The distance between the studs is vital – if you are covering the frame with plasterboard that is 9.5mm (⅜in) thick, the studs must be

a maximum of 40cm (1ft 4in) apart. However, if you are using 12.5mm (½in) plasterboard, the studs should be no more than 60cm (2ft) apart.

1 Use a joist detector to trace the position of joists and any cables or pipes above the ceiling surface.

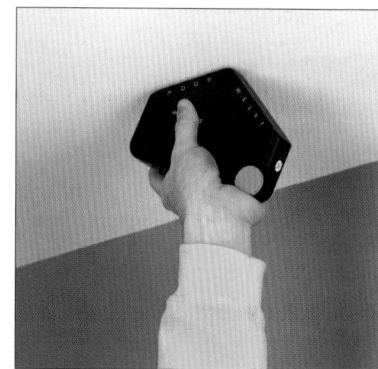

2 Having decided on the wall position, knock a nail into the ceiling close to the wall junction, at what will be the centre of the head plate position. Do the same at the opposite ceiling/wall junction.

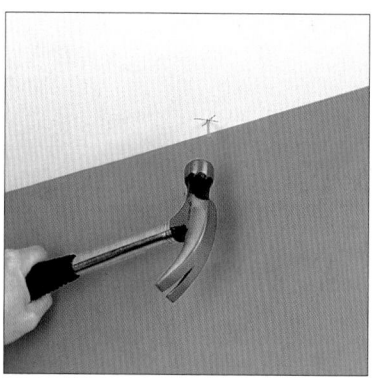

3 Attach a chalk line between the two nails and snap a guideline on to the ceiling surface. This line will

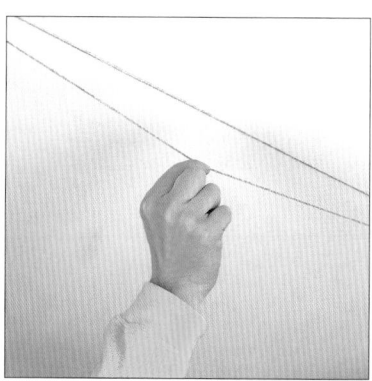

help to provide the exact position for the head plate.

4 Use a spirit level and pencil to continue this guideline down both walls at each end of the ceiling guideline. Continue the lines down to floor level.

5 Hold a stud section at skirting board level, and direct the wall pencil guideline so that it bisects the centre of the stud. Make a pencil guideline on either side of the stud, thus marking the skirting board. Remove the stud and cut out this section of skirting board in order to accommodate the sole plate. Repeat this process on the opposite wall. The guidelines should now indicate the

position of the head plate (ceiling), sole plate (floor) and wall plates.

6 Cut a timber stud to the exact length between the opposing walls. Position it, allowing the cut skirting board sections to accommodate each end of the timber length. Mark on this piece of timber (the sole plate), the exact position of any doors that may be required. Remember to allow for the door lining and the door frame.

7 Screw the sole plate into the floor at 40cm (1ft 4in) intervals. For concrete floors, drill and plug the holes before screw insertion.

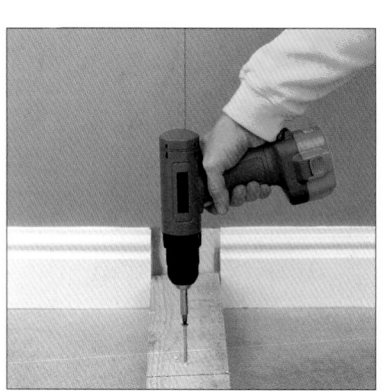

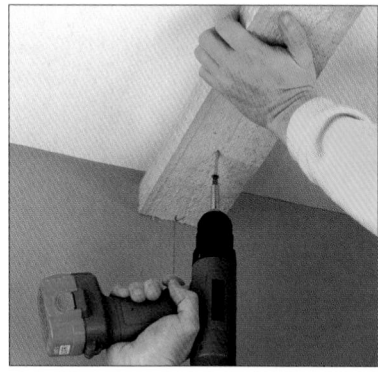

8 Cut a timber stud to the exact length between the opposing walls at ceiling level, and make a pencil mark bisecting the centre of the stud at each end. Align this mark with the wall guideline, before fixing the stud or head plate in position.

9 Cut two studs to the exact length between the head and ceiling plate on each wall and fix them into position.

10 Mark off along the sole plate at 40cm (1ft 4in) intervals to indicate the positions for

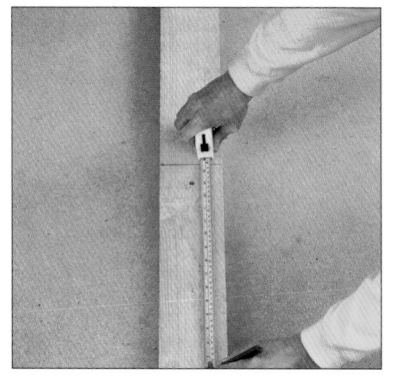

the vertical studs. If a door position has been marked, work away from each side of the door frame guidelines until you reach each wall.

11 Cut small blocks of timber and nail them in position at the side of each stud guideline. This is not essential, but it will help to make fixing the vertical studs in place much easier. The frame is now complete and ready to be filled in (see page 50 for the next stage).

USING A PLUMB LINE

It is also possible to create guidelines using a plumb line or bob. Once you have established the ceiling guideline (steps 1–2), attach the plumb line to each of the nails in turn and mark along, and at the bottom of, the line to gain a vertical guide. The plumb line may also be used from a central ceiling position to mark sole plate guidelines along the floor. Ensure that the plumb line is stationary before marking off.

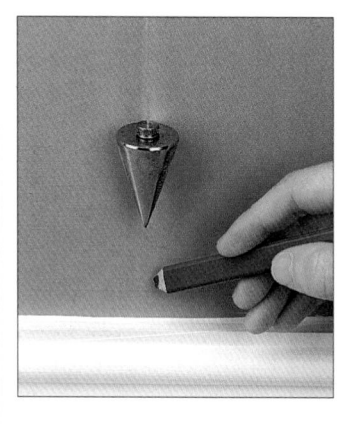

building a stud wall – 2

Once the outer framework of the stud wall has been installed, attention can be turned to filling in the framework and plasterboarding. Make a final check on levels of the frame and its positioning, because any slight adjustments are best made at this stage rather than later. See page 48 for a list of tool requirements.

filling the frame

1 Measure each vertical stud and cut the required lengths. Fix them at the base, holding them against the block supports to prevent them from moving. Use 10cm (4in) nails and knock or 'skew' them in at an angle on both sides of the stud, so that the fixings penetrate into the sole plate.

2 With the stud fixed at its base, hold a level against the length in order to find the precise vertical fixing

position in the head plate. Skew nails into each side of the stud and into the head plate.

3 Keep checking the level and adjusting the stud until it is precisely vertical, before securing it finally in place.

4 To make the door frame, cut a length of timber to the exact size between the two vertical studs on either side of the door opening. Remember to check the correct height measurement for the door (including the door lining), and nail the length in place, ensuring that it is level.

5 To add strength, fix a further length vertically between the door head and the head plate. Nails may be inserted into the base of the vertical stud, whereas at ceiling level the nails need to be skewed through the vertical length, into the head plate.

6 Extra strength will also need to be added to the full-length studs, so cut short lengths of timber to fit horizontally between them. These noggings should be positioned half way between the sole and head plates.

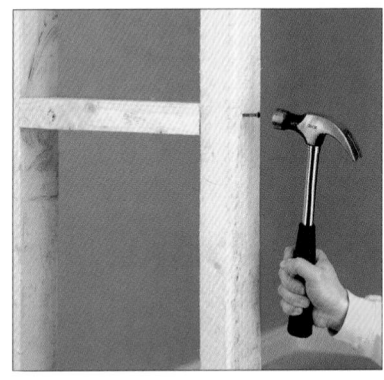

7 On completion of the framework, work on providing access for any services or electrical cables that may need to run through the wall. Drill holes through studs and noggings as required.

8 Thread cables through the holes drilled in the studs. (Check with a qualified electrician the exact cable requirements for the services you require.)

fixing the plasterboard

As discussed on page 48, ensure that you are using the correct depth of plasterboard according to the position of the studs. Bear in mind that if you are planning to use dry lining, the plasterboard should also have tapered edges (see page 84).

Invariably, sheets of plasterboard need to be cut to fit so careful measuring is required. As most ceilings or wall surfaces undulate slightly and are not completely square, the edge of plasterboard sheets will often need to be 'scribed' in order to produce a precise fit. This is most important at ceiling level and corners because the joint needs to be as tight as possible, whereas at floor level there is some leeway because skirting board will cover the joint.

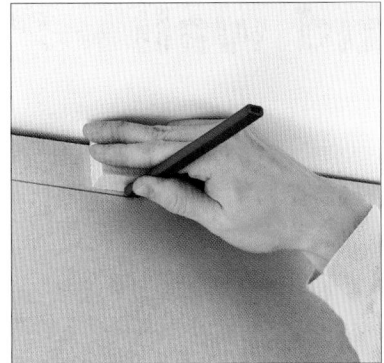

1 Holding the plasterboard sheet as close to the ceiling as possible (so that it touches), slide a small wooden block and pencil along the sheet, keeping the block resting against the ceiling surface. The pencil guideline produced will thereby mimic the profile of the ceiling, providing a guideline to cut the plasterboard for the perfect fit.

2 Use plasterboard nails to fix the sheets in place. Fixings should be made between 12mm and 25mm (½in to 1in) from the board edges and at 15cm (6in) intervals or centres along all edges and studs. Fix plasterboard around a door opening so that the join is above the centre of the door. Although this is technically more difficult to measure and cut, after dry lining or plastering, a central board join such as this will be less likely to crack than joints that run vertical from the door opening corners.

3 When one side of the wall is completely covered, drill the necessary holes in the plasterboard

for any electrical cables. Then, before plasterboarding the other side of the stud wall, install insulation blankets between all the studs. Finally, plasterboard the wall, ready for plastering (see page 86) and dealing with the door opening.

making an arch profile ⟋⟋⟋⟋

Arch profiles can be used as an alternative to traditional doors or square openings, adding greater character and providing a feature between rooms. Previously, such tasks involved a highly skilled procedure both to produce a framework for the arch and to finish off the surface with plaster. However, the manufacturing of arch formers has made the whole process much easier and quicker for DIY enthusiasts.

arch profile in a stud wall

tools for the job

cordless drill/driver

screwdriver

tape measure

hacksaw

hammer

filling knife

plastering trowel

Although arch profiles may be built on to existing wall openings, starting from scratch and building them into a new stud wall is much easier. This is because a new wall, if erected correctly, is more likely to be 'true' and 'square' compared to older walls

1 Most formers will have pre-drilled holes to accommodate fixings. Hold the former in position while drilling four pilot holes into the timber studs. Ensure that the front lip of the arch former is level with the plasterboard on either side.

2 Secure the former in place with wood screws. Use a screwdriver rather than a cordless drill/driver to tighten the screws, as overtightening could crack the plaster former. Greater control of movement can be achieved by using a simple hand tool in situations like this.

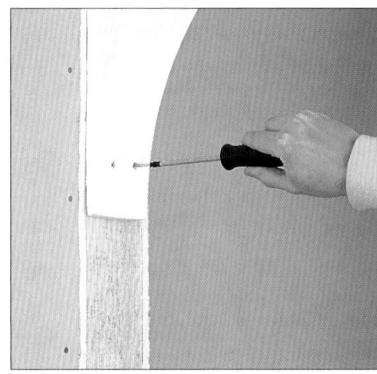

3 Measure and cut a piece of plasterboard to fit between the edge of the arch former and the floor for each side of the entrance. This is both to cover the wooden stud beneath, and to bring the surface up to the same depth as that created by the former. Fix the plasterboard in position with plasterboard nails, taking care not to damage the plaster.

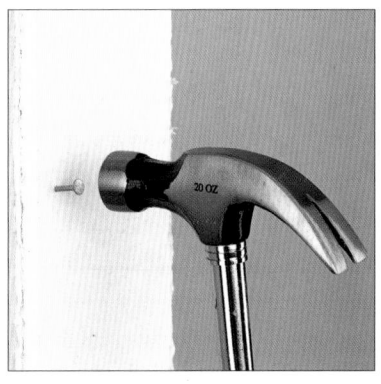

4 Cut angle bead to the correct length (former base to floor) and attach it on both edges of the opening. Fix the angle bead in position using plasterboard nails. Remember to ensure that the apex of each angle bead aligns precisely with the respective bottom corners of the arch former.

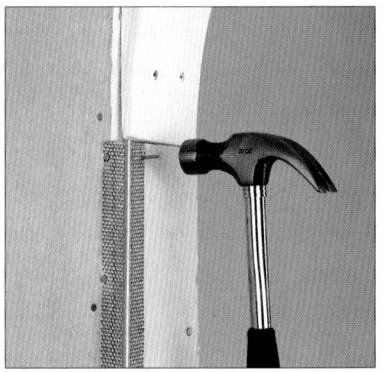

5 Repeat steps 1–4 to fit the second former and entrance lining around the arch. It is rare that the formers will join exactly – almost certainly gaps will occur between the top edges of the formers. To solve this, simply cut plasterboard to the appropriate shape and size and fix into position. Again, use angle bead to complete the edges.

👍

tips of the trade

Where the smooth former face meets the plastered edge of the entrance, it may be necessary to 'feather' the join with some fine filler in order to obtain a perfectly smooth arched profile. Once filled, use a fine grade sandpaper to finish the join.

6   When the formers, plasterboard lining and angle beads have all been positioned and aligned, fill the arch former holes with all-purpose filler or plaster bonding coat.

7   Tape the joints between the pieces of plasterboard, and between the board and the arch formers, with self-adhesive jointing tape.

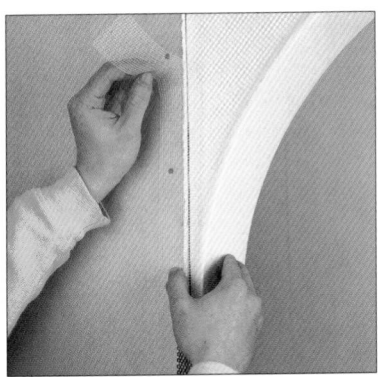

8   Apply plaster to the walls in the usual way (see pages 86–7), extending the plaster over and on to the arched formers. The actual arched face of the formers may not require plastering – this will depend upon the

type of former you have used. Once the plaster has been 'polished' and then left to dry, the arch is ready for decoration. With some formers, it may be necessary to apply two coats of plaster. This will depend on the depth of the former face in relation to the surrounding wall area. If the depth difference is more than 2–3mm (⅛in), apply two thin layers of plaster, rather than one thick coat.

tips of the trade

• **Dry lined arches** – An alternative dry lining technique can be used to produce an arch profile. Instead of using angle bead along the vertical arch edges, corner tape can be applied and jointing compound used. The internal area of the former can also be filled initially with plaster bonding coat, before being finished with jointing compound. This technique avoids using plaster across the entire wall surface.

• **Dealing with cracks** – In most cases, so long as the formers have been securely positioned and the arch has been plastered correctly, joint cracks are unlikely to appear. However, if hairline cracks do appear, and are not lost by refilling and painting, try covering the area with lining paper. However, be aware that large cracks may suggest that the arch profile has not been fitted correctly.

Arches add shape to rooms and soften edges, producing a relaxed and comfortable atmosphere, and link the decoration between two living areas.

making a serving hatch ⚒⚒⚒

Serving hatches provide ideal access for serving food from a kitchen into a dining area. Although they are still used for this purpose in many cases, they can also make attractive decorative features and may be constructed in a range of different styles. Building a hatch in a solid block wall or loadbearing wall will require greater endeavour (see opposite page). However, carrying out such a project in a non-loadbearing wall is a very straightforward exercise.

serving hatch in a non-loadbearing stud wall

tools for the job

joist/cable detector
pencil
spirit level
tape measure
dry wall saw
panel saw
hammer
cordless drill/driver
mitre block or mitresaw

1 Work out your preferred position for the hatch, then use a joist detector to find stud positions in the wall and also to check for services such as wires and pipes. Be prepared to make some small adjustments according to the position of the wall studs and these services. (It is almost certain that you will need to cut through some studs, but try to adjust your measurements so that the sides of the hatch correspond with the edges of the studs.)

2 Use a pencil and spirit level to draw a guideline on the wall to show the exact size of the hatch. It is essential to get dimensions and measurements as vertical and level as possible at this stage – this will help to make constructing the hatch quite simple when the necessary hole has been knocked through.

3 Use a dry wall saw to cut around the pencil outline. (This type of saw is used instead of a panel saw because its sharp point pierces the plasterboard easily.) If you come across a stud obstruction, use the very end of the saw to score the plasterboard until you penetrate through to the stud surface. Once

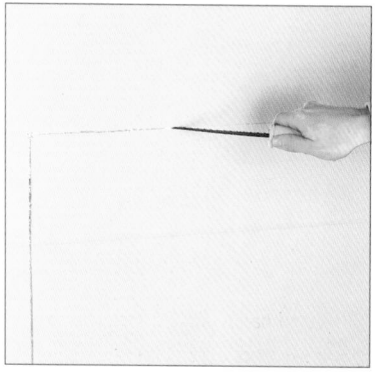

the plasterboard panel has been cut around, it may be removed and discarded. Repeat the procedure for the other side of the wall. If the wall was insulated, remove the insulatory blanket as required.

4 Remove noggings by first sawing centrally through them with the panel saw. Then lever out the noggings with a wrecking bar or hammer. If you try to saw too closely to the vertical stud, it is likely that you will come into contact with nail or screw fixings and damage the saw blade. Instead, remove such fixings with a hacksaw.

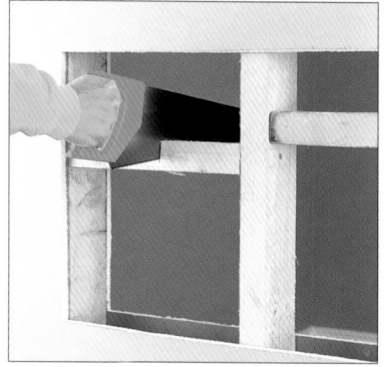

5 Leaving the central stud in place, cut and fit noggings to either side of it at the top and bottom of the hatch. It is best to use screws for this purpose, because trying to skew in nails with a hammer can push the noggings below the edge of the hatch, making them difficult to pull out of the wall and back into the required position. Provide pilot holes for the screws first, as this will help to avoid applying too much pressure on the noggings when fixing them in place.

6 Cut out the central stud, keeping the saw blade flush with the top and bottom of the hatch.

7 Line the hatch with 12.5cm x 2.5cm (5in x 1in) planed softwood. Nail measured lengths in position, beginning with the base followed by the top of the hatch and finishing with the two sides. Lost-head wire nails are best for fixing purposes, so their heads can be filled before decorating the hatch.

8 Use the mitresaw to cut architrave and fit it around the hatch on both sides to finish off the

project. Wire nails can again be used for fixing purposes. In addition to nailing the architrave through the front, use one smaller nail at each corner of the hatch, going through one section of architrave and into the adjacent section. This will help to pull the corner joints together and reduce the risk of any movement, which can potentially cause cracking.

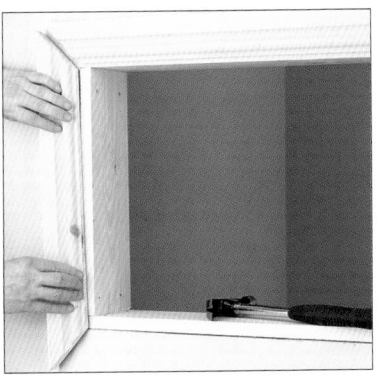

LOADBEARING WALLS

The illustrations shown here provide instruction for inserting a serving hatch in a non-loadbearing stud wall. However, if the hatch is to be inserted into a loadbearing wall, or a block or brick wall, the technique will need to be modified. In fact, the procedure is very similar to that of removing a loadbearing wall (see page 42). Clearly, the scale of the project will be reduced because you are dealing with a much smaller opening for a serving hatch. However, a lintel of some nature will be required – the size of which depends on the dimensions of the hatch. When removing blockwork, remember to wear the necessary protective equipment such as goggles, gloves and a hard hat.

A serving hatch provides a useful and attractive access point between two rooms. It can also draw light into dark areas of the home and makes a handy display area.

soundproofing walls ⫮⫮⫮

The best time to soundproof a wall is during its construction, but unless you are physically building a new wall yourself, this option does not often arise. Manufacturers have now come to recognize this rather basic problem and have, accordingly, developed a number of systems to make soundproofing existing walls a feasible and effective procedure, including better insulation slabs, which are now tested to a much higher standard.

By far the greatest need for wall soundproofing tends to arise with walls that you share with a neighbour.

soundproofing a party wall

tools for the job

wrecking bar
tape measure
pencil
panel saw
cordless drill/driver
spirit level
protective gloves
dust mask
hacksaw
sealant gun

Traditionally, soundproofing a party wall would usually mean building a new stud wall in front of the existing party wall, and using insulation blankets to fill the gap. The dimensions involved would almost certainly mean losing a sizeable area of your own room, as well as requiring some fairly major construction. However, the method below only encroaches 5cm–7.5cm (2in–3in) into the room space, and is therefore rarely noticeable in terms of the overall room dimensions. Proprietary plasterboard panels are used for this technique – these consist of two different thicknesses of plasterboard joined together, with another soundproofing layer sandwiched in between. Although this is the

ideal material, you can use normal plasterboard sheets so long as the bottom layer is of a greater thickness than the top layer. (This adheres to a basic soundproofing theory – when layering similar materials, never use the same depth of material twice.)

1 Use a wrecking bar to remove the skirting board from the base of the wall. Try not to damage the board as this can be re-used later, when the soundproofing is complete.

2 Starting at floor level, use a pencil to make a series of measurements along the corner of the wall, at 60cm (2ft) intervals. It is unlikely that the height of the wall will

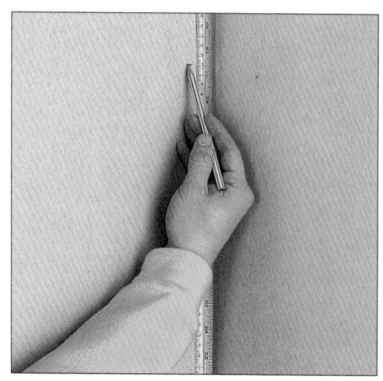

fit exactly into divisibles of 60cm (2ft), so simply make the last mark directly at ceiling level.

3 Cut a soundbreaker bar to the exact length of the wall you wish to soundproof, and fix it in position at floor level. Make sure that the open side of the soundbreaker is facing up, and that the fixings are made just above the floor level. Screw the fixings through the foam pads on the soundbreaker bar.

4 Position a second bar at the next measurement along, this time ensuring that the open side of the soundbreaker is facing down to floor level. Use a spirit level to ensure

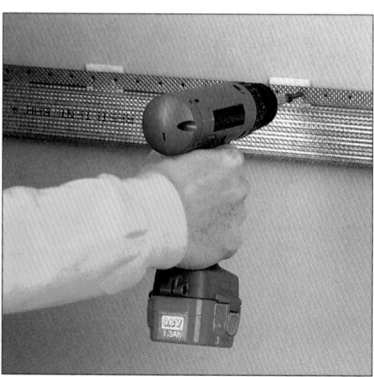

that the bar is positioned precisely level. Continue to fix soundbreakers at the marked-off intervals right up to ceiling level. All bars from the second one up should have the open side facing downwards.

5 Fit 120cm x 60cm x 10cm (4ft x 2ft x 4in) soundproofing slabs, beginning at floor level. Lip the bottom edge of the slab into the open side of the floor level soundbreaker, and fit the top edge of the slab into the open side of the soundbreaker above. So long as your measurements have been correct, a precise fit should be achieved. Wear protective gloves for this process as the soundproofing slab fibres can be irritating to the skin, and the bar edges can be sharp.

6 When the bottom section of the wall is complete, progress to the next level, inserting slabs in a similar fashion. Bear in mind that at this and subsequent levels, it is not possible to lip the bottom edge of the slab into the soundbreaker. However, the top edge will be lipped into the bar,

allowing the bottom edge of the slab to rest flush on the top edge of the bar below. Continue to fit slabs until the entire wall is covered.

7 Once trimmed and cut to fit, attach the double plasterboard panels to the wall. Using plasterboard screws, fix through the lower level of plasterboard and into the soundbreaker bar. Screws should be long enough to fix the board firmly to the bar, but not so long that they reach the original party wall. Otherwise, an automatic channel for sound transference will be created.

8 Lip the staggered edge of the next panel over the first, butting it up tightly to create a flush join. It may be easier to put marks along the previous sheet, identifying the exact position of the last fixing. These will indicate the position of the soundbreaker bars and therefore allow you to position the next fixing exactly. Continue to fit panels as required, fixing along the soundbreaker bars at 15cm–20cm (6in-8in) intervals.

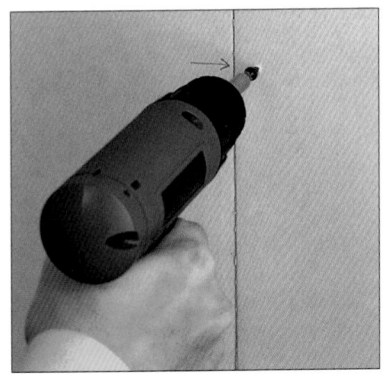

9 Finally, apply a bead of mastic around all the new joints made between the plasterboard panels and the existing floor, walls and ceiling. The wall may then be plastered or dry lined, its skirting reapplied, and decorated as required.

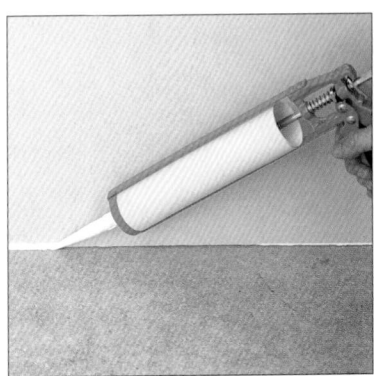

CARPET SOUNDPROOFING

Bear in mind that soundproofing efficiency will benefit from laying good quality underlay and carpet in the room. This situation may be further improved by using a specially designed acoustic flooring underlay system. Even though underlay and carpet are more generally concerned with the floor of a room, they will indirectly assist the soundproofing of a wall. This is especially the case if the floor is suspended, which enables noise to travel more easily from one room to another level. So deal with floor soundproofing issues at the same time as dealing with walls.

tips of the trade

Different tools will be required for marking and cutting different materials. For example, soundbreakers should be marked with a felt tip pen before cutting with a hacksaw. However, soundproofing slabs should be marked with chalk and cut with a panel saw – a dust mask is also vital for this process. Plasterboard panels can be marked with a pencil and cut with a panel saw.

building a block wall

Although stud walls (see pages 48–51) are easier to construct than solid block walls, there are some instances when a block structure may be more appropriate or even preferred. For example, in a house where all existing walls are of a block or brick construction, a stud wall may be rather out of character. Block walls also provide better soundproofing qualities and are better suited to supporting heavy objects or multiple fixings.

tools for the job

spirit level

pencil

tape measure

cordless drill/driver

spanner or plier wrench

hammer

gauging trowel

bricklaying trowel

club hammer

bolster chisel

goggles

protective gloves

1 Use a spirit level and pencil to draw a vertical line on the wall from the floor to the ceiling. This will be the line on to which the wall profile is attached, helping to 'tie in' the blocks to the existing wall structure. Profiles vary slightly in design but most will require holes to be drilled, ready for fixing. (Use the masonry bit specified by the manufacturers of the profile.) Hold the profile steadily in position on the wall surface and carefully drill through it into the wall surface beneath.

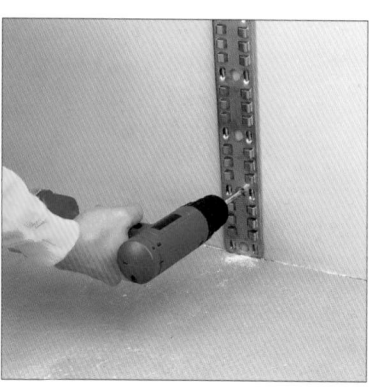

2 Plug the holes and insert the supplied fixings. Coach screws are often provided for this purpose, and are used in combination with a large washer to add extra strength and rigidity to the fixing. Position them by hand and tighten with a spanner or a plier wrench. Continue to add coach screws up the entire length of the profile. Once the profile is fixed in place, repeat steps 1 and 2 to fix the second profile to the opposing wall.

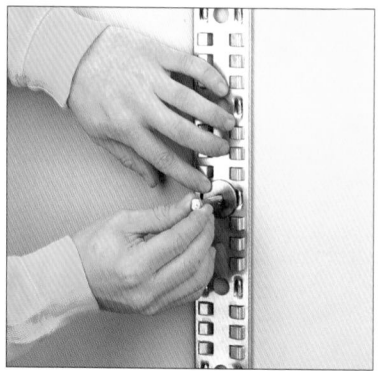

3 Attach a string line to the wall to one side of the profile. It should be in such a position that when the first block is positioned, the line will

safety advice

Block walls are quite heavy, so it is important to check that the weight is supported by the floor below. At ground level this is less of a problem, especially on a solid concrete base, but building on a suspended wooden floor is a different matter and you should seek professional advice. Also, when building on first floors or above, similar approval should be sought because joists may need additional strengthening.

correspond to the face of the block and slightly below its top edge. A block may be positioned 'dry' to gain the appropriate fixing point. The other end of the line should be attached to the corresponding position next to the other wall profile. This line will help with positioning the first layer.

4 Apply a strip of mortar to the floor, extending away from the profile, and of a width and length slightly wider than a standard block. Try to keep this mortar base a consistent but uncompacted level.

5 Take the first block and mould a cap of mortar on to one end using a gauging trowel. This process

is known as 'buttering' and is an integral part of the block- or brick-laying technique.

6 Lift and position the buttered end of the block tight up against the wall profile, while settling the base of the block into the mortar bed. The block weight will force mortar out from underneath it while finding a good, solid resting position.

7 Tap the block with the butt end of the bricklaying trowel to help it settle and check that the front face of the block just rests against the string line, and that it is level.

8 Use a spirit level to make any final adjustments, ensuring that the block is both level and vertical across the appropriate dimensions as required. After final positioning, continue along the floor adding blocks, checking levels and adjusting as necessary until the entire first course of blocks is complete. Trim excess mortar with a trowel as you progress and use it as the base for the next block, together with any extra fresh mortar that is required.

9 Apply a layer of mortar along the top of the first course of blocks to a similar depth as used at ground level. Also, use the ties provided by the profile kit to link into the profile itself and bed into the mortar layer.

10 The most essential rule of block wall construction is to ensure that mortar joints on adjacent levels never coincide. Therefore, before starting the second layer, cut a half block using a club hammer and bolster chisel. Always wear goggles when carrying out this

procedure to protect your eyes from flying debris. Use a sturdy surface to prevent the block from toppling.

11 Add the half block before continuing along with full blocks for the remainder of the course. Keep checking levels at regular intervals and move up the string line to correspond with the next block level. Never lay more than five courses of blocks in one session, and allow them to dry before progressing with further courses.

openings

It is likely that an opening of some sort will be required in the wall. Simply mark out the dimensions on the floor and build up to these guidelines, while leaving the opening block free. Once you have reached the required height for the entrance, a lintel will need to be installed at the top of the opening before you can continue adding blocks, and building up to ceiling level can be completed.

installing wall ventilation ⁄⁄

Effective ventilation is an essential part of any household construction, both for general efficiency and health and safety. Before double glazing and improvements to insulation, installing ventilation systems was rarely necessary because draughts were a 'natural' feature of most houses. However, increased efficiency of insulation in most modern houses means that artificial devices must be installed as substitutes for what was once an automatic system.

AREAS FOR VENTILATION
Key areas for ventilation include:

● **Bathrooms and kitchens** – Bathrooms are an environment in which moist air tends to pervade. Adequate ventilation is therefore vital to prevent mould or damp infestation, and condensation which can ruin decoration. Similarly, kitchens can be exposed to steam and condensation, as well as cooker fumes that need good ventilation. Both rooms tend to require mechanical ventilation, such as an extractor fan that actually takes air out of the room and to the exterior of the house.

● **Suspended floors** – Suspended or sprung floors require ventilating beneath them using air bricks in the exterior wall. Failure to install air bricks or allowing them to become blocked can cause problems such as dry rot.

● **Chimney breasts** – When a fireplace has been blocked off, it will be necessary to install a vent in the chimney breast to allow air circulation in the chimney void. The same ends can be achieved by installing air bricks on the external wall into the chimney void. However, the interior method tends to be easier to carry out and is equally effective.

● **Boilers and solid fuel fires** – These systems must be vented correctly to ensure that fumes are not allowed to build up inside the house. Always seek professional advice from a qualified engineer and get appliances checked regularly.

installing a through-wall vent

tools for the job

| joist detector |
| tape measure |
| pencil |
| core drill and bit |
| protective gloves |
| goggles |
| dust mask |
| hacksaw |
| sealant gun |

1 Mark off on the wall the centre point for the ventilation shaft. Check for any cables with the joist detector and ensure that the height and position of the hole adheres to any relevant building regulations.

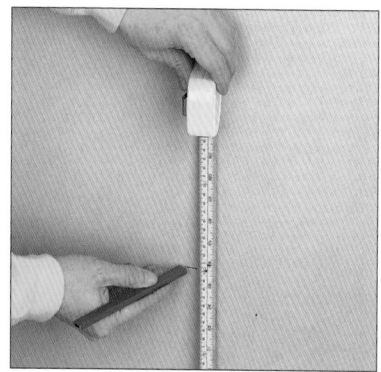

2 Attach the core drill bit to the main drill body, ensuring that it is correctly fitted in place. Read the guidelines provided by the manufacturer for this process as techniques vary with heavy duty tools.

3 Position the pilot drill point on the marked wall point and commence drilling. The pilot drill will make the initial hole in the wall to secure the core drill in place and allow the larger round core drill bit to begin cutting the hole in the wall surface. Be sure to hold firmly on to the drill as it is both heavy and can 'kick' as it bites into the wall surface. Goggles must be worn to protect your eyes from flying debris, and a mask is also important as the drill can generate a lot of dust as it it eats through the wall.

When the drill reaches the other side of the wall, there is a danger that it will blow out the exterior render or bricks, thus causing a larger hole than required, which will need repair. To prevent this from happening, the core drill can be used from both sides of

safety advice

It is important to get professional advice before installing or changing ventilation systems. This is vital when dealing with the requirements for fuels such as gas, oil or solid fuels as failure to vent correctly can endanger life.

the wall, so that the breakthrough point is inside the wall itself rather than directly on the outside. However, this will obviously require careful and accurate measuring and marking on both sides of the wall.

4 Remove the cut core by hand. It should come out in one or two large pieces depending on the wall make-up. If you are drilling through a cavity wall, ensure that no large pieces of the core fall into the cavity.

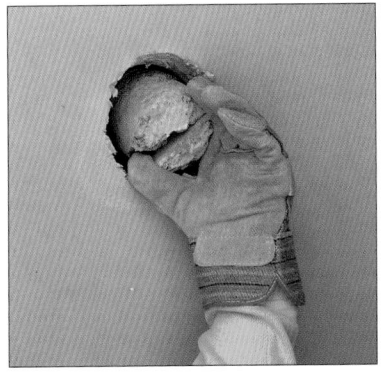

5 Line the hole with some ducting, cutting it to the right size with a hacksaw. The ducting is normally

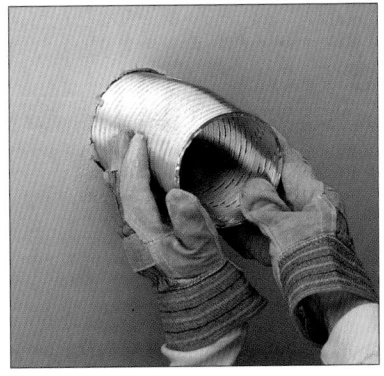

bought as part of a kit and the manufacturer's guidelines for positioning should be included.

6 Seal around the edge of the ducting with silicone, ensuring a good unbroken seal. Carry out this process on both the interior and exterior of the wall. (If areas around the edge of the hole broke away or became damaged while drilling, repair them with mortar followed by all-purpose filler, before applying sealant.)

7 Internally, fix a louvre vent to cover the hole. This must be a static ventilator made of metal or

plastic so that it cannot be closed off and inhibit ventilation. Plastic vents may be painted to match and therefore blend with the wall colour, making them a less noticeable feature.

8 On the exterior, fit a cowled cover over the hole. This enables a good throughflow of air while limiting strong gusts of wind. It also prevents rain from penetrating through the vent into the room.

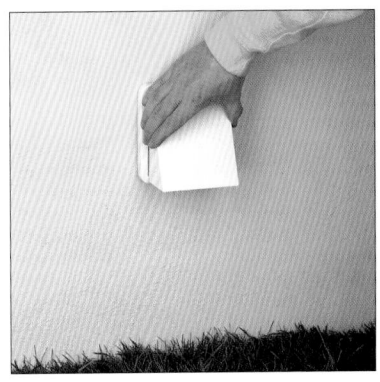

9 Again, seal around the cowled cover with more silicone sealant to ensure a completely rainproof seal.

building a glass block wall ///

Glass blocks provide an unusual alternative to more traditional wall structures, and produce a highly decorative finish that adds character to any room surroundings. They cannot be used for structural support, but they do fulfil the majority of roles required by most walls and make ideal shower walls or room dividers. Extremely versatile, they can even be used to construct curves – thus adding further interest to a wall surface and providing attractive, translucent properties.

tools for the job

spirit level
pencil
nail and line
hammer
cordless drill
gauging trowel
sponge

1 Use a spirit level and pencil to draw a precise vertical line on the wall surface, extending from ground level to the finished wall height. As with block walls (see pages 58–9), attach a string line at a height just below the top of where the first course of glass blocks will be, and where it will touch the face of the blocks. You may wish to hold a glass block in position to obtain the correct height and position measurements. Secure the line in the corresponding position on the opposite wall.

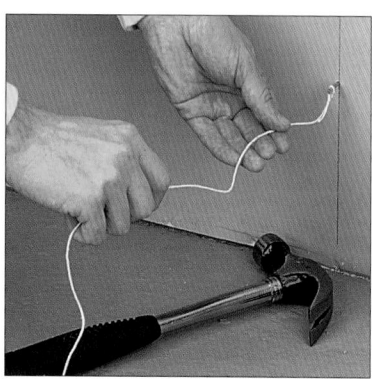

2 To add strength to the finished wall, it will be necessary to build a rigid steel framework inside the glass block structure. These steel rods need to be positioned every four to five courses (depending on the manufacturer's guidelines). In order to get the bottom course position for these rods, hold a block 'dry' in position at the base of the wall – on top of spacers – to ensure that it is at the correct height. Hold a steel rod on top of the block and mark the position at which it touches the wall surface.

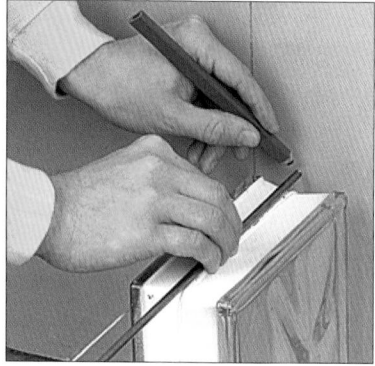

3 Remove the block, spacers and rod, and drill into the wall surface at the marked-off point. Measure the area required for the block and spacer, and mark off further points at which the rods will be inserted. Drill these holes at this stage rather than leaving till later.

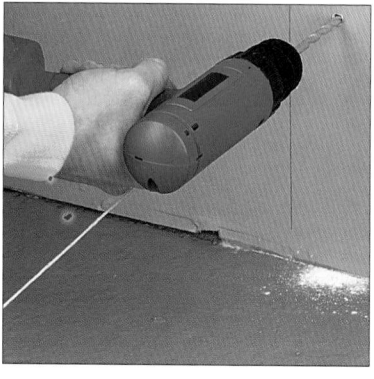

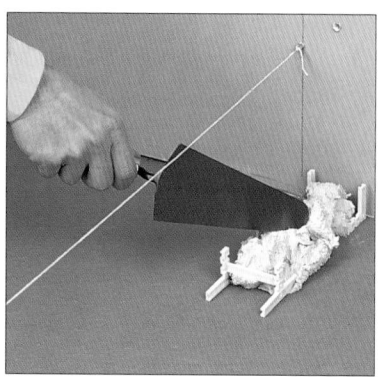

4 Mix up some mortar. (Use white cement as this produces a more pleasing finish with translucent bricks than the other, traditional types of mortar.) Use the spacers to position a block accurately. Then remove the brick and apply mortar to the area between the spacers.

5 Take a glass block and 'butter' one side with some mortar, ensuring a good even coverage, while trying to keep the mortar off the glass faces of the block.

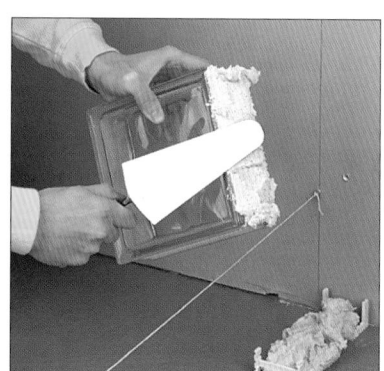

6 Position the block back on the spacers so that the buttered end is against the wall, with the adjacent edge bedding down into the

mortar on the floor level. Ensure that the block is level and vertical using the spacers – the block should rest against the edge of each spacer.

7 Position spacers and add blocks until the entire first course is complete. Use a spirit level to ensure that the block positions are precise. The top edge of each block should also rest against the string line. Insert a steel rod into the pre-drilled hole at the top of the first course of blocks.

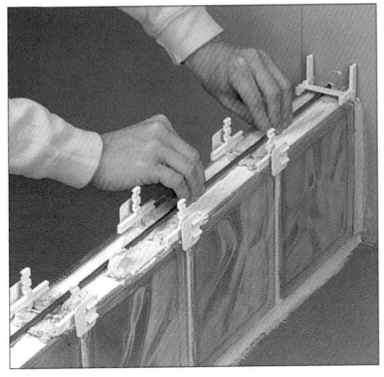

8 Once the wall is complete, remove the face plates of the spacers by twisting them.

9 Once the blocks have dried out, they can be grouted using a similar mortar mix as used for the building process. Work mortar into any gaps in the joints and smooth to a finish with a clean, damp sponge. The blocks will need wiping over several times to remove all mortar residue and leave a clean, bright glass block surface. If the wall is to be used in a

shower cubicle, use waterproof tiling grout, and seal the edge of the wall with silcone sealant.

wooden floors

When building on wooden floors, fix a wooden sole plate to the floor to act as the base for the block wall. Ensure that the wood is the same width as the glass blocks.

spacers

The spacers provided with glass block walls are designed so that they can be adapted to make both 'T' and 'L' shapes, and therefore deal with all requirements in a block wall construction. Simply snap off the parts of the spacer which you do not require.

Glass block walls make a very distinctive feature, helping to lighten rooms and creating an attractive, decorative finish.

installing a fireplace ↗↗

Fireplaces have always had a dual function – in addition to providing heat, they also provide a focal point and therefore contribute decoratively to the room as a whole. The advent of central heating meant that many fireplaces were blocked up, but their aesthetic value is now enjoying a revival and these features are reappearing. Solid fuel and gas fires require professional installation, but building a fireplace for aesthetic or ornamental purposes is relatively straightforward.

fitting a surround

Some of the most attractive modern fireplaces are based on a marble hearth and back panel design. Marble is a heavy stone and often requires two people for lifting and positioning. It is also fragile, so provide plenty of support while it is being positioned, and while you are waiting for any mortar to dry. The surround is either made of painted mdf or, as in this case, from stained softwood.

tools for the job

pencil & tape measure
gauging trowel
sponge
spirit level
pointing trowel
screwdriver
sealant gun
sponge

1 Having chosen your location for the fireplace, mark its central position on the wall surface.

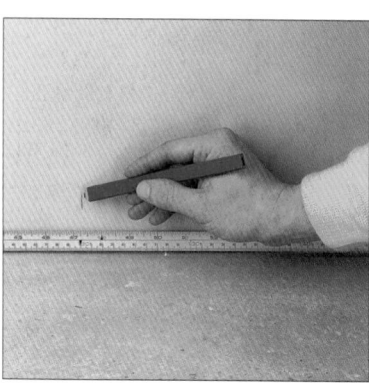

2 Taking measurements from the marked point on the wall surface, draw in the dimensions of the hearth on the floor. Use a gauging trowel to apply a number of blobs of mortar within the confines of this hearth guideline. Make sure the blobs are of a consistent size, so that when the hearth is positioned, it will sit and bed down as evenly as possible.

3 Lift the hearth into place and check that it is positioned central to the wall mark with a tape measure. Allow the hearth to bed down into the mortar. Check for any mortar squeezing out from under the hearth edges and remove with a clean, damp sponge before it dries.

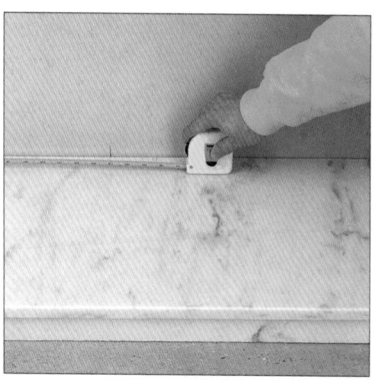

4 Use a spirit level to check the hearth positioning across all dimensions, side to side, front to back and diagonally, as it will not be possible to make adjustments later.

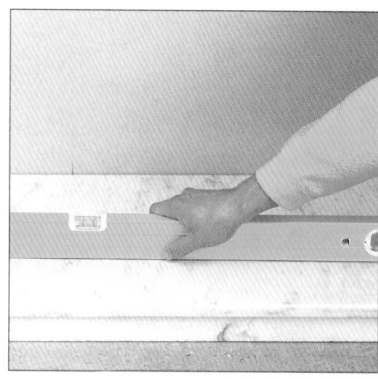

5 Add blobs of mortar to the back panel and position it centrally on the hearth. Allow the panel to secure to the wall surface, but do not press it finally into position. Check it is sitting vertically by using a spirit level.

6 Carefully lift the fire surround into position, pushing the back panel on to the wall until the surround is flush against the wall surface. This will also help to force the back panel into its correct position.

7 Remove the fire surround and seal around the edges of the back panel using some more mortar (a pointing trowel is ideal for this process). However, take care not to get any mortar on to the marble face – if this happens, remove it immediately with a clean, damp sponge before it dries.

8 Re-position the fire surround on the back panel. Secure it in place using glass plate fixings, which will help it to sit flush on the wall surface. Attach the fixings under the mantel shelf so that they will not be too conspicuous.

9 Finally, attach the internal brass surround to the back panel with some silicone sealant. The surround can be pressed into position by hand. Be sure to remove any excess silicone that squeezes out with a dry cloth, before it sets.

MORTAR CHOICE

Mortar made from white cement is ideal for marble fireplaces because of its aesthetic qualities. Fireplaces may also be positioned using bonding coat plaster, but when using light-coloured marble, bear in mind that the marble can become stained. Also, some marble types have transparent characteristics which will mean that the fixing material may be visible in places. For this reason, a light-coloured mortar is best as it should be less noticeable than many of the darker types of adhesive. White cement is generally available from good DIY outlets.

Once blended into the rest of the decoration, a fireplace can make a stunning impact on the look and feel of a room. Painting the internal 'fireplace' matt black creates the impression of an authentic old fire instead of a newly positioned reproduction.

altering the structure of a ceiling

When redesigning a room layout or planning a new colour scheme, it can be common to neglect ceilings or assume that their finish will be led by other design elements in the room. However, this does not have to be the case, and entering any renovation project should include close consideration of ceiling improvements and potential alterations. Therefore, appropriate heights, soundproofing, access and insulatory properties are all considered in this chapter, together with decorative ideas for finishing.

Different patterns and designs make suspended ceilings an unusual alternative to traditional ceiling finishes.

lowering a ceiling – 1

The most common reason for lowering a ceiling is quite simply the desire to reduce the height of a room for decorative or soundproofing purposes. High ceilings are most common in older properties, but this is not always the case and ceiling levels can be adjusted in any room – regardless of age – provided the practicalities of head clearance and final appearance are considered. A two-part process, the first step is to construct a framework for the plasterboarding.

making the frame

Before focusing on the ceiling itself, consider the existing wall construction. The new ceiling will be supported primarily by fixings to the walls in the room, and so the strength of these fixings is vital. For solid block walls, concrete anchors or frame fixings can be used with confidence as the strength of the fixing will be consistent on all wall areas. If you are fixing to stud walls, however, it will first be necessary to pinpoint the studs. Wall plates can then be fixed directly into the studs, rather than the surrounding, weaker plasterboard. Furthermore, for ceilings with a greater span than 2.4m (8ft), it will be necessary to attach timber hangers between the new framework and the existing ceiling, in order to provide extra support.

tools for the job

tape measure

pencil

spirit level

panel saw

cordless drill/driver

hammer

1 Having decided how far you wish to bring the ceiling level down, use a pencil and spirit level to mark out a guideline around the entire perimeter of the room. Never simply measure the distance at different points and join them together,

ensuring accuracy

Taking extra time to ensure accurate measurements, and that the joists are correctly aligned, will be highly beneficial when it comes to applying plasterboard to the framework. Even small discrepancies between joist levels will be accentuated once the plaster sheeting has been applied. It is also vital that the joists are not fixed in the hangers in a twisted position. Otherwise, when plasterboard is applied it will not fit flush against the bottom of the joist, resulting in weak fixings along the entire joist length.

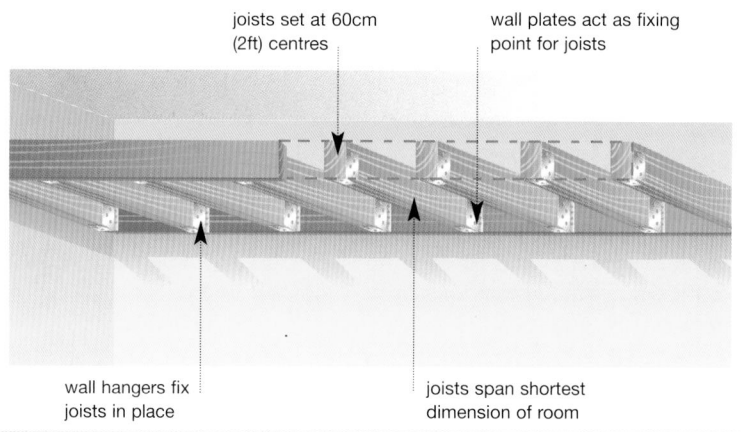

joists set at 60cm (2ft) centres

wall plates act as fixing point for joists

wall hangers fix joists in place

joists span shortest dimension of room

as slight undulations in most ceiling surfaces mean that these measurements do not provide a true level. It is better to mark off height at one point and use the level from that point on.

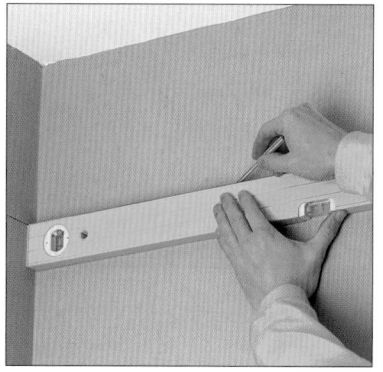

tips of the trade

Modern ceilings are normally 2.4m (8ft) high and manufacturers make most building boards to these dimensions. This is a good guideline when deciding on the height to set your ceiling. The timbers used for the frame here are 10 x 5cm (4 x 2in) but thinner joists can be used. However, thin joists will need to be fixed at closer intervals and timber hangers used to attach the joists to the existing ceiling. Plasterboard thickness can affect the position of joists. For 12.5mm (½ in) plasterboard, fix the joists at 60cm (2ft) intervals, for 9.5mm (⅜ in) plasterboard, the joists should be adjusted to intervals of 40cm (1ft 4in).

2 Fix lengths of 10 x 5cm (4 x 2in) sawn timber to each wall width with the bottom edge of each timber running precisely along the pencil guideline. Make fixings at 40 cm (1ft 4in) intervals along the timber. In this example, the wall plates are being attached with concrete anchors because the walls are solid block construction. If you are attaching to stud walls, use a joist detector to find the studs and therefore the ideal positions for fixing.

3 The joists for the frame should always span the room across its shortest dimension. Along the appropriate opposing wall plates, therefore, mark off at 60cm intervals to denote the position for the metal hangers, which will be used to support the joists.

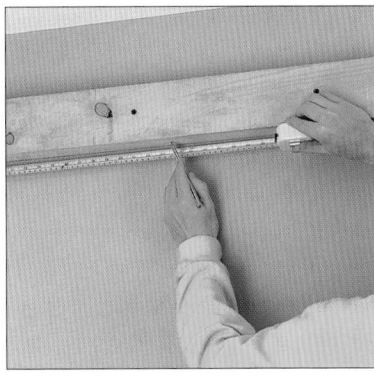

4 At each marked-off point on the two wall plates, nail a hanger in place – fix only to the underside of the wall plate for the moment.

5 Cut joists to the exact size between the opposing wall plates, positioning the cut joist inside the hangers. First, nail the hanger into the sides of the joist to clamp it in place. Then nail the hanger into the wall plate face for a secure, final fixing. Continue to attach joists to hangers across the rest of the ceiling framework.

6 To add extra rigidity to the framework, you can position some noggings between joists at staggered 1m (3ft 3in) intervals. The ceiling can now be considered ready for plasterboarding.

split level ceilings

Some people choose split level ceilings as an alternative to a complete ceiling level change. This is ideal for rooms in which high windows prevent the possibility of lowering the entire ceiling, or for people who want variation in the room height. The same basic system can be used to construct the frame, with some slight modifications to the main structure.

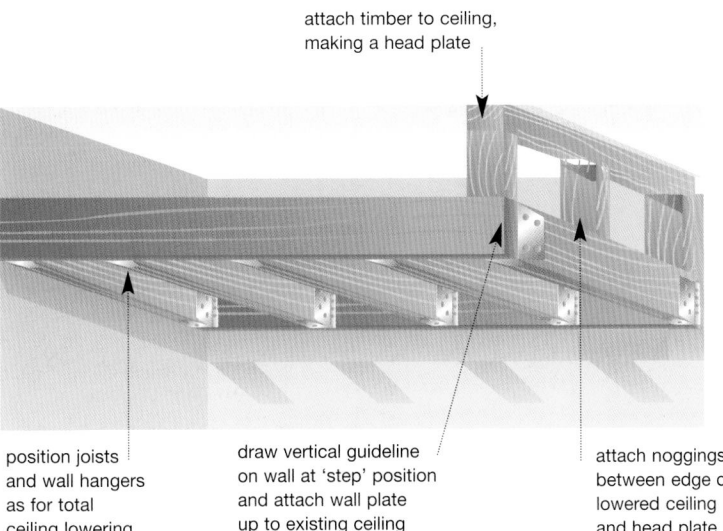

attach timber to ceiling, making a head plate

position joists and wall hangers as for total ceiling lowering

draw vertical guideline on wall at 'step' position and attach wall plate up to existing ceiling

attach noggings between edge of lowered ceiling and head plate

lowering a ceiling – 2 ⚒

Once the frame of your lowered ceiling is in place, plasterboard needs to be fixed in position, before dry lining or plastering can begin. Large sheets of plasterboard can be difficult to handle (see below) but laths are an ideal option in many instances. This is also the point at which additional features such as soundproofing or lighting fixtures should be considered. All of these tasks are quite straightforward, provided you plan ahead.

PLASTERBOARDING

If you are using regular-sized plasterboard, you will need to employ the assistance of a helper to lift and manoeuvre the boards. Nail the sheets at 150mm (6in) intervals along all the joists, while the joins between each board should be made half-way across the width of the joists. This will ensure that the edges of the two sheets join along a single joist.

plasterboarding with laths

Laths are much smaller and easier to handle than large plasterboard, which makes them better for manoeuvring and enables you to work alone. They are also ideal to use when joists are set at 60cm (2ft) centres because they tend to be supplied in 120cm x 60cm (4ft x 2ft) sheets, which means they do not require cutting, except for around the perimeter of the ceiling.

tools for the job

hammer

screwdriver (optional)

panel saw

protective gloves

1 Starting in one corner of the room, attach a single lath across three ceiling joists. Plasterboard nails are ideal for this process, or alternatively, plasterboard screws can be used.

2 Continue to add laths to the joists, staggering the joints so as to create a brick bond pattern. This means that as you reach the perimeter of the ceiling, you will need to measure and cut laths to fill the various gaps.

soundproofing

Lowering a ceiling also provides the perfect opportunity to add some soundproofing to the room. By inserting soundproofing slabs into the ceiling space before plasterboarding, you can make a substantial difference to the amount of noise audible from the room above. (An alternative

soundproofing technique is outlined on pages 74–5 where lowering the ceiling level is not an option.)

1 Weave 120cm x 60cm x 10cm (4ft x 2ft x 4in) soundproofing slabs between the top of the joists and the existing ceiling. If you have not been able to bring the ceiling down this far, use soundproofing slabs of the same size but with a 5cm (2in) depth instead of 10cm (4in). Rest the slabs in position, so that they are loosely joined but wedged securely above each joist.

2 Nail plasterboard sheets to the ceiling in the usual manner (see box). Bear in mind that it is important to use large sheets in this case, rather

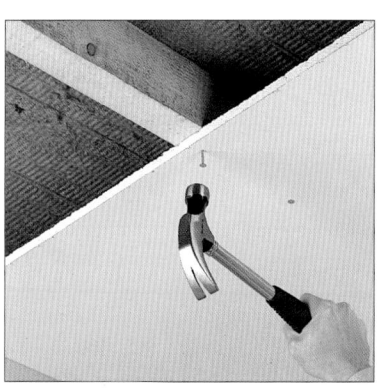

than laths, as the fewer the joins, the greater the soundproofing effect. Then apply a second layer of plasterboard (see step 5 page 74).

dealing with ceiling roses

safety advice

Before beginning any work on or around the ceiling rose, turn off the electrical supply at the consumer unit, and do not turn it back on until all the electrical work has been completed.

Ceilings tend not to have too many obstacles, and therefore lowering one can be a fairly trouble-free task. The main exception is a ceiling rose, which needs to be adjusted or lengthened in order to be of use for the new ceiling level. This work should be carried out after the new joists have been positioned, but before plasterboarding has begun.

tools for the job

screwdrivers (various)
cordless drill
hammer
pencil
tape measure

1 Unscrew the ceiling rose by hand, allowing the cover to slide down the wire to the fitting itself.

2 Unscrew the retaining screws that are keeping the rose plate secured to the old ceiling. Put the screws safely to one side as they will be needed again later.

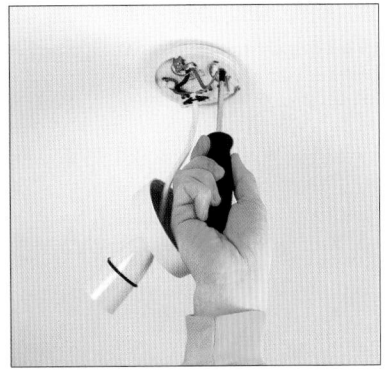

3 Release the electrical wires from the rose by unscrewing the relevant terminals, allowing the wires to drop free. The pendant should now be separate from the electrical cable, and can be put to one side.

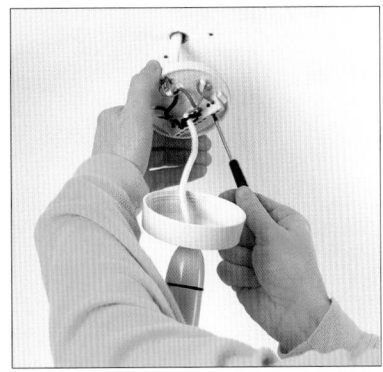

4 Use insulation tape to tape up each wire in the electrical supply cable. Ensure that each wire is completely separated from the others.

tips of the trade

It may be worth changing light fittings for flush-mounted spotlights, which will generally be less intrusive. However, always consult a qualified electrican before commencing work.

5 Plasterboard the ceiling until you come to a point where the old electrical cable is about to be totally obscured. Drill through the plasterboard directly below the cable, using a bit which is wide enough to accommodate the cable.

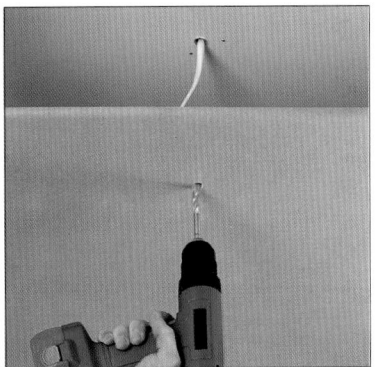

6 Pull the cable through the hole before continuing to apply plasterboard across the rest of the ceiling. If the cable is too tight in its original position and does not have the required excess to pull down to the new ceiling level, it will be necessary to add some extra cable to the existing one, joined with a junction box. Once the ceiling has been plasterboarded or dry lined, the pendant can be reconnected.

building a suspended ceiling ⁄⁄⁄

Suspended ceilings are traditionally linked with shopfitting, offices and commercial buildings. However, such ceiling structures are becoming increasingly popular in private dwellings. They are an ideal option for lowering ceilings, and require less structural work than alterations using joists and plasterboard. The tiles provided for suspended ceilings also tend to have both thermal and sound insulating properties and therefore make a useful alternative to traditional ceilings.

The construction of a suspended ceiling is a straightforward exercise so long as sufficient planning time has been allowed. It is worth drawing a scale diagram of the room in order to work out tile positioning and thus the ideal location for the main bearers in the framework (see diagram below).

tools for the job

| tape measure |
| spirit level |
| cordless drill/driver |
| hacksaw |
| side cutters |
| pliers |
| panel saw |

1 Draw a level pencil line around the perimeter walls at the prospective suspended ceiling height. Fix angle sections along this line at 40cm (1ft 4in) intervals. Fixings in solid block walls should be quite easy but you will need to follow the stud pattern (see page 68) on stud walls.

2 Fix angle brackets into the existing ceiling at measured intervals above the position where the main bearers will be.

3 Cut a section of hanger wire to a manageable length – 2–3m (6 –10ft) is suitable – and secure one end to a heavy object such as a workbench. Push the other end of the wire into a cordless drill and tighten the chuck until it is held securely in position. Slowly start the drill, causing the wire gradually to tauten until it is completely rigid. This will ensure that the wire has no slack and will make a rigid support when joined between the bearers and the ceiling.

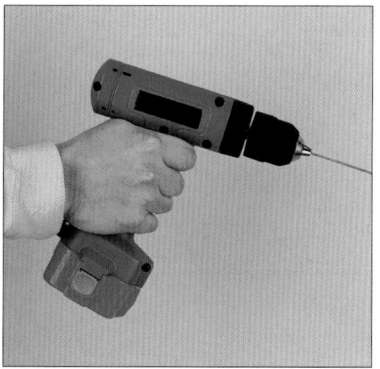

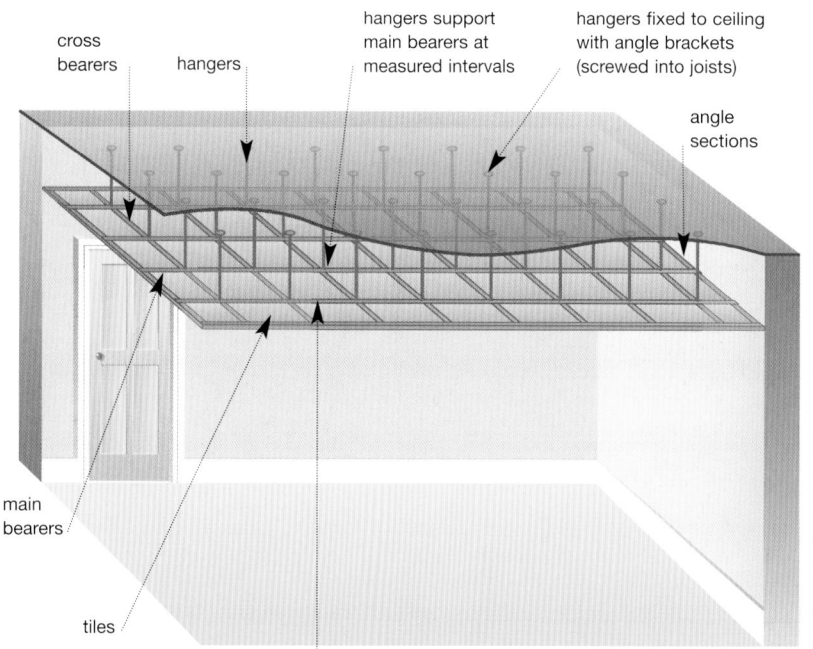

cross bearers

hangers

hangers support main bearers at measured intervals

hangers fixed to ceiling with angle brackets (screwed into joists)

angle sections

main bearers

tiles

bearer framework laid out so that cut tiles are an equal distance from wall around entire perimeter of room

4 Use side cutters to cut the wire down to the required lengths. Allow an excess of 10cm (4in) at each end of the length for attaching to the bearers and angle brackets.

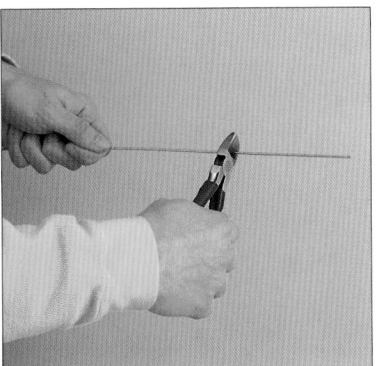

5 At each angle bracket, thread a section of wire through the bracket hole and tighten it in position by wrapping the end of the wire on to the main vertical section with pliers.

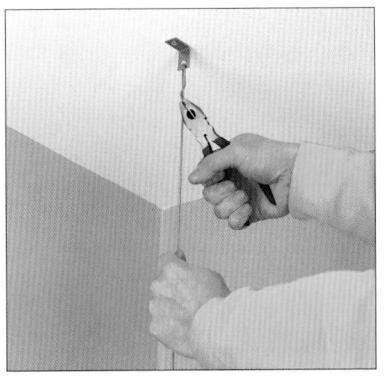

6 Position the main bearers on the angle sections. Thread the end of the hanger wires through the appropriate holes and wind the ends back on to the vertical length.

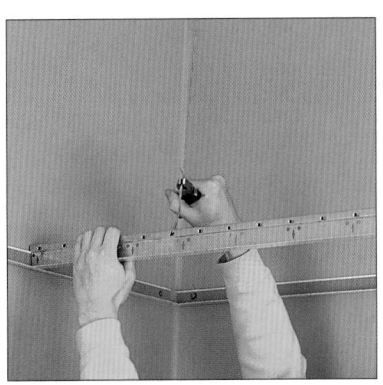

7 Fit the smaller cross bearers in position, at the appropriate intervals between the main bearers. The intervals should correspond to the tile dimensions.

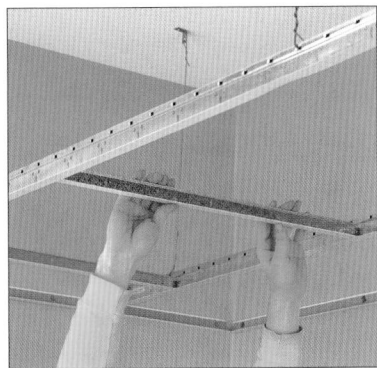

8 Simply drop the tiles in place, feeding them above the suspended ceiling level first and then lowering them into position between the bearers. There is no particular insertion order, but it is always best to position the full tiles first before working around the edges. (The edge tiles may be cut using a panel saw before they are fitted in place.) Some manufacturers provide clips that fit on top of the bearers to hold the tiles down in position.

Different patterns and designs make suspended ceilings an unusual alternative to traditional ceiling finishes.

---

tips of the trade

Main bearers need to be cut so that they can fit precisely between the angle sections on opposing walls. Mark off the length requirement on the bearer, and cut using a hacksaw.

soundproofing
a ceiling ⤢

If you are unable to combine soundproofing with lowering a ceiling (see page 70) it may be necessary to use other techniques for minimizing sound travel. One method is to lift the floor above and soundproof from above the ceiling in question. Alternatively, it is possible to work from below, taking the existing ceiling down and starting from scratch.

working from below

Soundproofing from below requires the removal of the old ceiling's plasterboard cladding. Once you have broken through the first piece of plasterboard, the task becomes a straightforward case of removing sections and sheets with a hammer or wrecking bar.

tools for the job

| claw hammer |
| wrecking bar |
| cordless drill |
| protective gloves |

1 Carefully remove the old ceiling with a wrecking bar. Then check between the joists for the presence of cables or pipes. Remove any remaining nails with a claw hammer – all joists must be free from obstructions before work begins so that new fixings can be inserted unhindered.

2 Starting on one side of the ceiling, fix soundbreaker bars across the joists at 40cm (1ft 4in) intervals. Fix the bars in place using drywall screws, ensuring that the screws are inserted through the felt pads and into the joist.

3 Weave 120cm x 60cm x 10cm (4ft x 2ft x 4in) soundproofing slabs above the soundbreaker bars and between the joists. Try to ensure that the slabs meet and join, above the bars. Continue to position slabs until the whole area is covered. Wear protective gloves for this process as the fibres in the slabs can cause skin irritation.

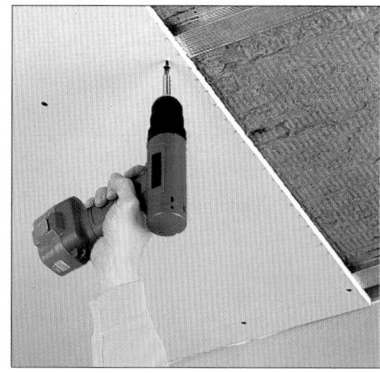

4 Fix 12mm (½in) plasterboard sheets to the ceiling using drywall screws. Fix the screws through the plasterboard and into the soundbreaker bars at 15cm (6in) intervals. Allow the screws to bite sufficiently to hold the plasterboard securely in place, but without the screwhead breaking into the surface and creating a weak fixing.

5 Fix 9mm (⅜in) plasterboard sheets over the first layer of plasterboard, staggering joints so that none of the second layer joints correspond with the first. Longer drywall screws will be required to penetrate both layers of plasterboard and fix into the soundbreaker bars. The ceiling may now be drylined or plastered in the usual way.

tips of the trade

Coving is a useful way to introduce an additional soundproofing seal around the edge of the ceiling (see pages 92–3).

If possible, working from above a ceiling is an easier option for adding soundproofing. Although this involves lifting a floor in order to gain access to the ceiling space, it tends to be less messy than taking a whole ceiling down. Soundproofing slabs are therefore slotted between joists from above, before the floor is relaid. However, where joist depth or the ceiling space is particularly large, sand pugging may be combined with sound insulation slabs to create a more effective soundproofing system.

tools for the job

bolster chisel

panel saw

hammer

cordless drill/driver

dust mask

protective gloves

1 Strip the floor back to the floorboards and remove the boards using a bolster chisel. Take care not to damage any of the boards as they will be repositioned once soundproofing is complete.

2 Cut sections of 5cm x 2.5cm (2in x1in) batten with a panel saw. Fix the lengths in place along the bottom of the joists, just above the plasterboard ceiling.

3 Cut and fit 12mm (½in) plyboard strips between the joists, fixing them in place by nailing through the ply and into the battens.

4 Line the face of the plyboard with a plastic membrane sheet. Tuck the membrane into the corners and allow it to encroach up to the top of the floor joists. Only nail in position at the top of the joists.

5 Carefully pour kiln-dried sand on to the plyboard between each joist, spreading out the sand into a layer about 5cm (2in) deep. A small piece of batten cut to the width of the

space between the joists makes an ideal tool for spreading the sand across the area and producing a consistent level.

6 Fit 120cm x 60cm x 10cm (4ft x 2ft x 4in) soundproofing slabs in between the joists and on top of the sand. The slabs may need to be cut to fit – use a panel saw and wear a dust mask when cutting. Protective gloves should also be worn whilst fitting the slabs. Then replace the floorboards – a thick underlay and good quality carpet will also add to the soundproofing effect.

safety advice

Remember that sand adds a great deal of weight to the ceiling, so check with a structural engineer that your ceiling will be able to cope with the load. Furthermore, this technique should not be used in ceilings containing water pipes. Any small leaks soaking into the sand over time will increase the weight further and could result in ceiling collapse.

insulating a ceiling ↗

Trying to make your home as energy efficient as possible provides benefits on a financial level and contributes towards protecting the environment. One of the simplest ways to increase energy efficiency is by ensuring that you have adequate loft insulation. This is easy to lay but requires some thought about how to deal with obstacles.

blanket insulation

Blanket insulation is the most commonly used form of loft insulation material as it is the simplest to handle and can be laid very quickly. Roll length measurements provided by the manufacturer make it easy to estimate the amount required. When measuring up, be sure to choose rolls that are the same width (or slightly wider) than the joist gap in your loft. This will help to avoid extra cutting.

tools for the job

protective gloves

dust mask

1 Roll out the insulation blanket between the joists. Do not compress it because much of its effectiveness is provided by maintaining its depth. Carefully tear the blanket by hand whenever a division is required.

2 Greater efficiency can be achieved by laying a second layer over, and at right angles to, the first. This technique obscures all the joists, so if you choose this option you may need to build access bridges in your loft.

loose fill insulation

Loose fill insulation offers an alternative to blankets. Although it can be used in most situations as a direct alternative, it is mainly used in lofts where there are a number of awkward spaces to fill, making it a more practical option than blanket insulation. It is made of similar material to the blankets, but has been shredded into smaller pieces.

tips of the trade

When installing loft insulation, do not cover any ventilation access. Most roof spaces are ventilated through grills or openings in the loft, or at the junction between the roof and exterior walls. Covering these areas can lead to damp and condensation problems, so keep filling safely away.

1 Pour the loose fill directly from the bag into the gaps between the joists.

2 Use a piece of batten, cut to the same length as the width of the gap between the joists, to even the loose fill out in the joist gap.

tips of the trade

Just as ventilation inlets must be kept clear of lagging, flush electrical fittings must also be given clearance, so that they do not overheat. Cut around flush fittings, leaving plenty of clearance between the insulation material and the fitting.

3 Insulation must always be on top of obstacles rather than below, so make some cardboard bridges for pipes, before covering over them with the loose fill.

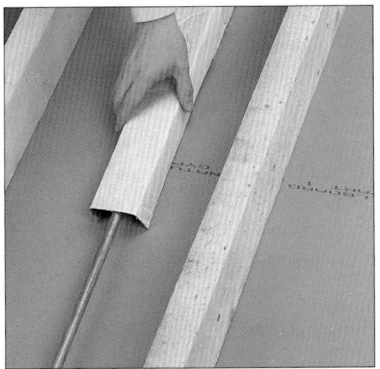

loft hatches

Loft hatches have to be movable, so it is clearly not possible simply to lay insulation over the top of the hatch. However, insulation is still necessary if it is to be effective throughout.

tools for the job

panel saw

hammer

protective gloves

dust mask

1 Cut four pieces of 12.5cm x 2.5cm (5in x 1in) planed softwood to the dimensions of each side of the loft hatch. Nail them in position to create a shallow box.

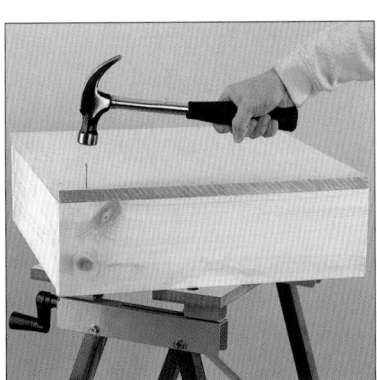

2 Insert a section of blanket insulation inside the box. Loose fill insulation may be used.

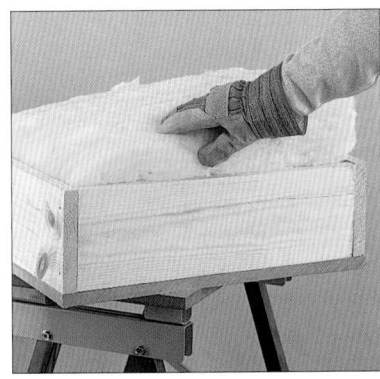

3 Cut a piece of plyboard to size, attach it to the top and position the box as the hatch.

DEALING WITH PIPES

Pipes situated between and below joist level are best dealt with as shown left. However, pipes situated above the joists need another method of insulation.

Fit pipe lagging over and around any exposed pipes, butt joining sections as required.

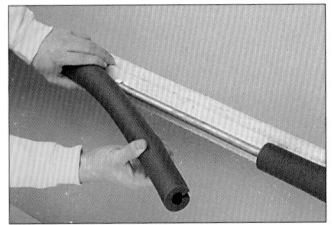

Where a junction is required, mitre the lagging so that a precise joint is achieved. Lagging can be cut using a craft knife or scissors.

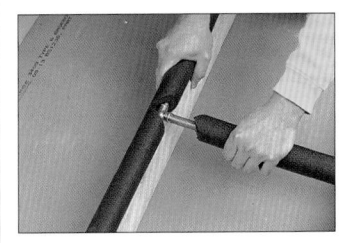

insulating water tanks

The growing popularity of combination boilers means that modern houses are less likely to have loft-situated water tanks. However, the majority of older houses still have water tanks which feed the various systems in the house. It is therefore important to ensure that the tank is insulated correctly.

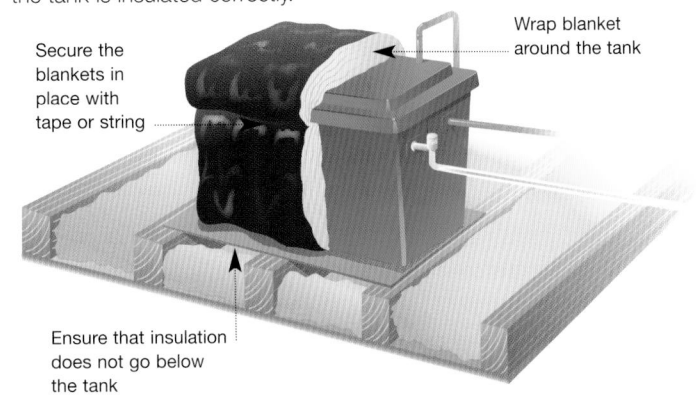

Secure the blankets in place with tape or string

Wrap blanket around the tank

Ensure that insulation does not go below the tank

building a loft hatch ⁄⁄⁄

Lofts are increasingly recognized as areas of under-utilized space. Many people now look to the idea of converting such areas into extra rooms, or improving the storage capacity in order to free-up other rooms. Most lofts have some sort of access built into the design of the house, but renovation may make it necessary to install a proper loft hatch.

cutting in a hatch

tools for the job

joist detector
tape measure
pencil
spirit level
plasterboard saw
panel saw
cordless drill/driver
hammer

Before beginning the process of installing a new hatch, it is important to make all the necessary calculations and judgements in terms of the suitability of its position. If ladder access is required, ensure that your chosen site has suitable provision for storing and/or supporting such equipment. Similarly, check to see what is directly above the proposed hatch, as all precautions must be taken to ensure that services will not be interfered with or disrupted.

Dimensions clearly require the hatch to be large enough to allow comfortable access for both yourself and any household items that need to be passed through the opening. The structure of the ceiling is vital because some joists will have to be cut in order to make room for the access area. It is therefore advisable to take some professional advice before embarking on the project, in order to ensure that the ceiling structure will sustain a loft hatch construction. In older homes, where joist depth tends to be more substantial, this is rarely a problem. In newer homes, however, joists tend to be thinner and so it is necessary to check the strength of the structure.

1 Use a joist detector to pinpoint the joist position on the ceiling. Mark out the proposed position of the hatch, ensuring that two of the opposing sides are directly below the edges of two joists. In this way, it will only be necessary to cut through one central joist to create the opening.

2 Use a dry wall saw to cut around the pencil guideline. On the two sides of the square that run in

the same direction as the joists above, try to rest the saw against the joists, thereby following directly along their edge. This should help to achieve an exact cut to the precise joist width.

3 Having removed the plasterboard 'hatch', use a panel saw to cut out the central joist. This will now provide access through the hole and into the roof space. Trim back the cut joist (from above) a further 5cm (2in) at either side of the hatch, so that when noggings are inserted to create the opposing sides of the hatch, they will be positioned back from the ceiling opening, and also supply a more rigid structure.

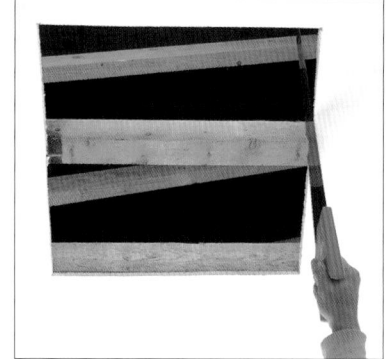

4 Use the panel saw to cut noggings to size, and then screw them in place to form the hatch frame. In addition to fixing the noggings centrally into the cut joists, it will also be necessary to fix in the corners. Skew screws through the noggings and into the joists at all four corners of the hatch frame using a cordless screwdriver.

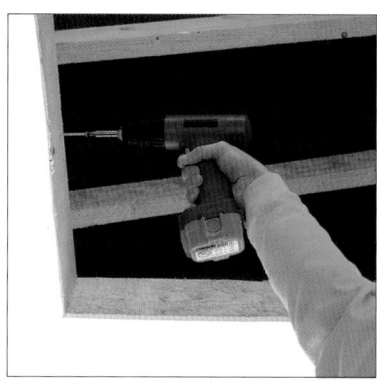

5 Cut 12.5cm x 2.5cm (5in x 1in) planed softwood to the internal dimensions of the hatch. Fix it in place by nailing or screwing directly through the lengths and into the joists and noggings. Ensure the bottom edge sits flush with the ceiling to produce a smooth lining upon which to attach the remaining hatch features.

6 Cut a 2.5cm x 0.5cm (1in x ⅜in) batten to the internal dimensions of the lining. Make a pencil guideline around the lining, half-way up its height. Then nail the batten in place, so that the bottom edge sits precisely on the pencil guideline. This batten will act as the ledge upon which the finished loft hatch will rest.

7 Measure and cut architrave to fit around the lining. Allow the architrave front edge to bisect the edge of the lining, in order to create a neat and balanced finish.

8 Tighten the mitred joints of the architrave by nailing further fixings at each corner, thus pulling the mitre into a secure, finished position.

9 Finally, cut a sheet of mdf (medium density fibreboard) to the dimensions of the hatch and drop it into place above the ledge created by the batten. This can be primed and decorated as required.

loft ladders

Access through a loft hatch can be made by means of a portable ladder or by a permanent, custom-designed ladder. Many manufacturers provide easy-to-install ladder systems, but make sure that your ladder is accessible and that the loft has enough clear storage capacity, without obstructing joists. If possible, choose your ladder design before building a hatch because many manufacturers stipulate particular dimensions and positioning in order to achieve the best access results.

ensure ladder has room to 'fold' in roof space – this will depend on design, so check with manufacturer's guidelines

fit required hinges to loft hatch

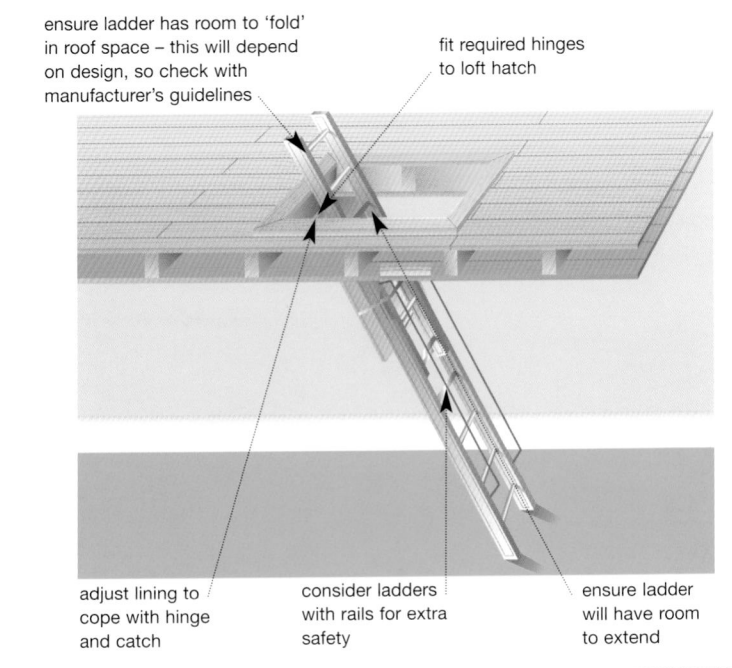

adjust lining to cope with hinge and catch

consider ladders with rails for extra safety

ensure ladder will have room to extend

constructing a slatted ceiling ⚐⚐⚐

Slatted ceilings offer a purely decorative option to traditional ceiling structure. They can be useful when trying to 'lower' a particularly high ceiling, and require less structural consideration than lowering the ceiling in its entirety (see pages 68–71). However, slatted ceilings do require a large quantity of wood and the jointing mechanism and measurements used in their construction need to be precisely accurate, in order to achieve the best possible effect.

tools for the job

pencil
spirit level
panel saw
combination square
mitresaw
chisel
wooden mallet
cordless drill/driver

1 Draw a level guideline around the perimeter of the room using a pencil and spirit level. This line will be the bottom edge of the slatted ceiling, and therefore its positioning should be considered carefully. Height suitability is really determined by the existing ceiling height in your home. Older, more traditional houses vary in ceiling height but modern houses tend to be about 2.4m (8ft).

2 Cut a piece of 7.5cm x 2.5cm (3in x 1in) prepared softwood to the length of the longest wall dimension. Use a combination square to make guidelines at 15cm (6in) intervals along the length.

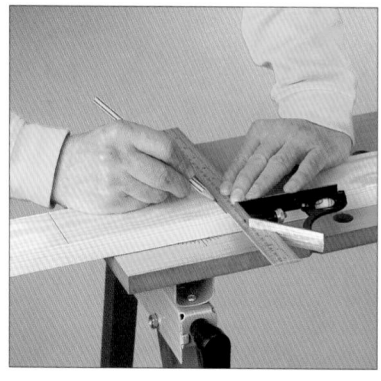

3 Pencil in a central bisecting line through an offcut of 7.5cm x 2.5cm (3in x 1in) prepared softwood. Hold the offcut next to each guideline on the full length in turn, marking a second guideline across the length to denote the width of the slats. Then, using the pencilled bisecting line on the offcut, mark where this line meets the pencilled guidelines on the full length on either side of the offcut.

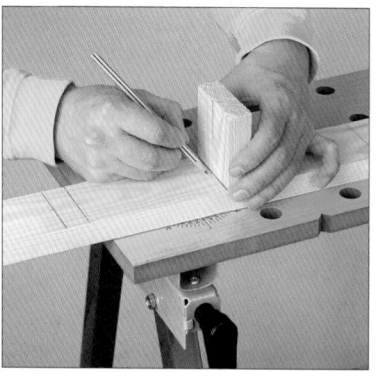

4 Use a mitresaw, set at the 90 degree angle, to cut down to the marks on each slat guideline on the length. Be exact with this cut, not allowing it to encroach further than the marked-off points.

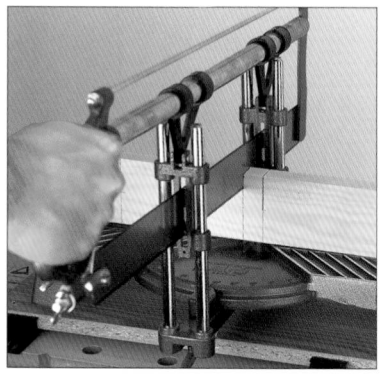

5 Use a chisel to cut out each sawn section of the length. Ensure that the chisel blade dimensions fit exactly between the sawn cuts so as to produce a precise, accurate finish. One light tap with a mallet on the chisel is usually enough to remove this small section of wood. Repeat steps 2–5 for the length of wood required for the opposing wall. It may pay to sand the cut-out area lightly to remove any rough edges.

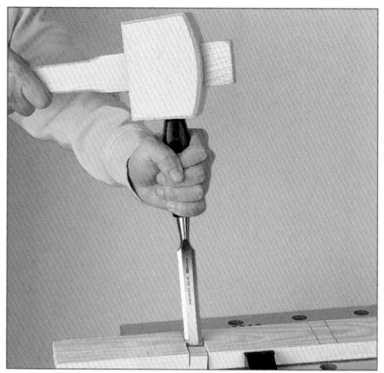

6 Screw the notched lengths into position on the wall, allowing the bottom, uncut edge of the lengths to run along the pencil guideline. Screw in fixings below every other notch using concrete anchor

screws or plugs and screws as required. On the two opposing walls – as yet untouched – fix full lengths of 7.5cm x 2.5cm (3in x 1in) prepared softwood between the notched lengths, flush against the wall.

7 Measure exactly between the opposing notches on the two opposing lengths (from wall to wall). Cut lengths of 7.5cm x 2.5cm (3in x1in) prepared softwood accordingly. At the ends of these lengths, measure in exactly the width of the length – 2.5cm (1in) in this case – and bisect the width of the length to produce an L-shaped pencil guideline. Cut this portion away, at each end.

8 Position the length between the appropriate notches, allowing the length to drop down into position.

9 A couple of knocks with a mallet may be required finally to position the length – pins should not be necessary. Repeat this process across the entire ceiling.

tips of the trade

For ceilings where the slat length is more than 3m you may need to add extra support. Fix a length of 50mm x 50mm planed softwood across the top of the slats, and attach it to the ceiling with 'hangers'.

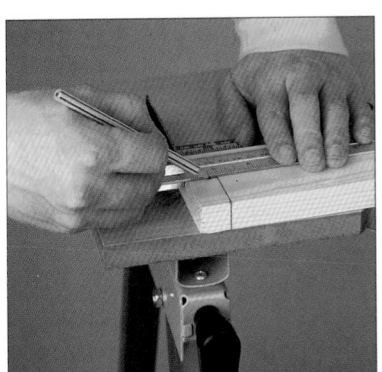

tips of the trade

Dropping the ceiling level will mean that ceiling-fitted lighting will also need adjusting. This may require the lengthening of pendants or fluorescent fittings. Alternatively, a switch to wall-mounted fittings could be an option. Consult an electrician before embarking on this work.

Painting the original ceiling above the slats can enhance the desired effect. The slats themselves can also be used as a system from which to hang further decoration.

cladding & lining

Once the basic structure of a room has been altered, further work is required to get the room ready for finishing touches and decorative features. In particular, it's important to achieve wall and ceiling finishes that are suitable for accepting decorative coatings. This chapter therefore explains the correct procedures for plastering and dry lining – both of which are essential skills in the construction finishing process. The remainder of the chapter looks at many other options of a more style-based nature, such as techniques for adding greater interest to wall or ceiling surfaces, in order to personalize the room and produce individual features and characteristics.

Decorative wall panelling makes an attractive finish in any room, especially when used on stairwells.

dry lining walls 📐📐📐

While previously it was explained how to create partitions and fix plaster sheeting to wall surfaces, it is also important to achieve some kind of smooth wall finish before decorative layers can be applied. The two most common types of wall finishes are plaster and dry lining. Dry lining is, in simple terms, a way of making a smooth join between plasterboard sheets. It provides a neat, professional finish.

dry lining

Although the basic structure of plasterboard is the same, there are slight design variations to help ensure a smooth finish. For dry lining, the plasterboard used for the wall surface should have slightly tapered edges. These edges work in conjunction with the jointing tape and jointing compound, enabling you to achieve a clean, smooth surface.

tools for the job

nail punch
hammer or screwdriver
scissors or craft knife
filling knife or scraper
sponge
coating knife
dust mask
dusting brush
side cutters

1 Before starting, check that all nail heads or screws are below surface level. Those which are sitting

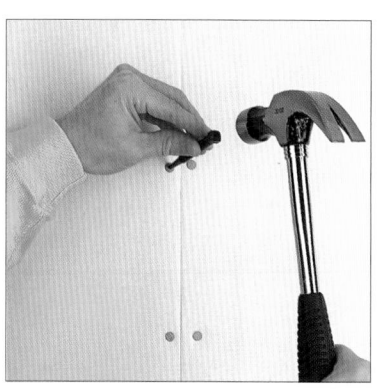

slightly proud of the surface may be knocked in using a nail punch and hammer. However, punch the nails only just below surface level – if they are inserted too far, the plasterboard may crumble and cause a weak fixing. Dry wall screws in plasterboard can be tightened with a screwdriver.

2 Apply self-adhesive jointing tape along the entire plasterboard, smoothing it into place and ensuring that there are no wrinkles or bumps in the tape surface. Cut the tape using scissors or a craft knife.

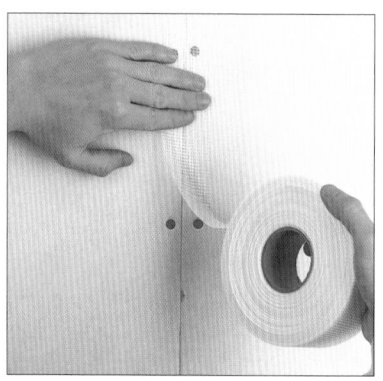

3 Use a filling knife (or scraper) to press the jointing compound into the length of the taped joint. Work

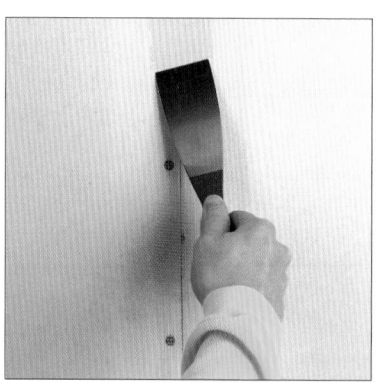

along the joint, making sure that the compound sits flush with the tape surface. Ensure that the whole joint is filled from ceiling to floor, re-working bits of the joint with more compound if you find it necessary.

4 Immediately after applying the compound, smooth any lumpy areas with a clean, damp sponge. Keep rinsing the sponge but be sure to wring it thoroughly, so that it doesn't become soaked. This is because excessive moisture can weaken the joint and cause cracking.

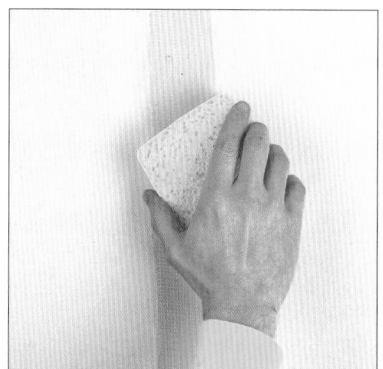

5 Use a coating knife to apply a wide band of compound down the filled joint. The knife should 'rest'

against the tapered sides. Then use a damp sponge to feather the edges of the compound and smooth the joint.

6 After completing all the joints, use a filling knife to add some extra compound over the nails or screw heads. Allow the compound to stand proud of the plasterboard surface.

7 Once the compound has dried, sand the joints and filled nail heads. (You can use abrasive paper wrapped around a sanding block or an electric sander.) Use very fine paper as anything coarse is likely to cause grooves in the surface.

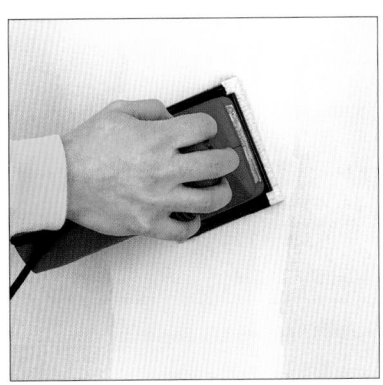

traditional tip

The technique described here uses self-adhesive jointing tape, which is a relatively new development. A more traditional method uses a jointing tape that is not self-adhesive. In this case, the compound is added to the join and then the tape applied over the top. Once the tape is in place, continue as before.

dealing with corners

Corners require a slightly different technique of application, but the principle of taping and joining sheets of plasterboard remains the same. Although the self-adhesive jointing tape used for flat wall surfaces can be used, it is easier to use specially designed corner jointing tape as shown here.

1 Use a dusting brush to remove any loose debris or material along the corner. Then apply jointing compound along, and to either side of, the corner junction. Ensure a good, even coverage along the entire length of the junction.

2 Apply corner tape along the junction, pressing it firmly into the jointing compound. Ensure that there are no ripples or bumps in the tape surface, and that the central crease of the tape runs directly along the corner junction apex. Cut the tape to fit with side cutters. (Scissors are insufficient because the tape contains wire strips.)

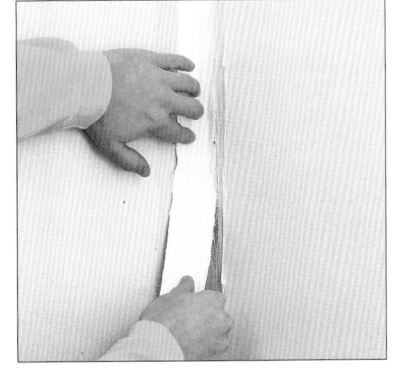

3 Remove excess compound from the corner with a filling knife. This also helps to secure the edges of the tape. Allow to dry before applying a second layer of compound to cover the tape. Once dry, this may be sanded to a smooth finish in the usual way.

external corners

Corner jointing tape is reversible, so it may be used in a similar fashion along external corners. Alternatively, an external corner trowel may be used for finishing purposes.

tips of the trade

• In order to achieve the best possible finish, make sure that tools are kept clean. This is especially important with the coating knife, which should be wiped down with a damp sponge after every few applications of compound.

• Remaining compound can be used as an excellent all-purpose filler. However, do ensure that it is stored in an airtight container.

• Always allow compound to dry at natural room temperature – excessive heat will cause cracking.

• Fine grade abrasive paper can quickly become clogged when finishing wall surfaces. To reduce wastage, use old medium grade paper that has been worn down on other tasks.

• Once sanded, seal the entire wall surface with a proprietary sealer before applying further decorative coats.

plastering a wall /////

Plastering is the traditional method for finishing walls. It is a highly skilled job but, with time and practice, it is possible to produce a good finish. Plaster can be applied direct to plasterboard, or it may be used to finish solid wall surfaces, but only after the appropriate render and preparation coats have been applied.

solid walls

tools for the job

mortar mixing equipment

paintbrush for pva solution

plastering trowel

gauging trowel

bucket

hawk

Whether block, brick or natural stone, such solid wall surfaces require a base coat of render before the plaster can be applied.

MORTAR MIXING

The secret behind successful rendering is to ensure the correct mortar mix and consistency for the rendering. The standard mix is composed of 5 parts builder's sand to 1 part cement, with plasticizer and waterproofer added according to the manufacturer's guidelines.

Add sufficient water to get the mix into a stodgy but smooth consistency, which will allow the mortar to spread across the wall surface easily, but without sagging and therefore losing its shape. Different walls have different absorption properties, so bear this in mind when mixing. Also, uneven surfaces may require a two-coat system, in which case the first should be a stronger mix of 4 parts sand to 1 part cement.

1 Before application, apply a coat of pva (polyvinyl adhesive) solution to the wall (5 parts water to 1 part pva) and allow it to dry. Use a plastering trowel to apply the render to the wall surface, with large, sweeping strokes. Press and smooth as you work, ensuring total coverage. Try not to worry about render that squeezes out and falls away on either side of the plastering trowel – the job is a messy one and this sort of excess is to be expected.

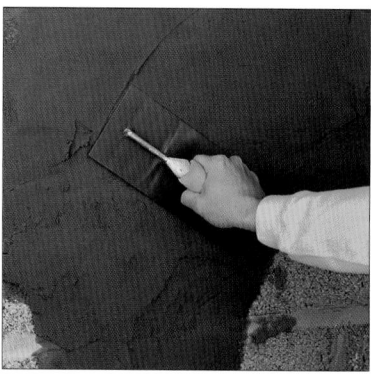

2 Smooth over the surface with a plastering trowel to create a flat finish. Then score the surface with the edge of a gauging trowel.

applying plaster

When a solid wall has been rendered and allowed to dry, the technique for applying plaster is very similar to that for applying plaster to plasterboard. The only difference is that plasterboard walls will need some preparatory work around the joints between different sheets. With a rendered surface, the wall simply needs to be wetted with pva solution before applying the plaster.

tools for the job

power drill & mixing attachment

plastering trowel

bucket

paint brush

scraper

1 Tape along all the joints between the plasterboard sheets using self-adhesive jointing tape. Press firmly in place, ensuring there are no wrinkles in the tape.

2 Mix multi-finish plaster into a smooth, creamy consistency by gradually adding water. If possible, use a power drill with a mixing attachment to stir the mix, as this will help to ensure a thorough blend. If you do use a drill, only engage the trigger when the mixing attachment is safely inside the bucket and plaster – starting the power drill and attachment outside the bucket can be extremely dangerous.

3 Apply the plaster across the wall surface using a plastering trowel. Spread the plaster evenly, pressing down as you move the trowel across the whole of the wall surface.

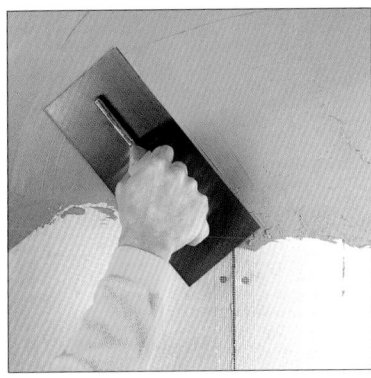

safety advice

As an alternative to taping joints with self-adhesive tape, traditional plastering scrim can be used. This dry tape needs to be applied using a plaster mix to secure it in place along the joints. Once dry, you can continue to plaster in the usual way.

4 When the entire wall is covered, smooth the plaster with the trowel to create a totally flat finish. Allow the plaster to dry to a firm but still wet-to-the-touch finish, and 'polish' the surface with a dampened plastering trowel. This process takes semi-dry plaster from the peaks on the wall surface and fills in the troughs, creating a smooth finish across the entire surface.

dealing with awkward areas

Every wall surface will normally have some sort of obstacle which hinders the free movement of the plastering trowel. Electrical sockets are perfect examples of problem areas, although the technique described here also applies to door and window frames.

1 In the tightest area, such as between the edge of the socket and the wall or door architrave, carefully smooth the plaster with a dampened paint brush.

2 Use a dampened scraper on the other corners and sides of the socket to produce a flat finish.

corners

Corners are commonly encountered when plastering, but generally create little problem so long as the correct procedure is followed. Professionals tend not to plaster adjacent walls on the same day, or, at the very least, they wait until one wall has set before starting the next. In this way, the plastering trowel can be used to scrape down tightly against corner joins, creating a well-defined edge. Alternatively, specialist corner plastering trowels may be used to achieve a finish in these areas.

BONDING COAT ALTERNATIVE

One alternative to render is to apply a bonding plaster coat directly on to block walls. This plaster is very different from finishing coat plaster, as it has a much coarser and more grainy consistency. Apply it using the same technique as for rendering, although follow the manufacturer's guidelines to ensure the correct mix.

panelling walls – 1 ⬈⬈

Wall panelling may either be applied directly over unfinished walls or on to a plastered or dry lined wall. The finish, which is normally wood-based, is designed to provide an attractive feature, although it can also help to prevent wall damage from chairs and furniture. Panelling generally requires a framework base which is made from lightweight battens.

making a framework

tools for the job

wrecking bar
pencil
tape measure
spirit level
panel saw
power drill
cordless drill/driver
hammer

For entire wall covering purposes, battens should be fixed at the ceiling/wall junction and ceiling/floor junction, with further lengths in between. For dado height panelling, the top batten should be positioned at the height to which you require the panelling to extend. One further batten should be positioned equidistant from the top and bottom battens.

1 Carefully remove the skirting board from the wall – the lengths can be reattached later.

2 Use a pencil and spirit level to mark a series of horizontal lines up the wall surface. Start at floor level, marking off every 45cm (18in) until you reach the required height.

3 Cut and fix battens along the guidelines. If the wall is masonry (such as this one) you will need to use a power drill to make pilot holes through the batten and into the wall, ready for screw fixing.

4 Use a cordless drill/driver to insert concrete anchor screws through into the wall surface. If you are not using concrete anchors, plugs and screws may be used as an alternative.

5 Hold a straight-edge (a piece of batten is ideal) across the face of the positioned battens. This will help you to check how 'straight' they are on the wall and to see whether the panelling will sit flush when attached. Undulating walls should be packed out by knocking some wooden wedges into the gap with a hammer. The first wedge may need balancing with a second wedge to keep the face of the batten flat and face-on to the wall surface. Once complete, re-check the straightness of the wall.

applying tongue & groove panelling

Tongue and groove is an effective way to produce a panelled wall finish. It may be applied from floor to ceiling, but it has greatest effect if it used up to dado level, as shown here. The thickness of the cladding varies – for this purpose, relatively thin lengths are ideal as they have no structural role and need only to be decorative.

repair & restoration

Not all constructional tasks involve the complete rebuilding of entire ceilings and walls. Indeed, most jobs are concerned with repairs and alterations to localized areas, such as restoring surfaces and areas of damage. This type of work is often quick to carry out but nevertheless important in maintaining or restoring the appearance of walls and ceilings. This chapter covers many of the more common repair projects which occur around the home, and provides instruction on the best means of dealing with damaged areas. Many of the methods used have been briefly mentioned in earlier chapters, but slight variations are often required when it comes to finding the best techniques for repairs.

121

Whether painted or stained, tongue and groove provides an attractive and hardwearing finish, to an entire room.

making minor repairs ↗

When preparing to decorate or finish a room, it is almost certain that some minor repairs or surface improvement will be required, regardless of the age of the ceiling or wall. All minor imperfections in such surfaces are relatively quick to repair but make an important contribution to the overall look of the room.

ceilings

tools for the job

hammer
nail punch
filling knife
craft knife
caulking blade
coating knife
lining fitch

Ceilings tend to avoid a lot of the wear and tear that walls receive because they are, quite simply, out of the way of much passing 'traffic' and potential damage. However, they do suffer damage from actions such as vibration – often caused by footsteps on the floor above. In many cases this never causes a problem, but sometimes persistent vibration can lead to minor damage in the ceiling surface.

popping nail heads

Nail heads can emerge from the ceiling surface for a number of reasons. In old ceilings, it may be because the nail was not knocked in properly and has loosened over the years. However, the problem is more common in recently plastered ceilings and indicates that either the plasterboard has not been secured firmly enough – which leads to a slight movement of the board itself – or that the nail is not inserted in a joist properly. The cure for either problem is very simple.

1 Punch in the nail head ensuring it is well below surface level. Alternatively, if the nail is loose, remove it with pliers and insert another into the joist close by.

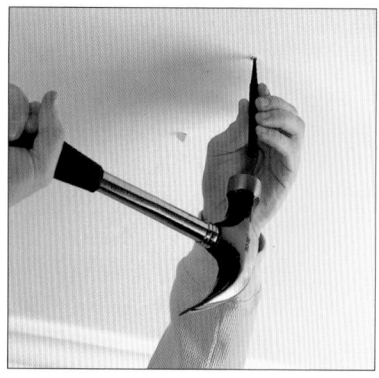

2 Use all-purpose filler to cover the hole. Allow the filler to dry and sand to a smooth finish.

ceiling cracks

As with popping nail heads, cracks can appear in both old and relatively new ceilings. The tendency is for cracks to follow the joint edges of the plasterboard sheets, which means that they are normally fairly straight and uniform in their course. However, this is no exact rule, and cracks may appear for any number of reasons. In minor instances, use all-purpose filler.

1 Use a craft knife to cut along each edge of the crack, removing loose material and shaping the crack into a small valley or fissure.

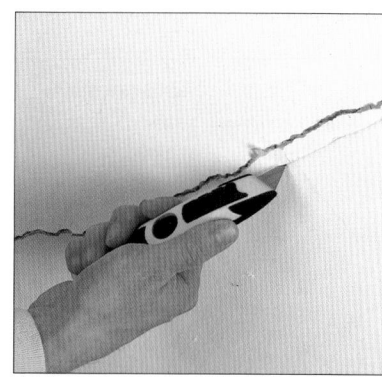

2 Use a filling knife to press filler into the crack, resting the edges of the filling knife on either side to produce a finish that is as flush as possible. For deep cracks, more than one application may be required. Allow to dry and sand to a smooth finish.

PERSISTENT CRACKING

Sometimes, however much filling is carried out, small hairline cracks will reappear in ceiling surfaces. Lining the ceiling can help to prevent the cracks from becoming visible, but if they crack the paper as well this suggests that there are structural problems, so seek professional advice.

walls

Walls do have the nail popping and cracking problems experienced by ceilings, but they are also prone to other damage as a result of general wear and tear. Again, most can be solved in a relatively short time.

dents and divots

Small knocks and scrapes are common on most wall surfaces and are basically unavoidable. Always repair any such marks before redecorating, to ensure a good finish.

1 For small holes, simply dust out any loose material and use a filler knife to apply all-purpose filler to the area. Allow to dry and sand to a smooth finish.

2 For larger holes, use the broad face of a caulking blade to apply the filler. For deep holes, try more than one application.

peeling tape

On dry lined walls (or ceilings) the tape used on joints may occasionally work loose and lead to a bulge in the wall surface. This may either be because it was not secured in place properly during wall construction, or it could simply be a sign of age. Whichever the case, it will need repairing before decoration can take place.

1 Tear back the defective area of tape and use a craft knife to cut it away at the place where there is still good adhesion between the tape and jointed wall surface.

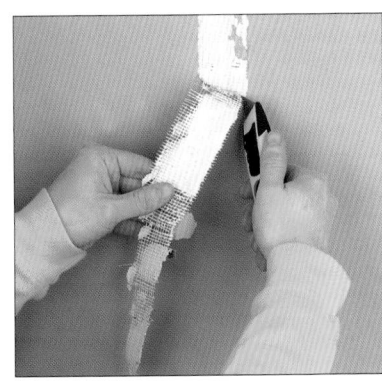

2 Reapply a section of self-adhesive jointing tape to the damaged area, following the same procedure as before.

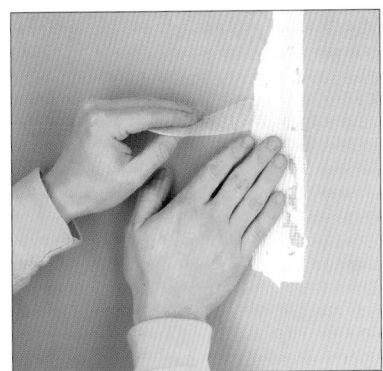

3 Use a coating knife to spread jointing compound along and over the joint. Allow it to dry before sanding the surface to a smooth finish with some abrasive paper.

wall & ceiling junction

The junction between the wall and ceiling is another area that can be prone to cracking. To repair standard junctions, use flexible filler or caulk as shown on page 108. Ornate joints such as cornice require more work.

1 Apply filler to the damaged area with your finger, making the filler sit slightly proud of the profile.

2 Use a wetted lining fitch to mould the filler into position. Allow to dry and sand gently.

improving ceilings ⟋⟋⟋

Making sure that a ceiling has a good surface for decorating may require more work than simply minor repairs. Severely sagging old ceilings can require demolition and reconstruction (see page 66) but some surfaces have other potential options. For example, applying a new plaster skim over a rough ceiling surface is one way of restoring it to a flatter finish. Alternatively, the projects considered below may be more appropriate to your needs.

old textured ceilings

Textured ceilings suit some people more than others. For this reason, you may find it desirable to restore a textured or patterned ceiling back to a flat surface. One technique for removing textured coatings is to use a wallpaper stripper. However, when using such appliances, pay close attention to the manufacturer's operating instructions and adhere to all the required safety procedures – goggles and gloves are essential protective equipment.

Alternatively, if the coating is particularly well stuck to the ceiling surface, it can be easier and less time consuming to simply plaster over the top of it. To do this, refer to the plastering techniques described in chapter 5, but you may also need to adopt the refining technique described below.

tools for the job

scraper
large paint brush or pasting brush
plastering trowel
mixing equipment

1 Use a scraper to knock off all the high points from the textured coating. The degree to which you have to do this will depend on the depth of finish but, generally, removing as much texture as possible will make the plastering process much easier later on.

2 Brush a coat of pva solution (5 parts water to 1 part pva) on to the textured surface to seal it and stabilize it in readiness for the plaster.

3 Mix up plaster (see page 87) and apply it to the ceiling with

a plastering trowel. A fairly deep plaster coat is required in order to 'take up' the roughness or texture on the ceiling, and therefore two coats of plaster may be needed.

THE TEXTURED OPTION

On badly cracked or rough ceilings, there is an option to use proprietary textured paint to help 'take up' the roughness or undulations of the ceiling surface. The texture produced is not the finish of standard textured coatings, but it is enough to fill minor cracks and provide a more even-looking finish, without going to the expense or time of re-plastering. It is worth bearing in mind that plastering a ceiling is by no means a job for the beginner and so textured paint is a serious and economic option for people with less experience.

using textured paper on ceilings

Just as lining paper can be used to smooth a ceiling surface, textured paper can be used to add pattern and interest to the ceiling surface.

The structure of this type of paper is three dimensional, so some care is required when hanging it. It may be necessary to line the ceiling first to achieve the best possible results.

tools for the job

chalk line
pasting brush
paperhanging brush
scissors
pencil
craft knife or scissors

1 Use a chalk line to gain a precise guideline across the ceiling surface. Secure the paper in the wall/ceiling junction, making sure that the edge of the length runs precisely along the chalk line.

2 Brush out the paper in the usual manner, applying enough pressure to secure it in position and to remove bubbles from beneath, but not so much pressure that the

pattern texture becomes crushed. Continue along the length to the other end.

3 Draw a pencil guideline along the wall/ceiling junction, peel the length back and cut along the guideline with a craft knife or scissors. Once trimmed, brush the end of the paper back in place and repeat the process at the other end of the length.

4 When joining lengths, take care not to crush the relief with the brush. Wipe off excess paste from the wall and paper surfaces as you work.

tips of the trade

Remember that textured paper needs a stronger mix of paste than normal paper because of its weight.

Textured paper offers a uniform, patterned finish which gives a greater focus to the ceiling and helps to distract the eye from undulations in the surface.

patching a ceiling

Ceiling damage is often caused by basic accidents – the removal of a floorboard, for example, followed by a misplaced foot. The damage can appear catastrophic, but repair is fairly straightforward. Even though ceiling structure itself may vary, the technique for repairing and filling a large area of damage remains the same. Essentially, the affected area must be patched with plasterboard before skimming the surface with plaster, ready for redecoration.

tools for the job

joist dectector
spirit level or straight-edge
pencil
pad saw
craft knife
claw hammer
cordless drill/driver
panel saw
filling knife
plastering trowel

1 Use a joist detector to help determine the exact position and direction of the ceiling joists. Alternatively, if the hole is very large, you may be able to insert your hand carefully through the gap and feel for the joists that way.

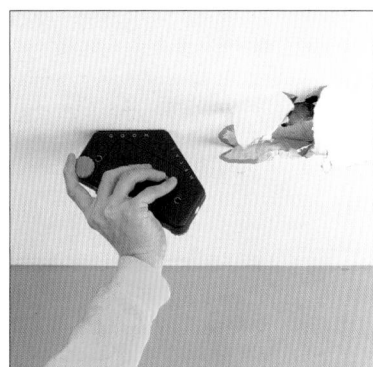

2 Use a straight-edge (such as a spirit level) and pencil to mark the area on the ceiling that will need patching. Create a neat, easy-to-cut shape, such as a rectangle – the dimensions should clearly be larger than the hole, and

should also extend to the centre of the joists on either side of the hole.

3 Cut through the plasterboard, or lath and plaster, using a pad saw. Along the joists it may be necessary to use a craft knife.

4 Use a hammer to remove any nails that are protruding from the joists. The wooden surfaces should be

safety advice

When cutting or sawing into a ceiling surface, always check that there are no pipes, electrical supplies or cables in the area of your work.

as flush as possible, to ensure that no obstructions will impede the insertion of the new plaster patch.

5 Cut two lengths of 10cm x 2.5cm (4in x 2in) sawn softwood to act as noggings on either side of the hole. Make sure that they are a tight fit, and use a hammer to ease them into place so that they extend into the ceiling space, while still leaving half the nogging visible along the cut edge of the hole.

6 Skew in screws at the corners of the noggings so that the screws go through into the existing ceiling joists, securing the noggings firmly into place. It is best to drill pilot

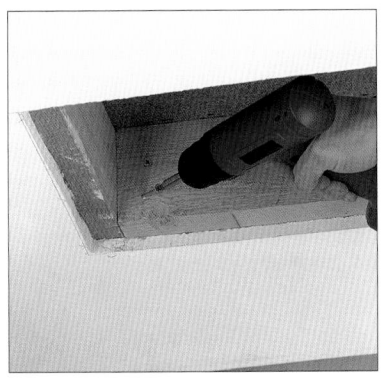

holes before inserting the screws, so as not to apply too much pressure to the noggings and risk pushing them further into the ceiling space.

7 Cut a piece of plasterboard to the exact dimensions of the hole. Ensure that the plasterboard you

tips of the trade

Another key cause of ceiling damage can be from the aftermath of a flood. Where water runs down through floor levels, it soaks the plaster sheeting, breaking it down and eventually resulting in an entire area breaking away. The repair procedure is the same as that demonstrated here, but some additional attention needs to be given to the decoration procedure. This is because water damage causes staining and if you apply water-based paint directly over a stain (even if it has totally dried out), the stain will continue to show through. It is therefore advisable to paint over the patch and surrounding area with an oil-based undercoat, before applying further coats of a water-based acrylic finish. This will help to seal the mark and prevent the stain from reappearing.

use is slightly thinner than the ceiling plasterboard depth. Fix it in place with plasterboard nails along the joists and the noggings.

8 Fill along the joints between the new patch and the surrounding ceiling surface with some bonding coat plaster. A filling knife is the ideal tool for this purpose – be sure to press the bonding coat firmly into the joint so that there are no gaps between the new section of plasterboard and the existing ceiling surface.

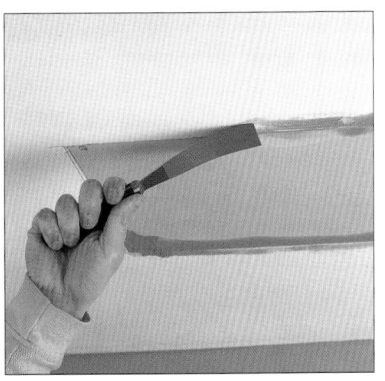

9 Mix up some multi-finish plaster and apply it to the patch using a plastering trowel. Try to bring the plaster level down to the same level as the ceiling, feathering the edges of the patch to the surrounding area. Running a dampened paint brush over the area of plaster that will extend on to the ceiling surface, may help to smooth the finish and provide a better surface to sand once the plaster has dried out. When finishing

off the new plaster skim, remember regularly to wet the blade of the plastering trowel as you smooth the surface before allowing it to dry.

Also remember that if the difference to be made up between the new plasterboard patch and the existing ceiling level is greater than 3mm (⅛ in), it is better to apply two thin coats of plaster rather than one thick coat. This is because during the drying process, a thick coat of plaster is likely to sag under its own weight, resulting in a very noticeable patch repair area.

PREPARING TO DECORATE

To achieve a good finish and make the patch as unnoticeable as possible, there are a few final procedures that will improve its 'invisible' effect.

● Fine sanding – Although a standard procedure for preparation, sanding is even more vital when trying to blend in a ceiling patch. The application of some fine filler, followed by further sanding, will improve the smooth nature of the final finish.

● Patch painting – When painting a patch, even if you are using an identical colour to that of the rest of the ceiling, the patch will invariably still show up against the rest of the ceiling surface. It is therefore best to prime the patch, apply a first coat of finishing paint and then apply the top coat over the patch and across the rest of the ceiling. This may sound extravagant, but it does tend to make the patch less noticeable in the overall finish.

● Lining – The best option is to line the ceiling after the patch repair. The thickness of the lining paper (1000–1200 microns is ideal) helps to smooth the ceiling surface further and reduces the likelihood of patch repairs remaining apparent. Once lined, the ceiling may be painted in the usual way.

making hollow wall repairs ⚒

Hollow walls are found in houses of all ages – modern homes often contain stud walls while older properties tend to have walls constructed of lath and plaster. In both cases, there is a void inside the wall which can cause problems when it comes to effecting a repair. When filler or plaster is applied to a hole in the outer plasterboard or lath and plaster layer, it tends to fall directly into the wall void unless some kind of support can be provided until it dries.

repair & restoration

128

minor lath repairs

In older properties containing lath and plaster walls, there can be a tendency for areas of plaster to work loose from the wooden laths and simply fall away from the wall surface. Broken laths can cause plaster to crumble, so repair them before beginning to re-plaster.

tools for the job

craft knife
dusting brush
scissors
screwdrivers
plastering trowel
gauging trowel

1 Trim around the edge of the hole with a craft knife. Carefully remove all the loose material until you get back to an edge where the plaster is still firmly bonded to the laths.

2 Use a dusting brush to clean down the laths, removing any dust and debris from their surface.

Pay particular attention to the bottom edge of the hole, where debris tends to collect.

3 Use some scissors to cut a piece of wire mesh to the hole size. Screw it into the laths so that it is fixed firmly. It may be easier to drill pilot holes in the laths before inserting the screws.

4 Dampen the hole with pva solution (5 parts water to 1 part pva) and apply plaster bonding coat to the hole, pressing it in place with a plastering trowel. Score the surface of the bonding coat with the edge of a gauging trowel. Ensure that the level of the bonding coat sits slightly below the level of the surrounding wall.

5 Once the bonding coat has dried, mix and apply some one-coat plaster to the patch, pressing and smoothing it in position, again with a plastering trowel. Allow it to dry before sanding to a smooth finish with some fine abrasive paper. You can then redecorate the wall in the usual way.

👍 tips of the trade

As an alternative to one-coat plaster, multi-finish may be used. However, one-coat plaster has a slight texture, so tends to produce a finish similar to the older lath and plaster walls. Multi-finish plaster, on the other hand, is much smoother and corresponds to the texture of modern finishing plaster.

stud wall repairs

Stud walls require a slightly different technique to that employed for lath and plaster, but again the emphasis is on providing support for the filler while it dries.

tools for the job

craft knife

dry wall saw

cordless drill

filling knife

1 Square off and cut around the edge of the damaged area with a craft knife. For thick plasterboard, it may be necessary to use a dry wall saw for this process.

2 Cut a scrap piece of plasterboard to a size slightly larger than the cut hole in the wall. Drill a small hole at its centre and thread a doubled over length of string

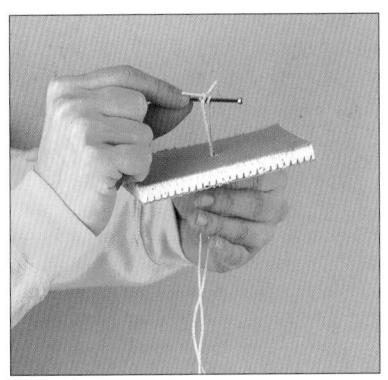

through the hole. On one side of the plaster sheeting, tie off the string on to a nail.

3 On the opposite side to the nail, apply some all-purpose adhesive around the edge of the piece of plasterboard.

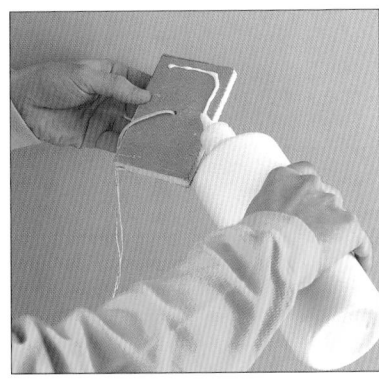

4 Push the plasterboard through the hole in the wall. Hold on to the length of string with your other hand so that the plasterboard does not fall into the void.

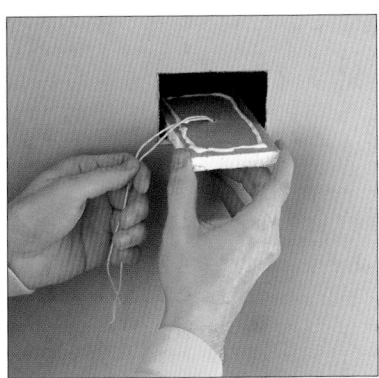

5 Carefully manoeuvring and pulling on the string, position the plasterboard patch so that it is held firmly up against the hole inside the wall, allowing the adhesive to adhere to the inner edge of the hole. Tie off

---

👍

tips of the trade

Dealing with surface damage is demonstrated on page 122, but if damage extends into the cavity of the wall, a different system is required.

---

the string on a piece of wooden offcut, thus holding the patch in position while it dries.

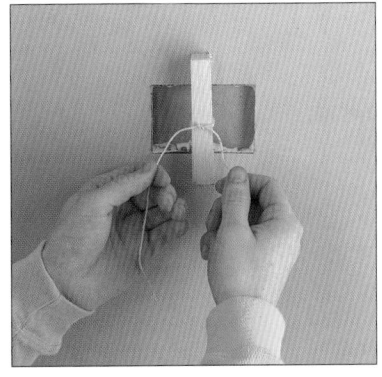

6 Once the adhesive has dried, remove the batten and cut the string. Use all-purpose filler to fill the hole – you will need more than one application for a good finish.

Large holes

For larger holes than those demonstrated here, it is possible to employ the same technique as for ceiling damage (see pages 126–7). In other words, trim the damaged area back to the vertical studs in the wall, creating a rectangular hole. Insert noggings horizontally along the top and bottom edge of the hole. Cut some plasterboard to fill the gap, nail it in place, and plaster in the usual way. The technique can be used on any holes that require filling – even old entrances. Simply insert studs and noggings as required, before fitting plasterboard and plastering.

making solid wall repairs ⤢⤢⤢

In many ways, solid wall repairs are easier to carry out than equivalent damage in hollow walls. This is because you do not need to worry about providing support while the plaster dries. However, it can still be challenging to produce a finish that blends with the surrounding wall area. Whether the damaged wall is brick, stone or block based, the same technique may be used for repair.

tools for the job

club hammer
cold chisel
protective gloves
safety goggles
dusting brush
old paint brush
gauging trowel
plastering trowel

1 Remove any loose debris from the hole. Use a club hammer and cold chisel to knock off any rough areas of old render or plaster. Always wear safety equipment such as goggles and gloves during this process, to protect yourself from bits of debris that tend to fly away from the wall surface.

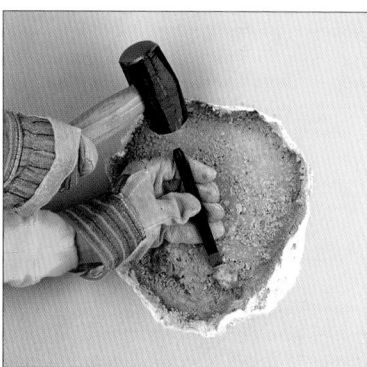

2 Use a dusting brush to clean out the hole as thoroughly as possible. Pay particular attention to the area around the edges, where dirt and dust tend to collect. Before any work can commence, all loose material must be cleared away so that the hole is totally dust free.

3 Mix up some pva solution (5 parts water to 1 part pva) and use an old paint brush to apply the solution liberally in the hole. Again, pay particular attention to the edges of the hole, allowing the solution to extend slightly on to the surrounding wall.

4 Mix up some bonding coat plaster, and press it firmly into the hole using a gauging trowel. Ensure that the bonding coat is moulded into all areas of the hole, and that it is brought up to a level which is slightly below that of the surrounding wall surface. You may find it easier to combine use of the gauging trowel with a plastering trowel to ensure an even surface finish.

5 Score the surface of the bonding coat, before it dries, using the edge of the gauging trowel. At the same time ensure that none of the bonding coat is pushed above wall level, as this will affect the finish when you apply the top plaster coat.

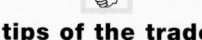

tips of the trade

If you do not have bonding coat and multi-finish plaster, it is possible simply to build up the patch with layers of one-coat plaster. This will not produce the same totally smooth, flush finish as that of multi-finish plaster, but its slightly rougher surface may be more appropriate on wall surfaces in older, less smooth properties.

6 Mix up and apply a coat of multi-finish plaster, using a plastering trowel to press it firmly into position. For holes of this size, rest the edges of the plastering trowel on the wall to the sides of the hole, thereby enabling you to produce a neat finish.

HOLE TYPES

● **Deep holes** – Where depth is greater than that shown above, it may well be necessary to apply a render coat to the hole before plaster can be applied. As always, it is better to apply thin layers rather than try to speed up the process with thicker ones. Over-application simply causes the render or plaster to bulge and makes it impossible to achieve a smooth finish when applying subsequent coats.

● **Shallow holes** – Where the top layer of plaster has blown away from the layers underneath, it may only be necessary to apply a single finishing coat. In such cases, however, it is common to find that if one area of top layer plaster has come away, this may be the case for most of the rest of the wall surface. Tapping the surface with the butt end of a trowel and listening for hollow reverberations will give some indication as to the stability of the surface. If the plaster is indeed 'loose', it is better to remove and re-plaster at this stage rather than redecorate and face a similar patching problem in the near future.

7 This finish can be further levelled-off by cutting a length of batten to slightly longer than the hole diameter, and gradually drawing the batten across the plaster surface, again making it as flush with the surrounding wall as possible.

8 Allow the plaster to dry off slightly. Then use an old paint brush to wet the surface of a plastering trowel with some clean water.

9 Smooth or 'polish' the plaster patch with the wettened trowel until a totally even and flush finish is achieved. Once the plaster dries, a light sand will be necessary to smooth the surface before redecoration can be carried out as required.

FINISHING OFF

● **Drying naturally** – The temptation when patching a small area is to try to 'force' the drying process by applying heat directly to the patch. This can have the effect of cracking the render and plaster, which will then require further repairs in order to achieve the desired finish. It is much better to allow the patch to dry naturally at room temperature so that any cracking can be avoided.

● **Priming** – Once dry, ensure that the newly plastered area is primed before further coats of paint are applied. A dilute acrylic coat (10 parts paint to 1 part water) is perfectly adequate for priming purposes in this instance.

● **Lining option** – On walls that may have a number of patch repair requirements, it may be necessary to consider lining the wall after repairs are complete, in order to smooth the surface further. On particularly undulating walls, woodchip or textured paper is a further possibility in terms of providing a more even wall finish.

repairing corners ⁄⁄⁄

Damaged internal corners can be treated in a similar way to open wall surfaces (see page 128) – plaster or filler is simply worked up to the corner junction and smoothed in place as required. However, external corners require slightly more work as there is a need to restore the actual profile of the corner itself. There are two main methods for carrying out this sort of repair, depending upon the extent or depth of the damage along the external corner itself.

minor corner repairs

Where a corner has been knocked or damaged in a small, localized area, it should be quite simple to restore the profile and sharp edge. It's worth bearing in mind that wall structure is not an important consideration because the same technique may be used on solid block or stud walls.

tools for the job

panel saw

hammer

filling knife

1 Cut a length of wooden batten, slightly longer than the length of the damaged corner section. The width of the batten should also be greater than the width of the widest point of damage on either of the two walls that meet to form the corner. Nail the batten in place on one wall, allowing its edge to run precisely down the corner edge. Make sure the nails can easily be removed later.

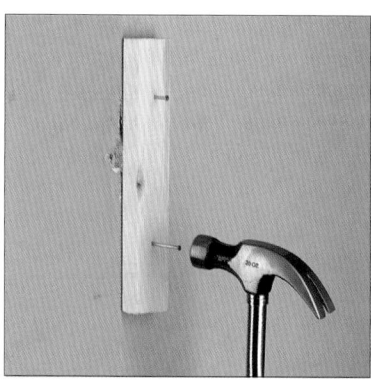

2 Mix up some all-purpose filler, employing a filling knife to press it firmly into the corner hole. Use the wall on one side and batten on the other to rest the edges of the filler knife, thereby creating a flush finish as the knife is drawn over the hole surface.

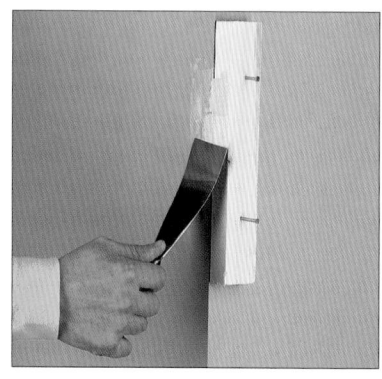

3 Allow the filler to dry, remove the batten, and reposition it on the adjacent wall, again running precisely down the corner edge. Fill the hole as required, bringing the level of filler up to and slightly over the level of the batten and surrounding wall surface.

4 Allow the filler to dry, remove the batten and sand the corner to a smooth and restored sharp edge. You

will also need to fill and sand the holes made by the nails when attaching the batten. If required, use some fine surface filler as a final measure to smooth any indentations that were not covered by the initial filler application.

complete corner repairs

Where damage is consistent along the complete length of a corner, it is more appropriate to repair the entire corner, rather than treat it in small areas. It is therefore necessary to make a more mechanical repair using angle bead to help restore the corner profile.

tools for the job

hacksaw

gauging trowel

plastering trowel

1 Cut angle bead to the required corner length using a hacksaw. (Tinsnips or side cutters may be used but a hacksaw tends to produce a neater and more accurate cut.)

2 Mix a small amount of multi-finish plaster; make sure it is a firm consistency. Apply the plaster with a gauging trowel along the edge of the corner at approximately 30cm (12in) intervals.

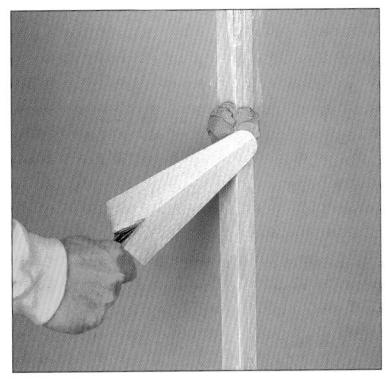

3 Press the length of angle bead into position along the external corner edge. Allow the plaster to squeeze through the mesh of the bead, so that there is good contact between the bead and the corner.

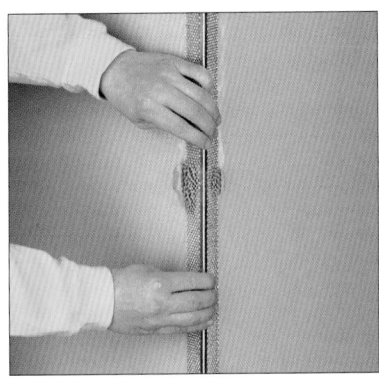

4 Use the edge of the trowel to remove excess plaster from the front surface of the bead. Make any

final adjustments in the bead position to ensure that it is vertical and running directly along the corner junction.

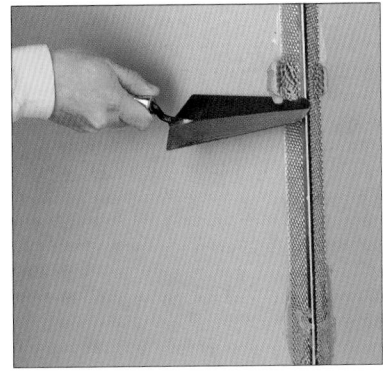

5 Once the plaster has dried and the bead is anchored in position, mix up some more multi-finish plaster and use a plastering trowel to apply it in a wide band along each corner edge. Use the metal edge of the angle bead to help guide the trowel down the wall surface, keeping an even coat of plaster covering the entire corner area. Apply a wide band so as to feather in the new plaster level with the existing wall surface. This is because applying plaster directly along the corner – and nowhere else – would provide an unrealistic appearance along its edge.

freehand corners

Although most external corners have a precise and rather sharp edge to them, in older houses this is often not the case, and a more rounded finish is clearly apparent. When repairing such corners, the precise apex to the corner is not necessarily required.

tools for the job

plastering trowel

external corner trowel

1 Use a plastering trowel to apply the plaster along the corner, moulding it into position along the corner edge.

2 Use an external corner trowel to run down the edge of the corner, making an even but not completely sharp edge to the corner. Wetting the trowel with clean water can make this process easier.

repairing wooden features ///

Wooden wall features often need repair and require quite different techniques of restoration compared to those for walls or plaster surfaces. Wood, whether in the form of panelling, skirting board or any other feature, tends to suffer from wear-and-tear such as general knocks, scrapes and splits. Minor knocks can be treated with the relevant filler, but more serious damage may require replacement sections of wood in order to restore the surface to an attractive finish.

skirting boards

The function of skirting board is to add a finish at the wall/floor junction, and to protect the base of the wall from any damage. Unsurprisingly, the skirting itself can become damaged over time and in need of repair. For short sections of damaged board, the most economical technique is to replace the entire length. However, on long stretches of skirting board this can be seen as wasteful, and inserting a replacement section is better.

tools for the job

wrecking bar & protective gloves

panel saw

mitre block

hammer

tape measure

damp cloth

nail punch

1 Ease the skirting board away from the wall using a wrecking bar to prise a gap between skirting

and wall. (Wear protective gloves for this process.) Position two pieces of cut-off batten behind the skirting and wedge the skirting board free from the wall surface.

2 Position a mitre block in front, and to one side, of the damaged section of skirting board. Cut down through the skirting board with a panel saw. Move the mitre block to the other side and then cut on the opposite mitre angle through the skirting board. Remove the damaged section.

3 Nail the skirting board back in position on either side of the gap you have created. Take accurate

measurements for the new piece of skirting you require and cut a length to fit, remembering to mitre each end correctly, so as to fit snugly in the gap.

4 Before fixing in place, test to see that your new section fits. Apply some wood glue along the cut edge of the new piece and position it, removing any excess adhesive with a damp cloth.

5 Fix the section permanently in place by nailing panel pins through the mitred join at either end of the new section. Three pins along each side should be sufficient. Punch in the pin head before redecorating the skirting.

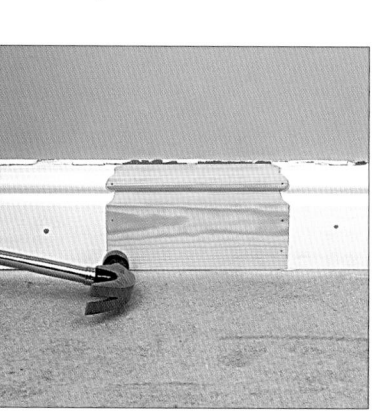

repairing tongue and groove

Damaged tongue and groove panelling presents a different set of problems because removing the panels – which have a concealed fixing mechanism – can be tricky. Some ingenuity is therefore required so that boards can be replaced, while avoiding any further damage to surrounding panels.

tools for the job

cordless drill

dry wall saw or padsaw

wrecking bar

claw hammer or pliers

panel saw

wooden mallet

chisel

1 Drill a hole to the side of the damaged board and along the joint it makes with the adjacent board. Choose a drill bit large enough to accommodate either a padsaw or a dry wall saw.

2 Use a dry wall saw or padsaw to cut through the join. Work up and down along the joint, until total separation between the two lengths has been achieved. Accuracy is not vital as the aim is simply to gain access to the damaged board in order to make your repair.

3 Use a wrecking bar to lever out the damaged board. You may also need to work a little on the other side of the board, because there will be other fixings holding the panel in place. However, with one edge loose, a combination of levering and easing should result in the board coming free. It is also worthwhile removing the board adjacent to the broken one, as the damage caused during cutting is likely to be noticeable.

4 After both boards have been removed, use a claw hammer or pliers to take out any pins or nails that may still be present in the exposed

battens beneath the tongue and groove cladding. Failure to remove them will hinder progress later.

5 Cut two new lengths of tongue and groove to size. Use a mallet and chisel to trim the tongue off one of the lengths – this is because damage caused in removing the old lengths may have affected the actual interlocking mechanism of the tongue and groove system. By removing the tongue on one length, it should then be possible to insert the strip into the existing panelling.

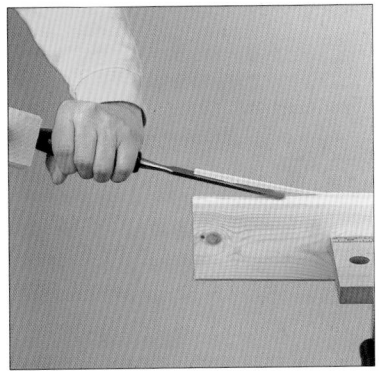

6 Interlock the two new sections into the panelling, and secure them in place with panel pins. The new panelling may then be primed and repainted.

tips of the trade

Tongue and groove is supplied in a range of thicknesses, so always check your requirements before purchasing replacement strips.

glossary

Acrylic – or water-based. Describes make up of paint or glaze used for open areas such as walls or ceilings.

Angle bead – metal, right angled strip used to create a sharp profile for external corners before plaster is applied.

Architrave – wooden surround applied around door frames or entrances to create finish.

Caulk – flexible filler supplied in tube and dispensed from a sealant gun. Must be smoothed to finish before it dries.

Cavity wall – wall composed of two layers. In effect, two walls separated by cavity or void. Common in construction of external walls of modern homes.

Chipboard – flooring material made of compressed wooden fibres, and supplied in sheets. Sheets normally joined with tongue and groove mechanism.

Colourizer – concentrated colour supplied in small tubes or containers, used to add colour to paint or scumble for paint effect purposes. Some are universal in that they can be added to both acrylic and solvent based paints or glazes.

Concrete anchor – screw designed to fix into masonry without the need for a wall plug.

Cornice – decorative moulding applied at wall ceiling junction. They are generally more ornate, and greater in depth than coving.

Coving – decorative moulding applied at wall ceiling junction.

Cutting in – term describing painting in the corners or at the different junctions on a wall surface or between walls and ceilings.

Dado – lower area of a wall.

Dado rail – wooden rail or moulding denoting the top of the dado and therefore dividing up the wall surface to a lower and upper area. Sometimes referred to as a chair rail.

Door lining – the wooden lining used to make up the internal part of a door frame.

DPC – or damp proof course, forms the barrier that prevents the penetration of damp from below ground level into the main structure of walls.

Dry lining – referring to the technique of combining plasterboard and jointing compound to create a wall or ceiling surface ready for decoration.

Eggshell – hardwearing paint that has a dull matt finish. Available in acrylic or solvent based forms.

Emulsion – acrylic or water-based paint used for open areas such as walls and ceilings.

En-suite – term normally applied to a bathroom that is directly adjacent to and serving one particular room. En-suite rooms are normally created through building a stud partition wall in a larger room to provide space.

External corner – the corners that stick out into the room.

Glaze – medium that colourizers are added to in order to create paint effects. Acrylic or solvent based alternatives. Sometimes referred to as scumble.

Head plate – wooden stud creating ceiling fixing or part of stud wall framework.

Hearth – area in front of and at the base of a fireplace.

Internal corner – the corners that point away from the centre of the room.

Jointing compound – similar to plaster or filler and used to join gaps between plasterboard when dry lining.

Jointing tape – tape used to join plasterboard sheets before plastering.

Joist – length of wood used in construction of ceilings and floors.

Dado rail: these rails are traditionally used to prevent chairs from damaging the wall surface.

jointing tape

Joist detector – sensor device used for finding position of joists in ceilings or walls. Some may also have different mode, which can be used to trace the position of electric cables or pipes.

Joist hanger – metal bracket used to bear the weight and position of joist ends in ceiling structure.

Junction box – box in which electrical cables are joined together.

Lath – wooden laths are lengths of wood used in the make up of old walls before the invention of plasterboard. Plaster laths are small plasterboard sheets.

Lining – term referring to the use of lining paper being applied to wall surfaces.

Lintel – supportive structure inserted above windows, doors or openings in walls.

Mdf – or medium density fibre board. Wooden based building board made from compressed wooden fibres.

Mitre – angled joint, normally involving two lengths joining at a right angle and therefore each piece requiring to be cut at a 45 degree angle.

Moulding – decorative length of plaster or wood used as a decorative detail on wall or ceiling surfaces.

Needle – length of wood inserted through a hole in a loadbearing wall to support the weight of the wall before the lintel is positioned.

Niche – moulded plaster feature, built into or inserted into wall surface to provide decorative display area.

Nogging – small length of wood used in ceiling, wall and floor structure to strengthen joist framework.

Open plan – home design where rooms are either spacious, or where smaller rooms have been knocked into one large one.

Party wall – shared wall that divides two properties.

Niche: a decorative plaster feature, built into a shallow wall recess, often used to display flowers, ornaments or statues.

Picture rail – wooden moulding positioned on upper part of wall. Traditionally used to hang pictures from. Now mainly used as purely decorative feature to break up a wall surface.

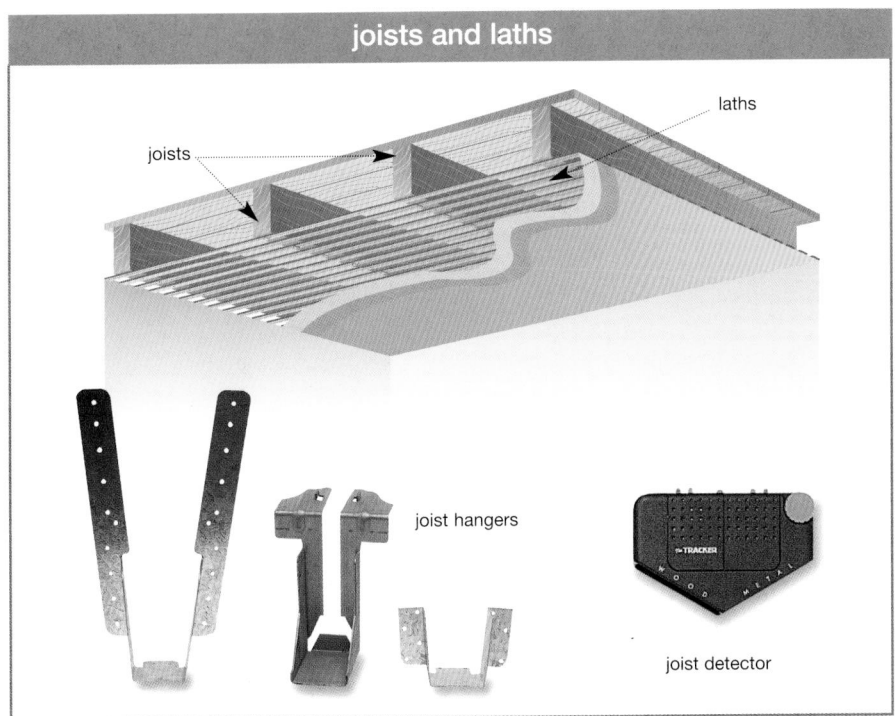

joists and laths

laths

joists

joist hangers

joist detector

Plasterboard – plaster layer compressed and enclosed or sandwiched between thick paper and manufactured in sheets to be used as standard building board for plaster surfaces or dry lining.

Plasticizer – a mortar additive, which makes mortar easier to use and work with.

Ply – thin veneers of wood bonded together to create building board. The grain of alternate layers or veneers tends to run at right angles to one another.

Polishing – referring to technique of finishing a plastered surface with a plastering trowel or float.

PVA – all purpose adhesive used to bind and/or stabilize surfaces. Use both concentrated and diluted.

Proprietary – referring to a material, tool or technique that relates specifically to one manufacturer or group of manufacturers.

Render – mortar based coat used as undercoat for plaster on solid block walls internally. Externally it may be used to form the finished surface, which may be left untreated or painted as required.

Rose – ceiling fixing for electrical light fitting. Also refers to plaster accessories used as ornate ceiling decoration.

RSJ – or rolled steel joists. Heavy duty lintels used when a loadbearing wall is removed and two rooms are converted into one.

Sand pugging – technique of sound proofing where sand is introduced into a floor space in order to insulate and reduce noise travelling between floors.

Scrim – traditional type of jointing tape used to cover joints between plasterboard sheets.

Sealant – any tubed silicone or mastic used for sealing along joints such as those between walls and window frames.

Skew – nailing or screwing at an angle through wood or masonry in order to provide a fixing.

Skim – applying top coat of plaster to wall surface.

Skirting board – decorative wooden moulding applied at base of wall.

Sole plate – wooden stud creating base or floor fixing for partition wall.

Solvent based – or oil-based. Term used when referring to the make up of paint or glaze.

Soundbreaker bar – metal strip attached to walls or joists, onto which plaster-board is fixed. Allows fixings to attach plasterboard direct to bar and not to wall.

Spacer – divider used between ceramic tiles to keep consistency of distance between each of the tiles.

Tongue and groove panelling: this type of wood panelling is useful for covering rough or uneven walls.

Split level – where a room has a step in either floor or ceiling levels.

Stud – wooden uprights used in the construction of a stud wall.

Stud wall – wall consisting of wooden studs and covered in plasterboard. Used as partition wall in houses. Finished with plaster or dry lined.

Subsidence – foundation problems in a house, which cause serious cracks and movement in its structure.

Tongue and groove – interlocking mechanism used to join some types of planking or building board.

Vinyl – protective covering on some wallpapers or additive used in paint, to improve their hardwearing and wipeable properties.

Wall plug – plastic or metal sheath, inserted into pre-drilled hole in wall to house screw insertion.

wall plugs

Wall profile – metal plate used to support and tie-in block or brick wall when a new wall is being joined to an existing one.

Wall tie – join internal and external layer of a cavity wall together.

index

a

access, equipment, 37
accessories, plaster, 94–5
accidents, 37
acoustic flooring underlay, 57
acrylic paint, 107
acrylic scumble, 107
adhesives, 29
    coving, 92–3
    dado rails, 98
    decorative panelling, 100
    wallpapering, 114
air bricks, 60
aligning floors, 46–7
all-purpose filler, 28, 108
angle bead, 26
    arches, 52
    removing a non-loadbearing
      wall, 45
    repairing corners, 132–3
angle brackets, 27
    suspended ceilings, 72, 73
angle section, 26
arches: pre-formed plaster
    arches, 26
    in stud walls, 52–3
architects, 32
architraves, 27
    cracks above, 39
    loft hatches, 79
    serving hatches, 55

b

bathrooms: en-suite, 22
    tiling, 105
    ventilation, 60
battens: dry lined walls, 17, 18
    loft hatches, 79
    panelling walls, 88–9
    tiling, 116
bearers, suspended ceilings,
    72, 73
beetles, woodworm, 41
blanket insulation, 76
block walls, 12
    bonding coat on, 87
    building, 58–9
    cavity walls, 17
    concrete blocks, 26
    cutting blocks, 59

glass blocks, 26, 62–3
    internal walls, 18
    lowering a ceiling, 68
    removing a non-loadbearing
      wall, 45
    solid walls, 16
    thermal insulation blocks, 26
boarding see tongue and
    groove
boards, 26
boilers, ventilation, 60
bolts, coach, 28, 58
bonding coat, 29
    arches, 53
    block walls, 87
    installing a fireplace, 65
    patching a ceiling, 127
    solid wall repairs, 130
bonding materials, 29
border tiles, 106
bottom plates: glass block
    walls, 63
    stud walls, 19, 49
brackets, 26, 27
brass screws, 28
breather paper, 17
bricks, 12, 26
    cavity walls, 12, 17
    internal walls, 18
    removing a non-loadbearing
      wall, 45
    solid walls, 12, 16
brushes, paint, 110
budgeting, 31
builders, 32–3
building boards, 26
building regulations, 31
building sand, 29
bulk buying, 31
butt joins, wallpapering, 114, 115
'buttering' mortar, 59

c

cables see electricity cables
    carpets, soundproofing
      rooms, 57
caulk, fitting dado rails, 99, 101
caulking blades, 109
cavity walls, 12, 13, 16, 17
ceiling roses, 23, 71, 95
ceiling tiles, 27
ceilings: construction, 13, 14–15
    coving, 92–3
    cracks, 39, 122
    damp problems, 41

dry lined, 15
    exposing roof rafters, 23
    insulating, 76–7
    joists, 13
    lath and plaster, 14
    loft hatches, 78–9
    lowering, 68–71
    minor repairs, 122
    ornate ceilings, 23
    painting, 110
    patching, 126–7
    plaster panelling, 94
    plasterboard, 14
    preparation for decoration,
      108–9
    slatted ceilings, 80–1
    soundproofing, 74–5
    split-level ceilings, 69
    suspended ceilings, 27, 72–3
    textured finishes,
      118–19, 124
    textured papers, 124–5
    top floor ceilings, 15
    wallpapering, 115
    wooden ceilings, 15
cement, 29
ceramic tiles, 106, 116–17
chalk lines, 48
chimney breasts: damp
    problems, 41
    ventilation, 60
chipboard floors, 14, 15
chisels, 37
circular cracks, 39
cleaning surfaces, 109
clout nails, 28
coach bolts, 28, 58
colourizers, paint effects,
    107, 112
colours: paint, 105
    paint effects, 112
colourwashing, 113
concrete: blocks, 26
    floors, 46–7
    lintels, 13
    screed floors, 13
concrete anchor screws, 28
construction, 12–19
    materials, 26–9
    tools, 25
corner jointing tape, 29, 53
corners: coving, 92, 93
    cracks, 39
    dado rails, 99
    damp problems, 41

dry lining walls, 85
    plastering, 87
    repairing, 132–3
    skirting boards, 96, 97
cornices, 23, 26
    fitting, 92–3
    minor repairs, 123
costs, 31, 32–3
coving, 26
fitting, 92–3
    minor repairs, 123
cowls, installing ventilation, 61
cracks: in arches, 53
    in ceilings, 122
    filling, 108–9
    testing, 38–9
    in walls, 123
cross-bearers, suspended
    ceiling systems, 27
curves, cutting tiles, 117
'cutting in', painting, 110
cutting tiles, 117
cutting tools, 37

d

dado, panelling walls, 88–9
dado rails, 89, 98–9, 101
damp problems, 40, 41
decorative finishes, 104–17
decorative rails, 98–9
dents, minor repairs, 123
dining areas, serving
    hatches, 54–5
disputes, with tradespeople, 33
divots, minor repairs, 123
doors: block walls, 59
    cracks around, 39
    lintels, 13
    stud walls, 49, 50
drawings, scale, 31
drip staining, damp
    problems, 41
dry lining: arches, 53
    ceilings, 15
    cleaning and sealing, 109
    minor repairs, 123
    walls, 17, 18, 84–5
dry partition walls, 19
dry rot, 40
ducting, installing ventilation, 61

e

eggshell paint, 107
electricity cables: lowering
    a ceiling, 71

power tools, 37
stud walls, 50–51
electric tools, 24
safety, 37
electrical sockets, plastering
around, 87
en-suite bathrooms, 22
equipment, 24–5
painting, 110
safety equipment, 36
for textured finishes, 118
wallpapering, 114
estimates, 32
expanding filler, 109
extension poles, rollers, 110
external walls, construction,
12, 16–17
extractor fans, 61
'extras', 32–3

f

fans, extractor, 61
fielded panelling, walls, 90–91
fillers, 28
bonding coat, 29
popping nail heads, 122
preparation for decoration,
108–9
repairing corners, 132
finances, 31, 32–3
fine sand, 29
finishing materials, 29
fireplaces, installing, 64–5
fires, ventilation, 60
first aid kit, 36
fixings: lowering a ceiling, 68, 69
mechanical fixings, 28
skirting boards, 97
suspended ceilings, 72–3
flexible filler, 108–9
floor plate, removing a
non-loadbearing wall, 44–5
floors: aligning, 46–7
building a stud wall, 49
chipboard floors, 14, 15
direction of floorboards, 12
glass block walls, 63
joists, 13
skirting boards, 96–7
soundproofing a ceiling, 75
underfloor construction, 13
ventilation, 60
flush joints, building a
stud wall, 51
formers, arches, 52–3

foundations, 13
frame fixings, 28
frame ties, screw-in, 28
frames: lowering a ceiling, 68
panelling walls, 88
freehand corner repairs, 133
fumes, ventilation, 60
fungi, dry rot, 40

g

gauges, tile, 116–17
glass blocks, 26
building walls, 62–3
glass plate fixings, marble
fire surrounds, 65
gloss paint, 107
glue, wood, 29
graph paper, scale
drawings, 31
grouting: glass block walls, 63
tiles, 117
guidelines, building a
stud wall, 48, 49
gypsum plaster covings, 92

h

hairline cracks, 39
hammers, 37
handmade tiles, 106
hangers see joist hangers
hatches: loft hatches, 77, 78–9
serving hatches, 54–5
hearths, installing, 64
hessian wallpaper, 106
hiring tools, 25
holes: filling, 108–9
hollow wall repairs, 128–9
minor repairs, 123
patching a ceiling, 126–7
solid wall repairs, 130–131
hollow walls, 18
cavity walls, 12, 13, 16, 17
repairs, 128–9
house construction, 12–19

i

infestation problems, 40–1
insects, woodworm, 41
insulation: ceilings, 76–7
materials, 27
sound/heat insulation tape, 29
soundproofing walls, 56–7
thermal insulation blocks,
17, 26
top floor ceilings, 15

internal walls, construction,
12, 18–19

j

joins, wallpapering, 114, 115
jointing compound, 28
arches, 53
dry lining walls, 84–5
jointing tape, 29
dry lining walls, 84–5
under textured finishes, 118
joints: block walls, 59
dry lined ceilings, 15
filling, 108–9
plaster ceilings, 14
stud walls, 51
joist detectors, 48
joist hangers, 26
lowering a ceiling, 68, 69
suspended ceilings, 72–3
joists, 12, 13
insulating a ceiling, 76
lath and plaster ceilings, 14
loft hatches, 78
lowering a ceiling, 68, 69, 70
plasterboard ceilings, 14
soundproofing a ceiling, 75
stud walls, 48
see also RSJs

k

kitchens: serving hatches, 54–5
tiles, 105
ventilation, 60

l

ladders, 37
loft ladders, 79
lagging pipes, 77
lath and plaster: ceilings, 14
walls, 12, 19
laths: lowering a ceiling, 70
repairing, 128
leaks, damp problems, 41
light fittings: lowering a
ceiling, 71
slatted ceilings, 81
wallpapering ceilings, 115
lines, chalk, 48
lining see dry lining
lining paper, 106
ceilings, 115
patching a ceiling, 127
solid wall repairs, 131
walls, 115

lintels, 13
block walls, 59
removing a loadbearing wall,
42, 43
serving hatches, 55
loadbearing walls, 12, 13
removing, 42–3
serving hatches, 55
local authorities:
building regulations, 31
planning permission, 30
loft hatches: building, 78–9
insulation, 77
loft ladders, 79
lofts: floors, 15
insulating, 15, 76–7
loose fill insulation, 27, 76–7
lost-head wire nails, 28
louvre vents, ventilation, 61
lowering a ceiling, 68–71

m

main bearers, 26
marble: fireplace surrounds, 64–5
tiles, 106
masking tape, 29
masonry nails, 16, 18, 28
mastic, soundproofing walls, 57
materials, 26–9, 106–7
matt acrylic paint, 107
mechanical fixings, 28
medium density fibreboard
(mdf), 26
fielded panelling, 90–91
tongue and groove, 91
metal lintels, 13
mineral wool, 27
mitres: coving, 92
skirting boards, 96, 97
mitresaws, 96
monitoring cracks, 38–9
mortar: aligning floors, 46
block walls, 58–9
cement, 29
fireplaces, 64–5
glass block walls, 62–3
mixing, 86
plasticizer, 29
mosaic tiles, 106
mouldings, 27
panels, 27
plaster, 23
rails, 27
movement, in walls, 38–9
multi-finish plaster, 29, 87

n

nails: clout nails, 28
   lost-head wire nails, 28
   masonry nails, 16, 18, 28
   plasterboard nails, 28
   popping heads, 122
   round wire nails, 28
   skirting boards, 97
   stud wall, 51
natural fibre wallpaper, 106
needles, removing a
   loadbearing wall, 42, 43
niches, 94–5
noggings: loft hatches, 78
   lowering a ceiling, 69
   patching a ceiling, 126–7
   serving hatches, 54
   stud walls, 50, 51
non-loadbearing walls, 12, 13
   removing, 44–5
   serving hatches, 54–5

o

oil-based paint, 107
oilstones, 37
one-coat plaster, 29
open plan rooms, 22
openings, building a
   block wall, 59
ornate ceilings, 23

p

painting, 110–11
   ceilings, 110
   cleaning and sealing
     paintwork, 109
   dado rails, 99
   paint effects, 107, 112–13
   paints, 105, 107
   patching a ceiling, 127
   solid wall repairs, 131
   textured finishes, 124
   walls, 111
panel pins, 28
panelling: cleaning and
   sealing, 109
   decorative, 100–101
   mouldings, 27
   plaster, 94
   repairs, 135
   walls, 88–91
papering see wallpaper
partition wall see stud walls
party walls, soundproofing, 56–7

paste, wallpapering, 114
patching a ceiling, 126–7
patterned wallpaper, 106
pendant lights: lowering
   a ceiling, 71
   slatted ceilings, 81
picture tiles, 106
pins, panel, 28
pipes, insulation, 77
planes, 37
planning, 21–3
planning permission, 30
plaster: accessories, 94–5
   arches, 53
   cavity walls, 17
   ceiling roses, 95
   cleaning and sealing, 109
   coving, 92–3
   cracks, 39
   hollow wall repairs, 128
   internal walls, 18
   lath and plaster, 14, 19
   mouldings, 23
   multi-finish plaster, 29, 87
   niches, 94–5
   one-coat plaster, 29
   panelling, 94
   patching a ceiling, 127
   plastering a wall, 86–7
   plastering over textured
     finishes, 124
   pre-formed arches, 26
   removing a non-loadbearing
     wall, 45
   repairing corners, 133
   solid wall repairs, 130–131
   undercoat plaster, 29
plasterboard saws, 54
plasterboard screws, 28
plasterboard, 26
   arches, 52
   cavity walls, 17
   ceilings, 14
   dry lining walls, 18, 84–5
   dry partition walls, 19
   hollow wall repairs, 129
   lowering a ceiling, 68, 70–71
   patching a ceiling, 126–7
   plastering, 86
   popping nail heads, 122
   removing a non-loadbearing
     wall, 44
   scribing, 51
   soundproofing ceilings, 74
   soundproofing walls, 56, 57

stud walls, 19, 48, 51
   textured finishes, 118
plasterboard nails, 28
plasticizer, 29
platforms, 37
plumb lines, 49
ply, 26
   soundproofing a ceiling, 75
polystyrene covings, 92
popping nail heads, 122
power tools, 24
   safety, 37
pressed panelling, 91
prices, 32–3
primer: painting walls, 111
   solid wall repairs, 131
problems, walls, 38–41
professionals, 32–3
profile cutting, skirting
   boards, 96
props, removing a loadbearing
   wall, 43
pva adhesive, 29
   plastering a wall, 86

q

quotations, 32

r

rafters, exposing, 23
ragging 'off', 113
rails, decorative, 27, 98–9
relief tiles, 106
render coat, 86
   cavity walls, 17
   external walls, 16
   internal walls, 18
repairs, minor, 122–3
rolled-steel joists see RSJs
rollers: painting ceilings, 110
   painting walls, 111
roof timbers, 12
roses, 23, 71, 95
round wire nails, 28
RSJs (rolled-steel joists), 13
   removing a loadbearing wall,
     42, 43

s

safety, 36–7
   building a block wall, 58
   cracks, 39
   removing a loadbearing
     wall, 43
sand: building sand, 29

fine sand, 29
sand pugging, soundproofing
   a ceiling, 75
sanding: filler, 108
   patching a ceiling, 127
satin acrylic paint, 107
saws, 24, 25
   mitresaws, 96
   plasterboard saws, 54
scale drawings, 31
screw-in frame ties, 28
screws: brass screws, 28
   coach screws, 28, 58
   concrete anchor screws, 28
   fixing skirting boards, 97
   plasterboard screws, 28
   soundproofing walls, 57
   standard screws, 28
   stud walls, 51
   wood screws, 28
scribing: plasterboard, 51
   skirting boards, 96–7
scumble, paint effects, 107,
   112
sealant guns, 108
sealants, 28
sealing surfaces, 109
self-adhesive jointing tape,
   29
self-levelling compound,
   aligning floors, 47
serving hatches, 54–5
shower cubicles, glass
   block walls, 63
silicone sealant: glass
   block walls, 63
   installing a fireplace, 65
   installing ventilation, 61
silk wallpaper, 106
skirting boards, 27
   block walls, 18
   brick walls, 18
   cavity walls, 17
   cracks below, 39
   damp problems, 41
   dry lined walls, 18
   dry partition walls, 19
   fitting, 96–7
   lath and plaster walls, 19
   removing a non-loadbearing
     wall, 44
   repairs, 134
   solid walls, 16
   stud partition walls, 19
   tiling walls, 116

slabs, soundproofing, 57, 70, 74, 75
slatted ceilings, 80–81
slopes, aligning floors, 47
sockets, plastering around, 87
softwood, 27
    building a stud wall, 48–9
    slatted ceilings, 80–81
solid fuel fires, ventilation, 60
solid walls: building a block wall, 58–9
    construction, 12
    external walls, 16
    internal walls, 18
    lowering a ceiling, 68
    plastering, 86–7
    removing a non-loadbearing wall, 45
    repairs, 130–131
soundbreaker bars, 26, 56–7, 74
sound/heat insulation tape, 29
soundproofing: ceilings, 74–5
    insulation slab, 27
    lowering a ceiling, 70–71
    walls, 56–7
spacers: glass block walls, 62, 63
    tiling, 116
split-level ceilings, 69
split-level rooms, 23
sponging 'on', 113
spray guns, painting walls, 111
stage payments, 33
stain block, painting walls, 111
staining, damp problems, 41
stairwells, decorative panelling, 101
stamping, paint effects, 113
starting work, 30–33
steel rods, glass block walls, 62, 63
step ladders, 37
stippling: paint effects, 113
    textured finishes, 118–19
stone, 26
    lintels, 13
    solid walls, 16
stud walls, 12
    arches, 52–3
    building, 48–51
    dry partition walls, 19
    lath and plaster, 19
    lowering a ceiling, 68, 69
    plaster sheeting, 19

removing, 44
repairs, 129
serving hatches, 54–5
supports: lintels, 13
    removing a loadbearing wall, 42
surfaces: cleaning and sealing, 109
    filling cracks, 108–9
surveyors, 32
suspended ceilings, 27, 72–3
suspended floors, ventilation, 60

t
tanks, insulating, 77
tapes, 29
    dry lining ceilings, 15
    dry lining walls, 84
    under textured finishes, 118
textured finishes, 29
    ceilings, 118–19, 124
    removing, 124
textured wallpaper, 106
    on ceilings, 124–5
    solid wall repairs, 131
thermal insulation blocks, 17, 26
tide marks, damp problems, 41
ties: cavity walls, 12, 13
    screw-in frame ties, 28
tile gauges, 116
tiles, 105, 106
    suspended ceilings, 27, 73
    techniques, 116–17
timber see wood
timber-framed houses, 12
timescales, 31
tongue and groove boards, 27
    ceilings, 15
    mdf, 91
    panelling walls, 88–9
    repairs, 135
    walls, 23
tools, 24–5
    painting, 110
    safety, 37
    for textured finishes, 118
    wallpapering, 114
top floor ceilings, 15
tradespeople, 32–3
transparent oil scumbles, 107

u
undercoat plaster, 29
underlay, soundproofing rooms, 57

v
varnishes, 107
ventilation, installing, 60–61
vinyl paints, 107, 111
vinyl wallpaper, 106

w
wall plates, lowering a ceiling, 68
wall plugs, 28
wall profile ties, 26
wall profiles, 26
wallpaper, 104, 106
    cleaning and sealing, 109
    dado rails, 99
    techniques, 114–15
    textured finishes, 124–5
walls: arches, 52–3
    block walls, 58–9
    brick-built houses, 12, 13
    cavity walls, 16, 17
    construction, 12–13
    coving, 92–3
    cracks, 123
    dado rails, 98–9
    damp problems, 41
    decorative finishes, 104–17
    decorative panelling, 100–101
    dry lining, 84–5
    external walls, 16–17
    glass blocks, 62–3
    hollow wall repairs, 128–9
    installing a fireplace, 64–5
    internal walls, 18–19
    lintels, 13
    lowering a ceiling, 68
    minor repairs, 123
    niches, 94–5
    open plan rooms, 22
    paint effects, 112–13
    painting, 111
    panelling, 88–91
    plaster panelling, 94
    plastering, 86–7
    preparation for decoration, 108–9
    recognizing problems, 38–41
    removing a loadbearing wall, 42–3

removing a non-loadbearing wall, 44–5
repairing corners, 132–3
serving hatches, 54–5
skirting boards, 96–7
solid wall construction, 12, 16
solid wall repairs, 130–1
soundproofing, 56–7
stud walls, 48–51
tiling, 116–17
timber-framed houses, 12
ventilation, 60–1
wallpapering, 114–15
wood cladding, 23
wooden feature repairs, 134–5
washers, 28, 58
water, insulating pipes, 77
water-based paint, 107
water damage, ceilings, 127
water tanks, insulating, 77
windows: cracks around, 39
    damp problems, 41
    lintels, 13
wire, suspended ceilings, 27, 72–3
wire nails, fixing skirting boards, 97
wood, 27
    building boards, 26
    cavity walls, 17
    ceilings, 15
    cladding, 23
    cleaning and sealing panelling, 109
    dado rails, 98–9
    dry rot, 40
    fireplaces, 64
    floors, 47, 63
    lintels, 13
    loft hatches, 79
    panelling walls, 88–91
    repairing wooden features, 134–5
    skirting boards, 96–7
    slatted ceilings, 80–81
    stud walls, 48–50
    timber-framed houses, 12
    woodworm, 41
wood glue, 29
wood screws, 28
wood stains, dado rails, 99
woodchip paper, solid wall repairs, 131
woodworm, 41
working platforms, 37

useful contacts

suppliers

Akzo Nobel Decorative Coatings Ltd
Crown House
Hollins Road
Darwen,
Lancashire
Tel. 01254 704951
decorative panelling

Area South Planning
Maltravers House
Petter's Way
Yeovil
BA20 1AS
Tel. 01935 462760

Aristocast Originals Ltd
14A Ongreave House
Dore House Industrial Estate
Handsworth
Sheffield S13 9NP
Tel. 0114 2690900
plaster accessories

B&Q DIY Supercentres
Tel. 0845 3002902

Dulux Decorator Centres
Tel. 0161 9683000

Feature Marble
Unit 5, Westex House
Winterstoke Road
Weston-super-Mare
Somerset BS23 3YS
Tel. 01934 614050

Fired Earth
Tel. 01295 812088
tiles supplier

Focus Do It All
Tel. 0800 436436

Great Mills
Tel. 01761 416034

Hewden Plant Hire
Tel. 0161 8488621

Homebase Ltd
Tel. 020 87847200

Lafarge Plasterboard Ltd
Marsh Lane
Easton-in-Gordano
Bristol
BS20 0NF
Tel. 01275 377773

Magnet Ltd
Tel. 0800 9171696
building materials

MGR Exports
Station Road
Bruton
Somerset BA10 0EH
Tel. 01749 812460

Milsom Contractors Ltd
28 Springfield Road
Wincanton
Somerset BA9 9BL
Tel. 01963 32811
suspended ceilings

Polyvine Ltd
Vine House
Rockhampton
Gloucestershire GL13 9DT
Tel. 01454 261276
paint effects, tools & materials

Screwfix Direct
Tel. 0500 414141
www.screwfix.com
tools & fixings

The Classic Cornice Co.
176 Garratt Lane
Wandsworth
London
SW18 4ED
Tel. 020 88740221

Tile Wise Ltd
12–14 Enterprise Mews
Sea King Road
Yeovil
Somerset BA20 2NZ
Tel. 01935 412220

Travis Perkins Trading Co. Limited
Tel. 01604 752424
building materials

Trim Acoustics
Unit 4, Leaside Industrial Estate
Stockingswater Lane
Enfield EN3 7PH
Tel. 020 4430099

Woods Insulation Ltd
Tel. 0800 9173926

associations

National Home Improvement Council
Tel. 020 78288230

Brick Development Association
Tel. 01344 885651

The Ready Mixed Concrete Bureau
Tel. 01494 791050

Timber Research and Development Association
Tel. 01494 563091

British Woodworking Federation
Tel. 020 76085050

Builders Merchants Federation
Tel. 020 74391753

Hire Association Europe
Tel. 0121 3777707

Federation of Master Builders
Tel. 020 72427583

Royal Institute of British Architects
Tel: 020 75805533

Institution of Structural Engineers
Tel. 020 72354535

Electrical Contractors Association
Tel. 020 73134800

Health and Safety Executive
Tel. 0541 545500

the authors

Julian Cassell and Peter Parham have run their own building and decorating business for several years, having successfully renovated a variety of large and small scale properties around the UK. These award winning authors have written a number of books covering all aspects of DIY, and their innovative approach has made them popular television and radio guests.

acknowledgements

We would like to thank the following individuals for supplying props, advice and general help throughout the production of this book – Michael and Sue Read, Mike O'Connor, Kevin Hurley, John and Margaret Dearden and June Parham.

At Murdoch Books (UK) we would like to extend our gratitude to all those people who have helped to put this book together, but special thanks to Angela Newton, Laura Cullen, Helen Taylor, Iain MacGregor and Natasha Treloar for their total professionalism and unerring ability to deal with whatever we threw at them.

Tim Ridley and Katrina Moore, once again made all the photographic sessions a pleasure to attend and, as always, a big thank you to them for the long hours, good humour and patience throughout the project. Finally, many thanks to Adele Parham for feeding the troops at a moment's notice and always being on hand to counsel two manic authors.

The Publisher would like to thank the following: Magnet Windows and Doors, Screwfix and A&H Brass Limited.

First published in 2001 by Murdoch Books UK
Copyright© 2001 Murdoch Books (UK) Ltd

ISBN 1 85391 869 5
A catalogue record for this book is available from the British Library.

All photography by Tim Ridley and copyright Murdoch Books (UK) Ltd except: p6, p7 and p8 (Elizabeth Whiting Associates), p9 (Murdoch Books®/Meredith), p22 and p23 (Murdoch Books®/Meredith) except p23 bottom right (Elizabeth Whiting Associates), p30 (Corbis), p31 bottom left (Corbis), p32 and p33 (Corbis), p40 and p41 Graham Cole, p55 bottom right (Elizabeth Whiting Associates), p63 bottom right (Elizabeth Whiting Associates), p73 bottom right (Elizabeth Whiting Associates), p93 bottom right (Murdoch Books®/Meredith), p99 bottom right (Murdoch Books®/Meredith), p104 and p105 (Murdoch Books®/Meredith), p119 bottom right (Elizabeth Whiting Associates), p125 (Murdoch Books®/Meredith)

CEO: Robert Oerton
Publisher: Catie Ziller
Publishing Manager: Fia Fornari
Production Manager: Lucy Byrne
Group General Manager: Mark Smith
Group CEO/Publisher: Anne Wilson
Commissioning Editor: Iain MacGregor

Design Concept: Laura Cullen
Senior Designer: Helen Taylor
Project Editor: Angela Newton,
Natasha Treloar, Alastair Laing
Photographer: Tim Ridley
Stylist: Caroline Davies
Illustrations: John Woodcock

Colour separation by Colourscan, Singapore
Printed in Singapore by Tien Wah Press

Murdoch Books (UK) Ltd,
Ferry House, 51–57 Lacy Road,
Putney, London, SW15 1PR
Tel: +44 (0)20 8355 1480, Fax: +44 (0)20 8355 1499
Murdoch Books (UK) Ltd is a subsidiary of
Murdoch Magazines Pty Ltd.

Murdoch Books®,
GPO Box 1203,
Sydney, NSW 1045, Australia
Tel: +61 (0)2 4352 7025, Fax: +61 (0)2 4352 7026
Murdoch Books® is a trademark of
Murdoch Magazines Pty Ltd.